# Homer Simpson Ponders Politics

# HOMER SIMPSON PONDERS POLITICS

## *Popular Culture as Political Theory*

Edited by
JOSEPH J. FOY and
TIMOTHY M. DALE

*Foreword by*
MARGARET WEIS

UNIVERSITY PRESS OF KENTUCKY

Scholarly publisher for the Commonwealth,
serving Bellarmine University, Berea College, Centre College of Kentucky,
Eastern Kentucky University, The Filson Historical Society, Georgetown
College, Kentucky Historical Society, Kentucky State University, Morehead
State University, Murray State University, Northern Kentucky University,
Transylvania University, University of Kentucky, University of Louisville,
and Western Kentucky University.
All rights reserved.

*Editorial and Sales Offices:* The University Press of Kentucky
663 South Limestone Street, Lexington, Kentucky 40508-4008
www.kentuckypress.com

17  16  15  14  13     5  4  3  2  1

Cataloging-in-Publication data is available from the Library of Congress.

ISBN: 978-0-8131-4147-3 (hardcover : alk. paper)
ISBN: 978-0-8131-4150-3 (epub)
ISBN: 978-0-8131-4151-0 (pdf)

This book is printed on acid-free paper meeting the requirements of the
American National Standard for Permanence in Paper for Printed Library
Materials.

Manufactured in the United States of America.

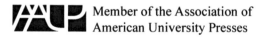 Member of the Association of
American University Presses

This book is dedicated to our parents.

# Contents

# FOREWORD

In describing what it means to be an author, Gary Paulsen once told me something I always remember: "We are the guy in the tribe who puts on the wolfskin and dances around the fire."

That ancient storyteller was an entertainer. He made the members of his tribe forget that they were shivering with cold or wondering where they might find the next meal. But he was doing more than entertaining. Through his tales, the storyteller was passing on tribal traditions, maintaining an oral history of his people, and instilling values that would enable them to survive.

He used the thrilling story of an exciting hunt to show the members of the tribe working together to bring down game. His description of a warrior's heroic death that ended up saving his people taught the value of self-sacrifice. The storyteller learned how to embellish the story in ways that stirred the emotions of those hearing it, so that they would remember it. If Homer had never told his tale, how many of us today would know about the fall of Troy?

As storytellers, we want our readers to enjoy our work, but we also want them to think about it. In fantasy fiction, the presence of different races such as elves and humans and dwarves gives the author the perfect opportunity to talk about racial discrimination. Not only is racial tension a good storytelling element; reading about the hurt and anguish and indignation suffered by an elf who is thrown out of the humans-only tavern can encourage readers to think about race relations in their own lives.

Since many adventurers often frequent taverns, my coauthor, Tracy Hickman, and I decided to make one of our characters an alcoholic. We did research on the subject and attempted to make our portrayal as accurate as possible. In writing about his struggles and the problems the other characters encounter trying to deal with him, we hoped to reach those readers who might find themselves in the same situation. We also wanted to encourage other readers to give serious thought to the issue.

Not only do human prejudices and fears, flaws and failings make for good storytelling; they serve to ground the fantastic in what the reader knows to be real, helping the reader suspend disbelief. One reason the Harry Potter novels are so successful is that they are about children in school. Never mind that in this school the children fly on broomsticks. The idea of being a kid in a classroom, having to deal with classmates and teachers, is something to which we all can relate.

Readers of books and those who write them will find much to think about in this interesting and entertaining book. I feel very privileged to have been invited to write the foreword.

And now, if you'll excuse me, I have to go find my wolfskin. It's time to tell a story.

Margaret Weis

## Introduction

# POPULAR CULTURE AS POLITICAL THEORY

### Plato, Aristotle, and Homer

*Joseph J. Foy*

> When people told themselves their past with stories, explained their present
> with stories, foretold their future with stories; the best place by the fire
> was kept for the storyteller.
>
> —*The Storyteller* (opening sequence)

In 1987 Jim Henson, most famous, of course, for his Muppets, created and
produced the first installment of *The Storyteller.* Combining live acting and
puppetry, Henson used this award-winning television series to recreate myth
narratives from around the world and, in the process, remind audiences
of all ages of the importance and power of the stories a society chooses to
tell. In each episode, the Storyteller (in the first season played by John Hurt
and in the second season by Michael Gambon) magically brought to life
tales of German, Russian, Celtic, Norwegian, and Greek traditions, each
one offering humanistic insights into questions of power, ethics, religious
belief, tradition, social hierarchy, the individual, and the "other." These tales,
which had been told throughout time and across cultures, served as a means
for dealing with the big questions that have long plagued communities of
people: questions about truth, justice, freedom, equality, and ethics. And
underneath the stories lay expressions of cultural values and frameworks
for understanding the world and our place within it.

American mythologist Joseph Campbell (1904–1987) describes myths like those presented in *The Storyteller* as "living inspiration of whatever else may have appeared out of the activities of the human body and mind," arguing that "religions, philosophies, arts, the social forms . . . boil up from the basic, magic ring of myth."[1] Campbell and other mythologists and folklorists, who ultimately address the common themes and symbols found through a cross-cultural comparison, use the popular stories shared within societies to reveal deeper insights into the messages they convey about the common philosophies contained in those societies.

It will likely come as no surprise to students of political theory, then, that myths—shared through stories, music, poetry, art, and sermon—have always been a way to communicate the principles and ideals of a society, as well as to frame and present insights regarding liberty, property, justice, rights, power, and community. Philosophers dating back to Confucius (551–479 BCE) praised poetic works like those contained in the Chinese *Book of Songs* (many of which were also, or later became, popular songs), noting that such poems are invaluable to moral education. Italian philosopher Machiavelli (1469–1527) turned to dramatization to present a philosophical allegory about virtue ethics and community: his play *La Mandragola*. More recently, Ayn Rand (1905–1982), a screenwriter-playwright turned novelist and philosopher, influenced countless conservative, libertarian, and Objectivist thinkers with her popular fiction novels *The Fountainhead* and *Atlas Shrugged*, and democratic socialist thinker and writer George Orwell (1903–1950) penned compelling critiques of Stalinism and the totalitarian state in *1984* and *Animal Farm*. These narratives, poems, and dramatizations, just like the shared myths passed down through time, express the dominant values, ideals, and beliefs that define political culture and pose allegorical thought-experiments that can guide our reasoning when approaching problems both personal and public.

## Popular Culture and the Modern Mythos

But where are our modern myths? Has civilization advanced beyond the need for stories and song to transfer cultural values and political philosophies across wide audiences of people? Do we still use dramatization and art to create a common cultural experience? Along with revolutions in democracy, education, production, and capitalization, modernity ushered in challenges to traditional social arrangements. With mass production and mass communication, technologies began to emerge that transformed the ways human beings interacted with one another. In the distant past, tribal associations and feudalistic arrangements tied people's identity to what was immediately present in their lives; then the ability to move more freely, communicate more openly, and engage in society more horizontally presented the conditions for modern nationalistic identities and eventually introduced pressures of globalization that began pushing against long-held cultural institutions. No longer was there a spot by a common fire where everyone gathered to listen as the storyteller told myth narratives or the balladeer sang songs to make sense of the world. Instead, people sought out entertainment in movie theaters and from radio and television programs; now they have Internet and other technologies as well. And yet, what is more and more apparent is that while technologies have changed and our methods of telling stories are different, we still share in fictional works as a means of framing the world around us and shaping a common culture. The acrid smoke of the campfire has been replaced by the whitish-blue glow of the film projector, but the organization of the world and the conveyance of values and beliefs through stories have endured.

For instance, Campbell describes how the same heroic myths that were shared for ages across cultures and traditions emerged in popular films like *Star Wars*.[2] He suggests that the *Star Wars* saga is "not a simple morality play" but a myth that reveals social truths about humanity, our place within social and political systems, and "the powers of life as they are either fulfilled or broken and suppressed through the action of man."[3] Describing the parallel journeys of Anakin Skywalker / Darth Vader and his son Luke, Campbell articulates how this film series weaves a tale that struggles with the same social and political and humanitarian questions told in classical myths, religious allegories, and narrative literature throughout the ages. *Star Wars*, Campbell notes, represents "not a specific historical situation . . . [but] an operation of principles."[4] He argues that a similar transference of these messages occurs in other venues of popular culture, from the smallest nursery fairy tale to "the latest incarnation of Oedipus, [and] the continued romance of Beauty and the Beast, [which] stand this afternoon on Forty Second Street and Fifth Avenue, waiting for the traffic light to change."[5]

## The Praisers of Homer

These stories that we share through mass media and common values that are shaped through consumer culture direct and shape our attitudes and perspectives related to our position as citizens within the state and as part of the world. Yet, many people are openly hostile to the idea of using popular culture as a vehicle for engaging in discussions about politics and political theory. Their criticisms range from the lack of sophistication and depth of popular culture itself to the ubiquitous nature of popular-culture books that are overrunning the shelves at local booksellers and working their way into the halls of academia. Popular culture is dismissed as at best a distraction and at worst a threat to the reasoned discourse and civic responsibilities necessary in contemporary democratic societies.[6]

Such a critique of popular culture's role in shaping attitudes and behaviors is not new. Plato (427–347 BCE) presented similar sentiments in several of his dialogues. For instance, in a conversation with Glaucon in book 10 of *The Republic,* Socrates denounces the role that art and poetry—the popular culture of Greek society at the time—play in shaping perceptions of truth and human affairs. Calling out the "praisers of Homer," Socrates contends that if we "accept the honeyed Muse, in song or poetry, pleasure and pain will be the twin kings in [our] city in place of established custom and the thing which has always been generally accepted as best—reason."[7] Put simply, artistry and poetics are intended to appeal to an arousal of passions and not of reason, and therefore they can pull individuals away from a rational pursuit of truth and into the realm of making decisions based on irrational, emotional urges. Socrates also contends within this and other dialogues that such artistry amounts to mere imitation (*mimesis*) of human affairs, and a poor rendering at that.[8] Human reason, which is complex and discursive, cannot be captured adequately by the artist who attempts to imitate and convey it through an unsophisticated mimicry. Likewise, since there is an ideal form of truth in the universe, according to Platonic thought, imitation cannot do it justice. Artists and poets present a false representation of the form; it cannot be packaged so crudely. The point was that the art produced by the poets of that age was misleading and potentially damaging to the politics of the just state because it distracted people from the truth and gave them a false sense of reality. So fearful of the disruptive and destructive power of popular culture is Plato (often seen as allowing his views to be presented through Socrates in *The Republic*) that he says such artisans ought to be either controlled to the benefit of the just state—wrapped up in his conception of the "noble lie" used to maintain order in society—or banished entirely.

And what would Plato contend given the ubiquitous nature of popular culture today? There is little doubt that he would condemn the nearly three hours each day—roughly 12 percent of the year—that Americans spend watching television (about half of the time that adults age fifteen and over in the United States devote to leisure) and the over $10.5 billion received at the box office in the United States in 2009 and again in 2010.[9] In particular, Plato would be critical of the diversity of popular culture available that is uncontrolled in terms of message. Films like *The Hangover* and its sequel (both of them among the one hundred top-grossing films of all time) glorify what he would almost certainly deem as the less noble aspects of human nature and behavior. Certainly, if Plato was skeptical of the intellects of his age who admired Homer the poet, "who has educated Greece," and declared that he was "worth studying both for our general education and for the management of human affairs,"[10] one can only imagine the scorn he would have for scholars who claim that Homer the Simpson is educating America and ought to be studied for insights into the social order and the human condition.

Aristotle (384–322 BCE), a student of Plato's, shared his teacher's assumptions that the artistry of popular culture amounts to imitation of an ideal form and that it possesses powerful rhetorical possibilities. However, unlike Plato, Aristotle embraced the arousal of passion through emotional appeal (*pathos*) as an important tool in the communication arsenal.[11] In fact, in his *Rhetoric*, Aristotle suggests that, among some audiences, it is difficult (if even possible) to produce conviction with mere facts and logic. Rhetoric, including the rhetorical power of persuasion through emotional appeals as presented through artistic media, serves as a method of persuasion in particular contexts where presentation of logic alone fails to inspire. Popular culture forms such as stories, dramatic works, poems, music, and visual artistry can, therefore, be a means of communicating and persuading and can work to engage and inform audiences in ways that logic and the presentation of fact simply cannot. Moreover, as Aristotle suggests, these forms go beyond mere presentation for the sake of entertainment or pacification: they are ways to communicate meaning. The creative talents behind contemporary popular culture are also conveying ideas and perspectives through the medium of entertainment.

## Popular Culture and the Many Promises of Political Thinking

Of course, what is important to remember is that Plato never suggests that popular culture is unimportant or that it does not play a highly influential role in shaping personal identity and communicating cultural values. On the contrary, if popular culture were ineffective in these ways, its purveyors would not be regarded as a threat. It is only because popular culture narratives are so powerful in conveying messages that resonate with audiences long after the credits roll or the song ends that they are so "dangerous." After all, Plato himself presents his philosophical works in dramatic dialogue akin to the script of a play, and his mentor Socrates tells allegorical stories like "Allegory of the Cave" and "Ring of Gyges" to explore questions about truth, morality, legalism, justice, and power. Plato also advocated the presentation of a "Noble Lie," a myth about the nature of the soul and its force in determining a person's place in society, to persuade people to accept their station and not disrupt what he considered the just ordering of the state.

The presumption of Plato is that there is only a singular form of the properly ordered state and that the only popular culture we ought to allow is that which perpetuates that vision. However, the history of political thought introduces a battery of prominent thinkers, each of whom contributes insights into notions of justice, equality, virtue, the properly ordered society, and the good life. This political theory canon surfaces in our popular culture narratives and is a part of our common, cultural conversation. We may not directly invoke Thomas Hobbes, but we wrestle with his assumptions about the state of nature and the power of the state when we read of the troubles of Katniss Everdeen and Peeta Mellark in Suzanne Collins's *The Hunger Games*. Whether or not we read Friedrich Nietzsche, we are presented with his arguments through the words of Voldemort, who tells Harry Potter at the end of *The Sorcerer's Stone* that "there is no good and evil, only power and those too weak to seek it." And as the chapters in this book illustrate, we watch Platonic philosophy in *Star Wars*, Aristotelian theories of community and virtue in *The Simpsons*, Machiavellian approaches to power in *The Godfather*, and contemporary Marxism in full 3D-effect in *Avatar*.

In part 1 of the book, authors use staples of American popular culture to examine classic treatments of civic virtue and the just society. In the first chapter, Dean A. Kowalski draws parallels between George Lucas's *Star Wars* universe and Platonic political thinking, and in chapter 2 Timothy M. Dale offers an Aristotelian counter to Plato's conception as presented through the community of Springfield in *The Simpsons*. Eric T. Kasper concludes this part with a look at Francis Ford Coppola's *Godfather* trilogy as a presentation of Machiavellian thought and reflections on power. Collectively, these chapters establish a foundation for considering the proper organization of society, as well as the role of the virtuous leader and the power of the state.

Part 2 explores the foundations and origins of the state, which help to provide insights about the purpose the state serves (or ought to serve) in establishing a framework for society. Susanne E. Foster and James B. South use Joss Whedon's space-western series *Firefly* and the companion film *Serenity* to highlight the importance of social-contract principles guiding perspectives on rational legalism and limitations on state authority. This is followed by Matthew D. Mendham's analysis of the popular sitcom *The Office*; in it he finds insight into the writings of another social-contract thinker, Jean-Jacques Rousseau, and of the famed Roman historian Marcus Cornelius Tacitus, who explore the pathologies and underlying theories of leadership within a republican system. In chapter 6, S. Evan Kreider examines Alan Moore's graphic novel *Watchmen* and contrasts the Kantian universalism of the character Rorschach with the utilitarian views of Ozymandias.

Part 3 confronts the limitations and possibilities of political life and the ways in which these challenges are presented in popular culture narratives. Mark C. E. Peterson shows how James Cameron's *Avatar*, the highest-grossing movie of all time, illustrates Marxist notions of alienation that one experiences in the materialist bonds of capitalist society. C. Heike Schotten deconstructs the Nietzschean critiques of modern thinking in the Disney/Pixar film *The Incredibles*, and Jamie Warner looks at the Foucauldian themes of power and discipline in J. K. Rowling's *Harry Potter* books. Denise Du Vernay concludes part 3 with an analysis of popular culture and the identity messaging that comes through many prominent forms of entertainment media.

Part 4 offers a look into the problems and promises of liberal democracy. In chapter 11, Carl Bergetz explains how the action-movie genre exposes the conservative political theory that constructs the iconic action hero in American cinema, glorifying illiberal themes and posing challenges to underlying assumptions made by democratic orders. In chapter 12, Mary M. Keys explores J. R. R. Tolkien's classic fairy stories and epic novel *The Hobbit* and finds commentary on virtue and Tocquevillian perspectives on liberal democracy. Finally, Joseph J. Foy examines the political and cultural transformation being ushered in by new media and social networking, which replace the singular storyteller with the voices of the many. Foy argues that elite control of discourse is disappearing as more and more people tell their own narratives—their own stories—in fulfillment of the democratic promise of liberal societies.

Ultimately, how we think about questions of rights, justice, equality, freedom, power, the state, and a host of other questions long debated in the field of political theory is just as profoundly shaped at the box office as in the classroom. How we conceive of ourselves in relation to the political system or feel and deliberate about the authority and legitimacy of institutions, actors, and outcomes in government is influenced and directed as much by the characters and complications of our television shows or the lyrics to our favorite songs as by traditional media or town hall debate. As political thinkers, we cannot dismiss the importance of philosophical messaging in popular culture. As citizens, we cannot presume that the storytellers of our age are not helping us to explain our past, understand our present, and foretell our future.

This volume is a testament to the notion that those conversations are happening within our popular culture, where the political theory canon is alive and well in our movies, our television shows, our music, our novels, and our media; in the myth narratives of modern America.[12] And so our story begins "a long time ago in a galaxy far, far away," where we turn for entertainment and, at the same time, learn more about our politics, our world, and ourselves.

## Notes

1. Joseph Campbell, *The Hero with a Thousand Faces,* 3rd ed. (Novato, CA: New World Library, 2008), 1.

2. Filmmaker George Lucas has often credited Campbell's book *The Hero with a Thousand Faces* for helping him focus his imaginative *Star Wars* universe into a more defined narrative about the journey of the hero. See Joseph Campbell and Bill Moyers, *The Power of Myth* (New York: Random House, 1988), xiii.

3. Campbell and Moyers, *Power of Myth,* 179.

4. Ibid., 177.

5. Campbell, *Hero with a Thousand Faces,* 2.

6. The arguments for and against popular culture as a pedagogical tool and a form of political discourse have been covered extensively in other works and need not be rehashed here. For a practical and theoretical treatment of the importance of popular culture scholarship in the field of politics and democracy studies, see Timothy M. Dale, "The Revolution Is Being Televised: The Case for Popular Culture as Public Sphere," in *Homer Simpson Marches on Washington: Dissent through American Popular Culture,* ed. Timothy M. Dale and Joseph J. Foy (Lexington: University Press of Kentucky, 2010), 21–35.

7. Plato, *Republic,* ed. G. R. F. Ferrari, trans. Tom Griffith (Cambridge: Cambridge University Press, 2000), 607a.

8. See the Platonic dialogue "Ion," in *Essential Dialogues of Plato,* ed. Pedro de Blas, trans. Benjamin Jowett (New York: Barnes and Noble Classics, 2005), 7–19.

9. "American Time Use Survey: 2010 Results, Bureau of Labor Statistics," U.S. Department of Labor, Washington, DC, June 22, 2011, www.bls.gov/news.release/atus.nr0.htm (accessed October 3, 2011); "Yearly Box Office," Box Office Mojo, http://boxofficemojo.com/yearly/ (accessed October 3, 2011).

10. Plato, *Republic* 606e.

11. Aristotle also describes the importance of *ethos* (an appeal to the authority of the presenter) and *logos* (an appeal to logic) in communication. See Aristotle, *Rhetoric,* ed. W. D. Ross, trans. W. Rhys Roberts (New York: Cosimo, 2010).

12. There are many other books that provide analyses of the political messaging of popular culture. See Joseph J. Foy, ed., *Homer Simpson Goes to Washington: American Politics through Popular Culture* (Lexington: University Press of Kentucky, 2008); Lilly J. Goren, ed., *You've Come a Long Way, Baby: Women, Politics, and Popular Culture* (Lexington: University Press of Kentucky, 2009); and Dale and Foy, *Homer Simpson Marches on Washington.* Likewise, there are popular culture and philosophy lists available from the University Press of Kentucky, Open Court Publishing, and Wiley-Blackwell Publishing. However, despite a few targeted works such as Anne Norton's *Republic of Signs: Liberal Theory and American Popular Culture* (Chicago: University of Chicago Press, 1993), this book is the first of its kind to examine the diverse political theory canon through the lens of popular culture.

**Part 1**

# CLASSICAL INSIGHTS AND CIVIC VIRTUE

# 1

# A Tale of Two Republics

## Plato, Palpatine, and Politics

*Dean A. Kowalski*

One doesn't often hear the names Plato and George Lucas uttered in the same sentence. We could muse, I suppose, that if the former solidified the intellectual importance of the ancient Greeks, the other solidified the cultural importance of modern geeks. But deeper connections exist, if one looks. Consider that both have authored politically charged tomes that have become classics in their respective fields. And each of these classics has quite a bit to say about the intricacies of, well, a republic.

It is admittedly unlikely that George Lucas had Plato's *Republic* open on his desk when he began penning the *Star Wars* saga. Nevertheless, the parallels are rather striking. By learning more about Plato's *Republic*, we achieve a novel and effective perspective for better grasping how Palpatine so efficiently transformed the Galactic Republic into the Galactic Empire, installing himself as emperor. Yet the Galactic Republic provides an interesting medium for better appreciating some of Plato's ideals, especially those pertaining to the locus of political power. So making connections between Plato's *Republic* and Lucas's Galactic Republic facilitates deeper insights into each.

## Society and the State

By the "state," political philosophers mean (roughly) a unified but structured society. Thus discussions of the ideal state invariably involve how, optimally, society should be structured. Who should preserve its well-being and direct its future, thereby possessing political power? How should the holders of political power be selected? How extensive should their power be? Should there be limits to that power, and if so, what should be done if the limits are violated? For that matter, should the state be structured to politically empower anyone at all?

These questions are difficult and therefore lend credence to the enterprise of political philosophy. But they have something else in common. Because each question explores aspects of how society should be ideally structured, but society is made up of individuals, they cannot be answered apart from a more basic question: what is best or optimal for the individuals making up the society? This is why the term *state* is often used interchangeably with *commonwealth:* what is in everyone's best interests—the common good—in terms of structuring society?

Thus discussions of the ideal state also invariably involve assumptions about human nature. This was also true in Plato's day. In the *Republic,* Plato uses his brother Glaucon as the mouthpiece for the commonly held view that human beings are driven by their desires for personal gain and satisfaction. Glaucon bolstered this contention with a story about Gyges, a shepherd who finds a magical gold ring. When the ring face is turned one way, its wearer becomes invisible. Gyges immediately utilizes the ring to fulfill all of his desires, including becoming king. Glaucon fears that any person would act this way. If there were no negative consequences for our indiscretions, why care about anything or anyone besides yourself? But, of course, magic rings are imaginary; consequences for moral and legal infractions are real. Moreover, being subjected to the whims of politically powerful individuals constantly seeking their selfish ends, especially if there is no way for you to obtain recompense or restitution, is not desirable. (Imagine living as a slave on Tatooine under Hutt rule.) Therefore, each of us implicitly strikes a bargain by agreeing to follow the laws of the state. Although it's sometimes about as much fun as kissing a Wookie, following state-sanctioned mandates keeps us civil, for the common good. This social arrangement is the best we can realistically hope for.

Plato spends a great deal of time and effort in the *Republic* arguing that the view Glaucon espouses is false. He agrees that most of us are driven by our baser, animalistic drives and that we often act on these desires. However, it isn't necessary that we do. There is more to human nature than merely its beastly (rancor) side. Furthermore, under the proper circumstances, human- ity can make important strides toward perfection. Human nature is perfected when the multiple facets of humankind act optimally, thereby achieving a sort of harmony among them. The ideal state should be structured so as to mirror, and reinforce, the ideal form of humanity. Plato's goal, as a social and political philosopher, is to explain just what that structure is and what circumstances must obtain to achieve it.

For Plato, everything within the ideal state functions optimally. Justice prevails when the citizens and the various factions of society all work harmoniously with one another. With no disputes or squabbles, everyone in the state is properly provided for and everyone is happy, which obviously is the common good. Plato believes that such an ideal state is synonymous with the just state. But when some citizens or factions act contrary to the way they should function, the state becomes disordered; injustice ensues and citizens of the state become unhappy. Therefore, Plato holds that there is a conceptual link between justice and happiness as they pertain to the commonwealth. A perfectly just state is perfectly happy. So, because everyone clearly wishes to be perfectly happy, the denizens of a commonwealth have a good reason to work toward the goal of living in a perfectly just state.

## The *Republic* Goes Galactic

Plato's architecture for a perfectly ordered state consists of three presuppositions. The first presupposition advises a division of labor. Some individuals seem better equipped for some jobs than for others. This is common sense. For instance, some people excel at running a business, such as Watto the junk dealer. Others possess the dexterity needed for piloting a podracer, such as the Dug Sebulba. But Watto cannot pilot a podracer, and Sebulba shows little aptitude for managing a business or bookkeeping. These fictional examples remind us of the reality that none of us is completely self-sufficient. Rather than forcing us to do everything for ourselves, why not encourage each to develop his or her own aptitudes? A division of labor is better for the state and its citizens.

Plato's second presupposition is that each citizen falls within one of three societal groups based on the person's natural aptitudes and abilities. Just as we might say a young Bith is a born jazz horn player, Plato extends this intuition into classifying kinds of people as "profit-loving" (producers), "victory-loving" (guardians), or "philosophical" (rulers).[1] The first faction is the most populous; it is made up of farmers, craftsmen, physicians, bankers, and merchants, among others. This class of citizens includes those who most efficiently provide the day-to-day goods, services, and sustenance for the commonwealth; they accomplish these activities most efficiently because they naturally excel at them.

Lucas's far-away and long-ago galaxy is replete with this group of denizens. There are moisture farmers on Tatooine, those in the Agricultural Corps (on Bandomeer and elsewhere), Corellian spice-runners, diner owners such as Dex on Coruscant, and Geonosian droid-makers. But there are also larger consortiums, for example, the Intergalactic Banking Clan, the Techno Union, and the Trade Federation. Furthermore, Lucas concurs with Plato that individuals pursuing these professions are (often) naturally suited to them. Neimoidians, for example, seem particularly adept to be part of, if not to lead, the Trade Federation; they are driven by greed and profit seemingly as a result of their very (insectlike) rearing. Note also how the Trade Federation secures the essential financial lifeblood of the galaxy by transporting goods and services to the Outer Rim, keeping planets like Naboo connected to the Core.

Plato's second societal faction, guardians, would today take in police officers, firefighters, members of the National Guard, and the military. This class of citizens is marked by their innate tendencies to be courageous and strong and to have a sense of adventure; they most efficiently provide protection for the commonwealth, defending it both from within (police, firefighters, the National Guard) and without (the army and the navy), because they naturally excel at the necessary activities.

The primary example of the guardian class in Lucas's *Star Wars* saga is none other than the Jedi. Given the prominent role of the Jedi, this may surprise some readers. But recall that the life of a Jedi is one of service to the Senate and to the Galactic Republic generally. The Jedi are peacekeepers, looking to always maintain balance in the Force. On rare occasions they act like the National Guard to quell some squabble or dispute, as when Qui-Gon Jinn and Obi-Wan Kenobi were sent to defuse the Trade Federation blockade of Naboo or Obi-Wan and Anakin were assigned to ensure the safety of Senator Amidala during her stay on Coruscant. The Galactic Republic lacked a standing military—at least until the clone soldiers were mobilized to defend against the threat of the Separatists and their droid armies. Thus, the Galactic Republic also has groups responsible for quashing internal and external threats to its safety.

Plato's third faction intriguingly arises out of the second. Initially, children with natural aptitudes for guardianship receive the same training.

But soon enough, a subgroup with particularly noteworthy intellectual gifts is identified. Those individuals receive very specialized academic and administrative training to become the governmental rulers and the societal leaders. Plato believed that this group would be rather small in number and that their training would last many decades. The exact political organization of this class is left rather unclear, but Plato advocated that they live in a sort of communal arrangement. They were to lack private property and not be concerned with wealth (416d–417b). The idea is to reinforce that they are to lead for the common good and not out of personal interest. In any event, this is the smallest class, made up of the most intelligent, rational, and self-controlled people—those best naturally suited to make difficult economic, social, and foreign policy decisions on behalf of the commonwealth.

Lucas's Galactic Republic also has political leaders of various sorts. But much unlike Plato, Lucas created political leaders that are something of a mixed bag. There is Supreme Chancellor Valorum, who serves as the chief of state residing in the capital city-planet of Coruscant. He seems to be an honorable man but is not a terribly effective leader. The Senate, also housed on Coruscant, comprises numerous representatives from all the star systems within the galaxy, not all of whom are forthright and well-respected. The Senate also includes delegates representing various special-interest groups, for example, Senator Lott Dod of the Trade Federation. The various star systems, in turn, benefit from their own local political structures. For example, Naboo elects a monarch serving for a limited term to safeguard the interests of its system.

The importance of Plato's first two presuppositions is now clearer. Each societal faction provides an essential feature of the well-ordered state: the producers provide all the necessities of life, including health care and financial services; the guardians protect the city from within and without; and the rulers provide governmental leadership. On this division-of-labor model, the state is well ordered, operating optimally, when each faction as a whole works at what it does best.

## Plato's Ideal State

Plato's third presupposition addresses the issue of how a state achieves and maintains perfection. Just as each citizen has one basic kind of latent but distinctive ability she is best suited for, Plato believes that each of the factions has a latent but distinctive characteristic it is most suited to exemplify. Yet, even as a Bith who is a "born horn player" must still hone his innate abilities to reach his full potential as a virtuoso Mos Eisely cantina player, each faction must strive to fully realize the characteristic it is fittest to achieve.

For the producers, the distinctive characteristic is moderation, or what Plato called "temperance." This societal faction should not produce too many or too few goods and services, lest the commonwealth become indulgent or impoverished. It seems unlikely that a starving army could properly defend the state against hostile invaders. It seems equally unlikely that the government could properly run the commonwealth without financial stability. Furthermore, this faction must not selfishly hoard its commodities or services, even though it is solely responsible for their production. Thus, the producers must understand, or at least accept, the need to share their produce with the other two factions for the overall good of the state, without resentment or delusions of grandeur regarding their role in the commonwealth. If the producers do not realize their proper role in society, they fail to exemplify their distinctive characteristic. Plato would say that they thereby become intemperate, and intemperance leads to social strife. An intemperate state is not well ordered and justice cannot prevail.

For the guardians, the distinctive characteristic is courage of conviction. This faction is to bravely defend the commonwealth from all threats to its well-being; the guardians should act as the loyal agents of the rulers, enforcing or enacting policy decisions. Plato relies on colorful analogies from the animal kingdom to convey the multifaceted role of the guardians; he writes, "Now will a horse, a dog, or any other animal be courageous if it is not spirited? Or haven't you noticed just how invincible and unbeatable spirit is, so that its presence makes the whole soul [self or person] fearless and unconquerable in any situation" (375b)? The guardians must also be strong, sharp-eyed, and loyal. Plato continues, "But surely they must be gentle to their own people and harsh to their enemies. Otherwise, they will not wait around for others to destroy them, but will do it themselves first" (375c).

Yet it cannot be overlooked that the guardians are quite intelligent. They must quickly recognize friend and foe and also understand how policy decisions may aid the former and protect against the latter.[2] Thus, for the guardians, being courageous is also being loyal to the state, and being loyal to the state requires correct convictions about when the state is in need of defense. When the commonwealth suffers from cowardice, disloyalty, or improper conviction in situations calling for bravery or loyalty, it is not well ordered and thus cannot be a just state.

For the rulers—those particularly talented and capable guardians—the distinctive characteristic is wisdom. The rulers must have knowledge of various topics. In addition to training in mathematics and harmonics, they must understand economic, educational, philosophical, and political policies of all sorts. Moreover, they must possess the sound judgment to discern how their knowledge ought to be enacted. They must know what sorts of public policies to enjoin and have a keen, intuitive sense for when changes in policy are needed. They must know what laws to enact and how severe the penalties should be if the laws are broken.[3] They must know when exceptions to laws should be made or when old laws should be replaced. They must know when a situation calls for a peace treaty or a declaration of war. And they must know when and how the guardians (the "national guard") should be summoned for domestic tragedies or natural disasters.

Plato tended to use the analogy of a ship captain to illustrate the role of a ruler in his ideal society. He writes, "A true captain must pay attention to the seasons of the year, the sky, the stars, the winds, and all that pertains to his craft, if he truly is to be a ruler of a ship" (488d). Plato clearly thought that rulers must not merely possess factual or encyclopedia-type knowledge. They must also be truly wise—fully aware of how their various pieces of knowledge fit together—to get the "big picture" for the benefit of everyone in the commonwealth, to make it take the proper course. A ship piloted by an unwise commander winds up like the *Executor*'s Admiral Ozzel—in turmoil with the life choked out of it. (Cue *Admiral* Piett.) Analogously, a state run by ignorant, imprudent, or shortsighted rulers suffers from continual political unrest. It will not function properly, and it cannot be just.

A perfectly just state, then, is one in which temperance, courage, loyalty, and wisdom prevail. When each distinctive characteristic is exemplified, the commonwealth enjoys perfect balance and harmony among its factions. Although the rulers and the guardians are unproductive regarding the daily necessities of life, the former provide sound leadership and the latter provide defense. Although the producers are not involved in governance or defense, they provide the sorts of goods and services without which the state could not survive. Thus, when the three societal factions work together to form a cohesive unit, justice obtains and the common good is secured.[4] Contemporary Plato scholar Julia Annas eloquently sums up the benefits of Plato's view: "Plato thinks that the point of a state is to make its members part of a political and cultural unity that brings out the best in everyone, because everyone will be guaranteed the place that best fits his or her talents."[5]

## Orchestrating Disharmony

Very little, thematically speaking, is perfect in Lucas's Galactic Republic. Yet things go horribly wrong once Palpatine succeeds Valorum as Supreme Chancellor. The Galactic Empire he institutes certainly seems unjust. But Plato would say that the injustice results from the irreparable disharmony Palpatine caused.

Plato would explain the success of Palpatine's political coup as the result of the Sith Lord's diverting the various Galactic Republic factions from their respective distinctive aptitudes. Palpatine transforms the Trade Federation into a political and military entity. He leaves the Jedi no choice but to become generals and field marshals—wagers of war rather than peacekeepers. He effortlessly turns the clone soldiers against their generals. He hastens the downward spiral of a crumbling Senate. The Clone Wars have the senators tied up in knots; they become obsessed with petty self-interested squabbles, all but forgetting the best interests of the Galactic Republic. These combined effects were obviously disastrous. As the Galactic Republic swiftly unraveled in Palpatine's insidious hands, Plato would have rhetorically asked: "Is there any greater evil . . . for a city [state] than that which tears it apart and makes it many rather than one?" (462a).

In the years leading up to *The Phantom Menace,* the Trade Federation struggles to defend itself from pirates and terrorists in the Outer Rim.[6] It requests additional judicial protection, but the Galactic Republic lacks the resources to provide it; furthermore, some of the raids occur in neutral space. Consequently, Lott Dod formally petitions the Senate for permission to strengthen the Trade Federation's defensive capabilities by upgrading its droid armies. Palpatine subtly influences Valorum to grant the request, but only if the Trade Federation accepts a new commerce tax on the currently free trade routes in the Outer Rim. This makes the Trade Federation a political player, embroiling it in various senatorial maneuverings.

Concurrently, Darth Sidious secretly works with Neimoidians in the Trade Federation Directorate, especially Viceroy Nute Gunray. Sidious, also financing Outer Rim terrorists, arranges for the assassinations of non-Neimoidians serving in the Directorate. This action solidifies Gunray's hold over the Trade Federation. It also leaves Neimoidian avarice completely unchecked. In an obvious act of intemperance, the Trade Federation upgrades its armies, but it protests the commerce tax by blockading and eventually invading Naboo—with its impressive new droid armies. The invasion signals the start of the Separatist movement and peril for the Galactic Republic.

The Separatist movement is emboldened under the charismatic leadership of former Jedi Master Count Dooku. Numerous star systems swiftly align themselves with Dooku, allowing him to sign treaties with various producer-class consortiums. The Jedi take note. Mace Windu, a senior member of the Jedi Council, somberly reminds Chancellor Palpatine: "You must realize there aren't enough Jedi to protect the Republic. We are keepers of the peace, not soldiers."[7] The Military Creation Act is partly a result of that advice. Some, such as (now) Senator Amidala, vehemently oppose it, and their voices are strong. Why threaten the Separatists with violence when you seek peace?

Concurrently, Obi-Wan serendipitously discovers an army of two hundred thousand cloned soldiers on Kamino, who were authorized ten years ago by Jedi Master Sifo-Dyas, acting under Palpatine's subtle influence. With civil war looming, the Senate responds by voting the Supreme Chancellor emergency powers to mobilize the clone army in the hope of putting down the Separatist stronghold on Geonosis. But the clones were genetically designed to take orders and not give them.[8] The Jedi become generals. They are soon spread all over the galaxy on disparate military missions. Focused on war, the Jedi's connection to the Force is altered; they are no longer singularly dedicated to maintaining its balance. Darth Sidious eventually initiates Order 66 to trigger genetically hidden psychology within the clones. As a result, the clone soldiers instantaneously mutiny against their generals; almost all the Jedi are assassinated by their formerly loyal troops. The clones now unquestioningly serve the Emperor.

Palpatine exerts far less effort at successfully imploding an already corrupt Senate. By the time of *Revenge of the Sith*, he has managed to manipulate various senators motivated by greed or self-aggrandizement, including Senator Orn Free Taa of Ryloth and the Vice Chairman of the Senate, Mas Amedda. Indeed, the Galactic Senate has become little more than a tool for widening the gulf between the privileged and the disenfranchised. This division is reflected in the structure of Coruscant itself. Most of its denizens eke out meager lives in the dank lower levels, while the senators live far above in the posh upper levels. Furthermore, Palpatine exploits this arrangement to oust Valorum. Various self-interested senators hide behind the rule of law and public decorum to derail Valorum's efforts, thereby making him appear ineffective. When he cannot prevent the invasion of Naboo, Amidala sounds the vote of "no confidence." Becoming Supreme Chancellor, aided with some timely emergency powers, Palpatine has all he needs to bring all of his Sith-borne plans to fruition.

## Plato Surveys the Galactic Republic

Plato's commentary on Palpatine's clandestine maneuverings might begin mundanely with the guardian and ruler classes. Plato was clear that the guardians had to be rather intelligent in order to properly protect the state. The vast majority of the guardian class—the clone soldiers—were genetically designed to be Palpatine's trump card against the Jedi. They were ultimately puppets, a tool that he could implement by almost literally flipping a switch. Plato was also clear that the rulers should be the intellectually elite of society, instilled with valuing the common good in all their decisions. This might describe solitary figures like Bail Organa or Padmé Amidala, but they represent a small minority of the Galactic senators. In fact, the various political leaders of the Galactic Republic hark back to the greedy sailors in Plato's ship-captain analogy, those who quarrel "with one another about steering the ship, each of them thinking that he should be captain even though he's never learned the art of navigation. . . . They're always crowding around the shipowner, begging him and doing everything possible to get him to turn the rudder over to them. And sometimes, if they don't succeed in persuading him, they execute the ones who do succeed or throw them overboard" (488c). This scenario is eerily reminiscent of the individual senators piloting their own "repulsorlift" balconies, trying to get the Chancellor's attention in order to change the course of the Republic.

Plato would also probably question the size of the Galactic Republic. If the state is too small, it cannot be self-sufficient. If the state is too large—say, the size of a *galaxy* that can be traversed only with the help of hyperspace lanes—the prospects of discord are great. Moreover, note how the Senate Building itself, containing 1,012 detachable balconies, represents the Galactic Republic's mammoth size and overwhelming diversity. With so many different voices all clamoring to be heard, it is unlikely that any sort of unity could be maintained. Thus Plato advises that the rulers be fully cognizant of the size of the state (*polis*); it may continue to grow, but not past a certain point, at least not if it is to remain unified (423b). Plato was seemingly most concerned about the state becoming divided into two, especially with respect to economic status. As the state grows, presumably some but not all will grow wealthy. A conflict of interests will result, leading to much political unrest and ultimately upheaval. Palpatine exploited the Galactic Republic's lack of unity, especially the avarice of those who wished to retain and enhance their wealth at the expense of others, such as those on Naboo, who had little financial recourse.

But Plato's most strident criticism of the Galactic Republic would no doubt be its commitment to democracy. Plato's negative view of democracy may insult our current sensibilities. Nevertheless, he begins his critique with a series of rhetorical questions: "First of all, aren't they free? And isn't the city full of freedom and freedom of speech? And doesn't everyone have license to do what he wants? . . . And where people have this license, it's clear that each of them will arrange his own life in whatever manner pleases him" (557b). Contemporary readers may not feel the force of Plato's questions, but Plato worries that there is too much personal freedom in a democracy. On the one hand, such liberty is indicative of a plurality of values, which leads to disunity. Disunity can only lead to civil strife. Rather than doing what they are most naturally suited for, given their natural talents, citizens do whatever they want, including nothing at all. Society quickly breaks down. On the other hand, Plato believes that unity is ultimately preserved through his meritocracy: only those who are best suited to govern should lead. And lead they must, since the state requires wise guidance to keep it functioning optimally. But in a democracy, those that are most suited to govern need not govern. Furthermore, a democratic citizenry may come to adore and follow a leader who merely "tells them that he wishes the majority well" (558c). This situation can only invite various "sailors" to clamor for the "rudder" even though they have no aptitude for "navigation"; and society faces shipwreck.

Through an account that eerily echoes Palpatine's political ascendancy, Plato argues that "democracy's insatiable desire for what it defines as the good also destroys it: freedom" (562b). By prizing freedom to the extreme, citizens become so wary of losing it that they will empower any flatterer who seems willing to preserve it for them. This protector of the people—"their special champion"—is publicly revered and politically empowered (565c). Soon, their special champion requests "that the people give him a bodyguard to keep their defender safe" (566b). (Bring in the clones—say, aren't you a little short for a storm trooper?) The people's champion continues to charm the citizenry and publicly denounce absolute power. But soon he "stirs up a war so that the people will continue to feel the need of a leader" (566e). (Cue the "temporary" emergency powers.) Eventually, he will have to do away with "anyone who is courageous, high-minded, intelligent, or rich" in order to keep political power. (Let's see: Wookies besieged in trees, Mace windowed, Yoda swamped, Gunray's Mustafar morbidity.) "The champion" will continue to purge the best citizens from the commonwealth, thereby becoming its destroyer. And the Supreme Chancellor becomes Emperor.[9]

In short, Plato warns that we must guard against what we *seemingly* want most and instead be vigilant about what is *actually* best for us. Sometimes a democracy isn't best. How would the family unit function as a democracy? Analogously, our true interests are best served when political and social unity is preserved by each of us performing those duties we are most fit to accomplish, with the wisest of us offering guidance to those who need it. Only then does the state function optimally; only then is the state truly healthy. If we don't follow what is best, we may find ourselves echoing Vader: "Yes, my master."

## Jedi Philosopher-Kings and Balance

Plato is sometimes criticized because his account of the ideal state is too unrealistic to be put into practice. The significance of this criticism is debated among scholars. Some argue that Plato's *Republic* offers an ideal that we should strive to emulate; even if it forever remains unobtainable, working toward it will reap great political and social benefits. Others flatly argue that a theory that cannot be put into practice is next to useless.

Without presuming to resolve this debate, we can observe a novel connection to it via the *Star Wars* saga. The Jedi are trained in ways very similar to the training of Plato's rulers. The unique talents of each are identified in early childhood. The respective "younglings" are taken from their homes to undergo highly specialized physical, intellectual, and ethical training, away from the temptations of mainstream society. If all goes well with a padawan's apprenticeship, the padawan eventually becomes a member of the Jedi Council. If all goes well with a guardian's training, the guardian eventually becomes a "philosopher-king."

Plato believes that the ascendancy of the philosopher-king is crucial to an ideal state and, indeed, human flourishing; he writes: "Until philosophers rule as kings or those who are now called kings genuinely and adequately philosophize, that is, until political power and philosophy entirely coincide . . . cities [states] will have no rest from evils . . . nor, I think, will the human race. And until that happens, the constitution [commonwealth] we've been describing in theory will never be born to the fullest extent possible" (473d–e). However, Lucas's Jedi—even the likes of Yoda and Obi-Wan—invariably shun political power.[10] It seems that such power is too tempting; it leads one to the dark side. In this way, Lucas seemingly sides with Plato's detractors that even the best of us—no matter how well trained or intellectually gifted—is corruptible.[11]

Plato believed that his philosopher-kings, once they had attained genuine knowledge and virtue, would never swerve from their role as *benevolent* monarchs. They would always do what is right and good, taking everyone's best interests into account. But Lucas seems to believe that no one—not even the Jedi—is that resolute. If Plato's detractors are correct about this, then Plato's system seems particularly troubled, because it cannot operate without philosopher-kings guiding the state. Moreover, Lucas's decision to have the Jedi answer to the Senate, always serving to maintain balance in the Force, makes more sense. As the Jedi strive to keep far from the shadow of darkness without being blinded by the light, they and the Force remain balanced.

The operatic *Star Wars* saga is many things. It is a story about good and evil, folly and redemption. But perhaps among its various messages is the benefit of a society with a system of political checks and balances. Perhaps there is room for rule of law, assuming that it doesn't become a social and political straightjacket. Even though the Galactic Republic became overly encumbered in its plurality of voices and values, this doesn't necessarily mean that the ultraunity of Plato's *Republic* is the only alternative. Moreover, the downfall of the Galactic Republic doesn't obviously serve as an indictment of democracy in all of its forms. Yet Plato has a point, in that any political leader should strive to become learned, wise, and virtuous. Thus, as political padawans, we should "mind what we have learned"; we must keep balance as we continue to explore and refine our path toward political excellence. Save us it can.[12]

## Notes

1. Plato, *Republic*, trans. G. M. A. Grube (Indianapolis: Hackett, 1992), 580d–581e. See also 455b–c. Hereafter, all references to the *Republic* will be made parenthetically in the text. Plato tended to call his second group "auxiliaries" and the third "guardians." However, for reasons that will become apparent, it seems more convenient (and informative) to refer to the second group as "guardians" and the third as "rulers." (Yet

it seems pretty clear that Plato would scoff at the suggestion that his "guardians" should be called "rulers"; see 463b–c.)

2. Plato offers his "noble hound" analogy to illustrate this point: "When a dog sees someone it does not know, it gets angry even before anything bad happens to it. But when it knows someone, it welcomes him, even if it has never received anything good from him. . . . It judges anything it sees to be either a friend or an enemy on no other basis than that it knows the one and not the other (376a–b).

3. Plato controversially extends this directive to include the use of propaganda ("noble falsehoods") and censorship to ensure that the producers have correct beliefs about how to behave—all for the overall good of the commonwealth. See, for example, 377–78 and 414b–415a.

4. Plato liked to describe justice in the state in terms of physical health. The state prospers in exactly the same way the body prospers, namely, when all its internal organs are functioning properly and harmoniously. The kidneys must clean the blood at the rate the heart pumps it, and the lungs must oxygenate it accordingly. Just as this arrangement is most beneficial for the animal, the harmonious arrangement of the various factions of society is most beneficial for the state. That which is optimally best for the state equates with its perfect health. When the state is perfectly healthy, perfect happiness reigns within its borders. See 444e–445b; see also Plato's *Charmides*, in *The Dialogues of Plato*, trans. Benjamin Jowett (Oxford: Oxford University Press, 1953), 10–11.

5. Julia Annas, *An Introduction to Plato's Republic* (New York: Oxford University Press, 1981), 301.

6. The backstory to *The Phantom Menace* relies on James Luceno, *Star Wars: Cloak of Deception* (New York: Ballantine Books, 2001).

7. Patricia Wade, *Star Wars: Attack of the Clones* (New York: Scholastic Books, 2002), 13.

8. Obi-Wan is informed by a Kaminoan cloner that the clones are "totally obedient, taking every order without question. We modified their genetic structure to make them less independent than the original host." Ibid., 90.

9. This is not to say Plato believed that democracy necessarily devolves into tyranny or despotism in exactly this way for exactly these reasons. Plato's views on the transitions between various forms of government are actually rather convoluted. See Annas, *Introduction to Plato's Republic*, 294–305.

10. It's true that in the larger *Stars Wars* universe of the Old Republic, the Jedi seemingly accepted more political power. Some even became Supreme Chancellor. However, this practice was not without its social and political difficulties, and it was eventually discontinued. See Ryder Windham, *Star Wars Jedi vs. Sith: The Essential Guide to the Force* (New York: Ballantine Books, 2007), 56–57.

11. Plato's famed student Aristotle was among Plato's detractors on this point. See, for example, Aristotle, *Politics*, trans. W. D. Ross, in *The Basic Works of Aristotle*, ed. Richard McKeon (New York: Random House, 1941), 3.15. He offers a detailed criticism

of the *Republic* at 2.1–5. Interestingly, Plato also eventually came to have doubts about the prospects of anyone becoming the sort of philosopher-king his meritocracy required. He revisited these issues in the *Laws*, one of the last books he wrote.

12. My sincere thanks go to Nicholas Bruce for sharing with me his vast knowledge of the *Star Wars* saga, offering insights well beyond his years. I have no doubt that he will one day take his own philosophical padawan; on that day, balance will be truly brought back to the Force once and for all.

# 2

# ARISTOTLE'S POLITICS AND THE VIRTUES OF SPRINGFIELD

## Community, Education, and Friendship in *The Simpsons*

*Timothy M. Dale*

The title sequence for *The Simpsons* television series has become a cultural icon. White clouds move in a bright blue sky, and the unmistakable yellow lettering emerges from behind the clouds as a chorus sings the name of the family after which the show is named. The scene then moves down from the sky to overlook the town, including the nuclear plant, the city hall, and the Springfield tire fire, before arriving at the school (where Bart is writing sentences of punishment on the chalkboard). The city of Springfield is featured prominently as the setting for the show. By the time the title sequence is complete and the members of the Simpson family have raced from their various places in the town to meet on their couch in front of the television set, we have surveyed much of Springfield and have been introduced to most of the characters living in the town. This focus on the town at the beginning of every episode of *The Simpsons* is a reminder that this longest-running television show is about more than just the family at its center. It is also a story about a city and the community of people who inhabit it.

The Greek philosopher Aristotle would describe episodes of *The Simpsons* as stories about a "constitution of people," held together by mutual values, common experiences, and shared friendships. Aristotle might also see the community of Springfield as exemplifying many of his observations about political communities and the virtues and practices that keep them bonded together. The community of Springfield is certainly flawed, but

Aristotle famously recommends that our political theories must begin with a practical account of those who live within a society and include an investigation into why political regimes succeed or fail. Approaching the city of Springfield the way Aristotle would, we find that the city is successful because it is held together by common goals and shared values. The adventures of its citizens exhibit Aristotle's insights about the nature of political regimes, the value of education, and the integral role of friendship for keeping a city intact and cultivating virtuous citizens.

## A Political Theory of Springfield

If we approach *The Simpsons* asking about its politics, on first glance we would likely observe its most overt political messages. Politicians are incompetent and corrupt, media are sensationalistic and lazy, citizens are easily persuadable, and many people are eager to manipulate others for their own gain. At this surface level, *The Simpsons* frequently offers poignant and effective political and social satire, reflecting in the town the absurdity and injustice its writers find in the world.[1] Several episodes involve political campaigns and other explicit references to the American political system, and these episodes usually include a critique of the corruptibility of elected officials and the unsophisticated gullibility of citizens. Through the overt messaging of its narrative, political commentary in *The Simpsons* often takes direct aim at our conventional politics; it contains many insightful, forthright, and mocking portrayals. These satirical depictions of society and politics are linked to a deeper concern about the purpose of community and the nature of relationships within it. Because of this, we have to dig below the surface of the parody of politics to find the political theory at the heart of the series.

Underneath the familiar irreverence of *The Simpsons* toward political and social life, the show contains an innate understanding of the goodness of human nature. Through the action of any given episode, the characters learn that they can depend on one another, and the family and the city find order through the redemption that is in place at the end of every episode. In this way, almost every episode of *The Simpsons* is a story about disorder. The narrative action is usually driven by a character or characters who find themselves out of their normal place in the family or in the town, and the resolution involves bringing the family or the town back into order. The political theory of *The Simpsons* is about applying the basic goodness of human beings in an effort to stabilize the ethical, political, and economic order of the Simpson family and the city of Springfield.

*The Simpsons* thus contains a political philosophy parallel to that of Aristotle, who also maintained that the primary purposes of politics are to cultivate virtue and maintain order in a society.[2] For Aristotle there is not one consistent answer to the question about which kind of authority structure is best for accomplishing these tasks, however. This is because different societies and different people require different political regimes. Some people might be particularly good at ruling themselves, for example, and therefore a regime that allows them to participate in government is preferable. Another society may contain people who desire honor and recognition from others, so that society's best government would bestow honors for good behavior. Aristotle's recognition of differences among people leads him to recommend that governments be judged by what is the "best possible," as opposed to the "best overall."

For Aristotle, despite the existence of several acceptable forms of government, patterns across different regime types can be identified. He explains that governments can rule in the interest of the common good, or they can rule in the interest of themselves (those in power). These regimes can be further divided according to how many people rule in accordance with their ruling principle (one, few, or many). The best regimes rule in the common interest no matter how many people are in charge, and the regimes are identified as monarchies, aristocracies, and constitutional polities. Aristotle believes that any regime that rules in the interest of the common good is acceptable. The problem is that regimes tend toward their deficient forms. No matter who has authority, over time authority will be used by those who have it to pursue self-interest. A political regime is unhealthy, according to Aristotle, when the good of one or a few is held higher than the good of society.

Turning to look at the politics of Springfield with Aristotle in mind, we find that *The Simpsons* contains a similar account of the fate of well-meaning political endeavors. In the episode "They Saved Lisa's Brain,"[3] Lisa's frustration with the stupidity of the town's citizens leads her to join a group of Mensa members. After being bullied out of a rightful gazebo reservation, the Mensa group goes to confront the Mayor about the town's stupider residents controlling the political system. The Mayor, who misunderstands the Mensa members when they storm into his office and declare "The jig is up, Quimby!" leaps out the window to escape what he thinks are corruption charges. Lisa and the members of Mensa soon discover that the town charter declares that in the absence of a mayor, a "council of learned citizens" will rule. When they, the smartest members of the town, take over, Lisa describes their goal as to "use the power of good ideas to change things for the better"—which includes eliminating green stoplights (everyone moves faster for yellow) and renaming the jury the "Justice Squadron," which meets at the "Municipal Fortress of Vengeance" (to make it sound more appealing). The group soon begins to fight among themselves, however, as each member wants to pursue his or her own pet project. When presented at a town meeting, the group's ideas, including a shadow-puppet theater and Comic Book Guy's seven-year breeding plan (based on the Vulcan society in *Star Trek*), cause a violent backlash. Fortunately, Stephen Hawking appears to rescue Lisa from the violence. He shames the naive approach of the "council of geniuses," saying, "I wanted to see your utopia, but now I see it is more of a Fruitopia."

In this episode the town learns Aristotle's lesson about the tendency of even well-meaning regimes to devolve into self-interest and conflict. The common good cannot be trusted to a single person or group of people for very long. The solution to this problem, according to Aristotle, is to create a "mixed regime" wherein several groups of people contribute to decision making. Aristotle compares this mixed regime to a feast, where the number of people and the different contributions they bring add to the stability of the government.[4] The aim of the mixed regime is to sustain a political order that will help its citizens live the best possible life. For Aristotle, the best possible government is one that effectively combines the pursuit of excellence with the behavior of which people are capable.

One of the requirements of stable and effective political structures observed by Aristotle is that people fulfill particular roles within that structure according to their natures.[5] Disorder emerges when people or societies attempt to do things that are outside their natural tendencies or capabilities. The city of Springfield operates according to this Aristotelian principle. All of the characters in *The Simpsons* have particular roles to perform in the town, and Springfield falls into disorder when characters step outside of their naturally defined roles. When Homer runs for political office in "Trash of the Titans," for example, he wins election as sanitation commissioner but fails at the job. Homer is so terrible, and his policies cause so many problems, that the city of Springfield has to literally move (all of the buildings and people) to a different location. The disorder introduced by

Homer's election is corrected when he is removed from office and the town is returned (relocated) to its original position.

Homer's moving out of his normal position within the social order is a common source of disorder, but other characters' changing roles cause disorder as well. In "Bart vs. Lisa vs. the Third Grade,"[6] conflict is created when Bart and Lisa move into the same class. Not only is the sibling relationship disrupted, but the disruption makes it all the way to the governor, whose flag contest is ruined by the competition between Bart and Lisa. The situation is resolved when Principal Skinner moves the two back to their respective classrooms at the end of the episode.

The principal, Seymour Skinner, is involved in his own role dislocation when, in "The Principal and the Pauper,"[7] he is discovered not to be the real Seymour Skinner. In a case of stolen identity, the character Seymour is actually Armin Tamzarian, an imposter who stole the identity of a war hero. When the real Skinner appears after decades as a prisoner of war, Tamzarian leaves town in disgrace and the real Skinner takes over as principal. The town hates the new principal, however, and the episode ends with the town banishing the real Skinner by tying him to a chair on a train. A judge then declares that the old Skinner will have his old job and that no one may mention the name *Tamzarian* again "under penalty of torture."[8] In episodes like this, the town experiences disorder and discomfort when a character or characters are removed from their natural place. Order can be restored only when everyone finds her or his native place within the structure of the town.

Thus, the political theory at the heart of *The Simpsons* prefers order over disorder and maintains the goodness of its characters according to the roles that they play in the broader community. What makes a worthy social order for the people of Springfield is close to Aristotle's description of a good constitution that promotes the common interest and creates a community in which the whole is greater than the parts.[9]

## Education and the Virtuous City

One of the primary political problems for Aristotle, as for the citizens of Springfield, is that members of a community do not always recognize or understand what is in the common interest. A key concern for a political regime is therefore to educate people toward virtuous behavior.[10] The school serves as a central location in much of the action of *The Simpsons,* and it is here that Bart and Lisa learn many of their lessons about civic responsibility and how to behave toward others.

It is at school, for example, that Lisa learns to treat the social outcast Ralph Wiggum with respect after breaking his heart in the episode "I Love Lisa."[11] Bart also learns many moral lessons at school. In the noteworthy episode "Bart Gets a 'Z,'" he plays a prank on his teacher by spiking her drink and causing her to lose her job.[12] When she learns that Bart is the one who was responsible for her lost job, she declares that Bart is the only child she has ever met who was "bad on the inside." Stricken with guilt, Bart decides to confess to the principal and accept his punishment with the hope of getting his teacher her job back. In these episodes school is where grade-obsessed Lisa and hopeless hoodlum Bart learn lessons about compassion and are revealed to have much more complex natures than the superficial way their characters first appear.[13]

The children of Springfield are not the only ones who receive an education under its regime. Adult citizens, too, find many learning experiences, sometimes at the hand of Lisa and other times by a design of tradition. In "Lisa the Iconoclast"[14] Lisa discovers that the town founder and hero, Jebediah Springfield, was actually a pirate who was the enemy of George Washington. While attempting to report the truth about the town's history, Lisa realizes that the memory of Jebediah and the lesson his memorial teaches the town ("A noble spirit embiggens the smallest man") are more important than the truth. Here Lisa learns the lesson that Aristotle promotes as key to the success of a community: the purpose of stories and community celebrations is to make people strive to be better. In accord with Aristotle's (and Lisa's) view, the people of Springfield need to rely on tradition to help them practice virtue, and it is through tradition, including the founding story of the town, that citizens learn values like courage, nobility, and generosity.

Aristotle would go further with the people of Springfield to emphasize that moral character comes about through habituation and exercise. People do not learn virtue through reasoning or deliberation, but through the actual practice of virtues. The practice of virtues, according to Aristotle, teaches people that virtue lies in the avoidance of extremes. The virtue of truth-telling, for example, is the "mean" between the extremes of brash honesty and deceit.[15] In the case of Jebediah Springfield, Lisa makes the virtuous decision to *not* disclose the true identity of the town's hero. The truth in this case is that the town is made better by the myth of Jebediah. In the case of all moral actions, there is a middle ground, and practice with these actions is what makes us virtuous.

## Friendship and the Virtuous Citizen

The existence of friendship within a society is just as important as institutions and traditions of education for the practice of virtuous behavior and the development of excellent citizens. For Aristotle, the shared objectives inherently pursued in a friendship are essential for the development of other virtues and indispensable for the formation of community. Friendship assists in the process of finding the "mean between extremes" (the basis for all virtues) because a friendship requires partnership and compromise. Friendship is also the foundation of community because it is the basis on which people collaborate for common purposes.[16] Ultimately, friendship helps to make people and communities good because people want to treat friends well, and the practice of doing good things for friends habituates us in virtuous behavior that will extend outside of the friendship.

Aristotle also believes that friendship within a society contributes to political stability. Friends are more likely to be patient with each other, and the understanding that exists within a friendship makes it easier to develop compromises. Friendship is even useful when it comes to common defense—friends are more likely to want to defend each other, and they can better coordinate activities pursued for the common interest. Correspondingly, Aristotle observes that friendship is often held in even higher regard than justice, because the bonds of friendship cause people to act in good ways toward each other without external guidelines or rules.[17] Well-developed friendships are the glue that holds society together.

We find the kind of friendship admired by Aristotle prevalent in the city of Springfield. Almost every significant character in *The Simpsons* has a significant friendship with another. Within these friendships the characters complement each other's personality, and in many cases the friends help each other learn things about themselves. Friendships in Springfield also often help the friends make good decisions; it is frequently the advice or actions of a friend that bring a "disordered" person back into the normal order.

Homer Simpson has several such friendships with other characters, but none perhaps are more significant than his friendships with Barney Gumble, the barfly; Ned Flanders, the evangelical Christian neighbor; and Marge, Homer's wife. On the surface, and in most episodes, Barney is the supportive drunk at the other end of the bar, Ned Flanders is the constant source of annoyance who lives next door, and Marge is the patient mate who is always there for support and charitable words of encouragement. When these friendships are featured in episodes, however, we are given a deeper look into the friendships, their meaningfulness, and how they help Homer realize and exercise virtue.

In the episode "Mr. Plow,"[18] Homer decides to buy a snowplow and becomes a hero in the city for the plowing service he provides to pay for his new form of transportation. Barney asks for Homer's advice about how he can become successful, too, and the advice he receives leads Barney to form a rival snowplow business that is more effective than Homer's. Barney's success leads to Homer losing all of his customers (and the key to the city, which is taken from him and given to Barney). When Homer decides to plot revenge against Barney, he sends him to a dangerous place to plow, and Barney becomes trapped by an avalanche caused by one of his burps. After seeing his trapped friend, Homer regrets his actions and rescues Barney. The two friends decide to work together as plowing partners, and Homer declares, "When two best friends work together not even God himself can stop them!" God sees this as a dare and causes all the snow to melt, forcing Homer out of business and returning the town to normal. Although Homer is susceptible to rivalries with his friends, he also maintains a deep commitment to their well-being, and he learns in episodes like "Mr. Plow" that the bonds of friendship are meaningful and important for his happiness.

Homer's friendship with Ned Flanders is more complex. Superficially, Homer views Flanders as his arch-nemesis, mostly because he is jealous of the perfect life that Flanders seems to lead. Feeding Homer's apparent hatred is the cheerfulness with which Flanders approaches all interactions with Homer. In "Homer Loves Flanders,"[19] however, these roles reverse. Flanders wins tickets to a football game that Homer desperately wants to attend and invites Homer to go with him. Homer has a great time at the game and decides that Flanders is his best friend. Homer's overbearing gratefulness annoys Flanders, causing Flanders to declare that he is beginning to hate Homer. Homer's pursuit of Flanders's company drives Flanders to the edge and ultimately prompts him to yell at Homer in the middle of church. The shocked congregation embarrasses Flanders, but Homer comes to his defense and convinces everyone that Flanders deserves another chance. Even though the relationship quickly returns to normal (Homer is back to

HOMER SIMPSON PONDERS POLITICS: POPULAR CULTURE
AS POLITICAL THEORY; ED. BY JOSEPH J. FOY.
                              Cloth     264 P.
LEXINGTON: UNIV PR OF KENTUCKY, 2013


ED: UNIV. OF WISCONSIN-WAUKESHA. COLLECTION OF
NEW ARTICLES.

  **ISBN** 0813141478      **Library PO#** FIRM ORDERS

                                    **List**     35.00   USD
   8395 NATIONAL UNIVERSITY LIBRAR   **Disc**     14.0%
   **App. Date**   5/07/14   SOC-SCI     8214-08 **Net**     30.10   USD

SUDJ. POLITICS & CULTURE--U.S.--20TH CENT.


CLASS JA75.7          DEWEY# 306.20973      LEVEL GEN-AC

---

**YBP Library Services**


HOMER SIMPSON PONDERS POLITICS: POPULAR CULTURE
AS POLITICAL THEORY; ED. BY JOSEPH J. FOY.
                              Cloth     264 P.
LEXINGTON: UNIV PR OF KENTUCKY, 2013


ED: UNIV. OF WISCONSIN-WAUKESHA. COLLECTION OF
NEW ARTICLES.

  **ISBN** 0813141478      **Library PO#** FIRM ORDERS

                                    **List**     35.00   USD
   8395 NATIONAL UNIVERSITY LIBRAR   **Disc**     14.0%
   **App. Date**   5/07/14   SOC-SCI     8214-08 **Net**     30.10   USD

SUBJ: POLITICS & CULTURE--U.S.--20TH CENT.


CLASS JA75.7          DEWEY# 306.20973      LEVEL GEN-AC

"hating" Flanders the next week), in this episode Homer's virtue is cultivated and displayed through his friendship with Flanders.

The most significant relationship that Homer has is with his wife, Marge. Throughout *The Simpsons* series, Marge demonstrates an enduring and unconditional devotion to her husband, and he frequently expresses his gratitude for her fidelity and compassion.[20] Marge is especially useful to Homer as the understanding friend who encourages him after his plans go awry. Homer attempts to be just as supportive for Marge, but this support occasionally backfires. In one such episode, "The Twisted World of Marge Simpson," several levels of their friendship are demonstrated.[21] Here, Marge is thrown out of an investment group, the Springfield Investorettes, for refusing to take high risks. Homer encourages Marge to start her own business, and she starts a pretzel business that is less than successful. In support of Marge, Homer makes a deal with the Mob to make Marge's business profitable, but the plan backfires when mobster Fat Tony demands 100 percent of the profits. When the Simpsons refuse to pay the Mob, they are rescued by the Investorettes, accompanied by Japanese organized crime. Homer's devotion to Marge is demonstrated in this episode, along with Marge's ability to forgive. The honesty of Homer's confession allows them to work together as a couple toward a solution and brings them closer together.

Aristotle recognizes the partnership of marriage as a significant "institution of friendship" that advances civility, decency, and a common social life.[22] Homer's relationship with Marge keeps him grounded in reality and usually prevents him from engaging in completely antisocial behavior. But even Marge is occasionally capable of selfish and disorderly behavior. Nevertheless, it is through their relationship that one always manages to recover and redeem the other.

## Friendship and the Divided Soul

Another characteristic of the friendship between Marge and Homer, and other partnerships we find in *The Simpsons,* is that one person in the relationship typically represents the "rational" approach while the other is driven by appetites and desires. This dualism is a direct reflection of Aristotle's depiction of the soul as being divided into two parts, the rational and the nonrational.[23] For Aristotle, these parts of the soul are both essential to its functions, but the rational must be developed out of the nonrational. He sees the nonrational as a natural immaturity of the soul and believes that through education the rational emerges. The rational part, then, should rule the irrational, both in the individual and in the well-ordered society.

Other key partnerships of other characters correspond to the same relational split between rationality and irrationality that we find in Marge and Homer's relationship. Lisa and Bart also illustrate the pairing of rationality and appetite, as does the relationship between Waylon Smithers and Montgomery Burns.[24] In each of these cases, one of the characters in the relationship is the voice of reason for the other, whereas the character embodying appetite is often the source of adventure, but also disorder. The tension between these different character types usually creates friction between the characters, but it is also the force of attraction that keeps them bound to each other. In part this attraction allows one of the pair to live vicariously through the other. The attraction also exists because the nonrational character recognizes that he or she needs the reasoning character to resolve problems and reestablish order. In these cases, the characters of Marge, Lisa, and Smithers, insofar as they are coupled with their corresponding partner, are reliably able to rein in the disorder that the appetites of the others tend to bring about.

Following the Aristotelian model, embedded in *The Simpsons'* depiction of these pairs is a critique of the gendered way in which Aristotle conceives of rationality and irrationality. For Aristotle, a male is more naturally fitted to rule than a female because the rationality of men is naturally more developed than that of females and because men naturally have the ability to command more authority than women.[25] For the relationships in *The Simpsons,* the opposite is true. In each case the female (or feminine) side of the pair is the one most grounded in reason, and it is the male who is a slave to his appetites. Homer is susceptible to being tempted by any desire that is immediately apparent to him, and Marge provides the balance and influence of reason.[26] Bart's appetite for making mischief gets him into frequent trouble, and although Lisa is often frustrated by her older brother, she takes pride in her ability to offer advice to get him out of that trouble. The millionaire Burns is most inclined to pursue his appetite for money, but Smithers offers a voice of reason, tempering Burns's greed with a concern for the long-term stability of his business and an attentive view toward public relations.

For the key characters in these relationships, the balance between reason and appetite is essential for preserving order, both within the friendship and in the city of Springfield. It is not possible, or desirable, to eliminate the appetites, since the "trouble" caused by their pursuit provides many opportunities for the town and delivers much of the richness it enjoys. It is essential, however, for reason to keep the appetites under control, since the disorder that exists without the force of reason would break the relationships and the city apart. From an Aristotelian perspective, the paired relationships in *The Simpsons* serve as a metaphor for the soul, for which desires are followed but in which reason is respected.

Furthermore, from Aristotle's point of view, the different parts of the soul each have something crucial to offer. Aristotle argues that it is foolish simply to consider generalities when describing the good soul,[27] since the virtues are better enumerated to account for the many contexts and situations that require different kinds of actions and different forms and applications of virtue. Thus, in Aristotle's account, the moderating force of reason provided by Marge, Lisa, and Smithers is important for the pursuit of virtue, just as there is an important place in the soul and in the city, given particular purposes and circumstances, for the appetites of Homer, Bart, and Mr. Burns.

## The Well-Ordered Springfield

Through *The Simpsons'* mix of characters and the adventures that occur in the program, in every episode the town of Springfield moves from disorder back to order. The overt messaging in *The Simpsons* that seems cynical about conventional politics and social relationships is intelligible only on a foundation of a political theory that aims at something better. Even in the episodes about the fundamental dysfunction of citizens and politics, the system ultimately works, and *The Simpsons* usually offers a defense of the effectiveness of conventional political structures.[28] Within its order the community of Springfield is stable because all of the different characters, and their relationships with each other, hold it together. Each person has a specific role and place for which she or he is well suited. Moreover, the city of Springfield is stable at its core because the family, namely the Simpsons, is its cornerstone. Different members of the family are good at different things, allowing the family to pursue a common interest with the strengths of each member added to the pursuit.

As a family in which all members participate in its management, and a family that includes a diversity of virtues among its members, in the final analysis the Simpson family serves in part as a critique of Aristotle. In his *Politics* Aristotle notoriously defends the subordination of women and children within his conception of "nature."[29] Contrary to Aristotle's depiction, the Simpson family offers a strong case that a relationship of justice within a family is more parallel to the just organization of the political order. In *The Simpsons* we find a family that is a community of people whose different natures promote the overall well-being of the family. Homer occasionally asserts himself as the "head of the household," but the virtuousness of his decisions is usually questionable and needs to be tempered through interventions by other members of the family. *The Simpsons* suggests that the same logic Aristotle applies to the mixed regime in the political community can also apply to that of the family. Using Aristotle's statement about the ideal constitution, we see that it pertains to the Simpson family as much as it does to the political order: the best life for a city (and for human beings) should be judged "neither by a virtue that is beyond the reach of ordinary people, nor by a kind of education that requires natural gifts and resources that depend on luck, nor by the ideal constitution, but by a life that most people can share and a constitution in which most city-states can participate."[30]

The crucial question to ask from the perspective of Aristotle's ethics and politics remains: is Springfield happy? For Aristotle happiness is life's highest possibility and is the condition that means a purpose has been fulfilled. The goal of an individual life, and the goal of a city, is to be good at what it is supposed to do and to practice the virtues that will achieve this kind of happiness. While it is true that Homer (and other citizens in Springfield) represents a hedonistic view of happiness, episodes do not conclude with this view being rewarded. The source of disorder through the action of each episode is the pursuit of appetites and characters moving outside of their proper place within the social order. Happiness in Springfield returns at the end of every episode because people are placed back into the natural order of the town, given the exercise of different virtues by the characters who intervene through the course of the story.

In this way, *The Simpsons* holds an Aristotelian mirror to our ethical, social, and political lives and presents us with reflections of ourselves and our social and political order. Political theory presented in a performance as entertaining, profound, and relevant as *The Simpsons* should cause us to reflect on the following questions: What is the proper authority structure for the kind of people we find ourselves to be? Are our values and purposes reflected in our political order? What are the sources of disorder in our society, and how do we recover from them? How do we promote virtue, both in personal relationships and through political and social structures?

Answering these questions requires an investigation into who we are, what we value, and how we want to live our lives. Aristotle and *The Simpsons* recommend that we be honest and realistic as we consider these questions, and Aristotle pushes us to actively pursue the best possible life for ourselves and our society. Motivated by the pursuit of excellence, we should engage in political theory striving for a life that is better, in the context of what is possible for us to achieve.

## Notes

1. For discussions of social dissent and political messaging in *The Simpsons,* see Matthew Henry, "Gabbin' about God: Religion, Secularity, and Satire on *The Simpsons,*" in *Homer Simpson Marches on Washington: Dissent through American Popular Culture,* ed. Timothy M. Dale and Joseph J. Foy (Lexington: University Press of Kentucky, 2010); and J. Michael Blitzer, "Political Culture and Public Opinion: The American Dream on Springfield's Evergreen Terrace," in *Homer Simpson Goes to Washington: American Politics through Popular Culture,* ed. Joseph J. Foy (Lexington: University Press of Kentucky, 2008).

2. Aristotle, *Politics,* trans. C. D. C. Reeve (New York: Hackett, 1998), 1252a.

3. Season 10, episode 22.

4. Aristotle writes that "a city-state consists of many people, just like a feast to which many contribute, and is better than one that is a unity and simple. . . . A large quantity is more incorruptible, so the multitude . . . are more incorruptible than the few." *Politics* 1286a.

5. Aristotle describes the city as a "composite of many parts," and these parts are the "natural material" out of which the city is built. *Politics* 1274b38, 1325b40.

6. Season 14, episode 3.

7. Season 9, episode 2.

8. Ken Keeler, on the DVD commentary, explains, "This [episode] is about a community of people who like things just the way they are. Skinner's not really close to these people—you know, he's a minor character—but they get upset when someone comes in and says, 'This is not really the way things are,' and they run the messenger out of town on the rail. When the episode aired, lo and behold, a community of people who like things just the way they are got mad. It never seems to have occurred to anyone that this episode is about the people who hate it." Ken Keeler, commentary for "The Principal and the Pauper," in *The Simpsons: The Complete Ninth Season,* by Dan Castellaneta, Julie Kavner, and Nancy Cartwright (Beverly Hills, CA: 20th Century Fox Home Entertainment, 2006), DVD.

9. Aristotle, *Politics* 1279a30.

10. Ibid., 1337a. For Aristotle, education is the best way to preserve a regime, should be the primary concern for a society, and should suit the particular constitution.

11. Season 4, episode 15.

12. Season 21, episode 2.

13. The voice of reason and conscience, in more episodes than any other character, is Lisa, who provides frequent moral lessons to members of her family and others in Springfield. With her saxophone by her side, Lisa is also closely associated with music. This is a significant point for an Aristotelian interpretation of *The Simpsons*, since education in music is important for promoting virtue, according to Aristotle. *Politics* 1340a.

14. Season 7, episode 15.

15. Aristotle, *Nicomachean Ethics,* trans. Terence Irwin (Indianapolis: Hackett, 1999), 1103a15–20, 1104a20–25, 1107a35–40, 1108a20–25.

16. Ibid., 1167a25. Aristotle uses the term "concord" here to refer to the condition of friendship in which the citizens in a city "agree about what is advantageous, make the same decisions, and act on their common resolution."

17. Ibid., 1155a23–25.

18. Season 4, episode 9.

19. Season 5, episode 16.

20. In "A Streetcar Named Marge" (season 4, episode 2), Homer outwardly wonders why Marge does not deserve someone better than him, and in "The Last Temptation of Homer" (season 5, episode 9), even when tempted by the "perfect woman" for him, Homer endearingly admits that he has already found Marge, who is the perfect woman for him.

21. Season 8, episode 11.

22. Aristotle, *Politics* 1280b35.

23. Aristotle comments: "As soul and body are two, so we observe that the soul also has two parts, the irrational part and the part possessing reason, and that the states which they experience are two in number, the one being desire and the other intelligence; and as the body is prior in its development to the soul, so the irrational part of the soul is prior to the rational. And this also is obvious, because passion and will, and also appetite, exist in children even as soon as they are born, but it is the nature of reasoning and intelligence to arise in them as they grow older. Therefore in the first place it is necessary for the training of the body to precede that of the mind, and secondly for the training of the appetite to precede that of the intelligence; but the training of the appetite must be for the sake of the intellect, and that of the body for the sake of the soul." Ibid., 1334b20.

24. In the episode "Blood Feud" (season 2, episode 22), Mr. Burns refers to Smithers as the "gentle ying to his [Burns's] raging yang."

25. Aristotle, *Politics* 1259b, 1260a13.

26. In "Secrets of a Successful Marriage" (season 5, episode 22), Homer completely collapses after Marge kicks him out for sharing personal stories about their marriage with his adult learning annex class.

27. Aristotle, *Politics* 1260a25.

28. In "Mr. Lisa Goes to Washington" (season 3, episode 2), for example, Lisa confronts the corruption of politics by writing an essay about it, but she loses the essay

competition. The episode ultimately resolves Lisa's disillusionment, however, because the corrupt representative is thrown in jail and the system is proven to work.

29. Aristotle, *Politics* 1259b.

30. Ibid., 1295a.

# 3

# "KEEP YOUR FRIENDS CLOSE BUT YOUR ENEMIES CLOSER"

## Machiavelli and Michael Corleone

*Eric T. Kasper*

In Mario Puzo's bestselling novel *The Godfather,* published in 1969, he told the story of a fictional mafia family in America. The book was famously made into a successful and award-winning film, *The Godfather* (1972), as well as a sequel-prequel, *The Godfather Part II* (1974), and a sequel, *The Godfather Part III* (1990). These movies relate the saga of the Corleone crime family, including the transition of power from one generation of the family to the next. The main character in all three films, Michael Corleone, quickly becomes the embodiment of the political philosophy of Niccolò Machiavelli in *The Prince.* Although at first Corleone is repelled by the seamy underbelly of the "family business," a series of violent events in *The Godfather* turn him from an idealist to a consequentialist who thirsts for political power. Indeed, examples of Machiavellian realism occur in many of Michael Corleone's words and deeds throughout the *Godfather* film franchise.

Niccolò Machiavelli wrote *The Prince* nearly five hundred years ago to the Florentine ruler Lorenzo II de' Medici, apparently to serve as a political how-to manual for the royal ruler. Machiavelli's overarching goal in the work is the attainment of Italian unity, but the book can also teach the reader much about power politics. Machiavelli, considered by many political theorists to be the first modern political philosopher, emphasizes the notions that the ends justify the means and that one must be willing to use force if necessary to achieve one's political goals. In other words, Machiavelli tried to describe how politics really occurs, not how it should be. It is for this reason that Machiavelli is not only a proper noun today—the term *Machiavellian* is now a derisive and pejorative adjective that represents "the view that politics is amoral and that any means however unscrupulous can justifiably be used in achieving political power." This chapter uses *The Godfather's* Michael Corleone as a teaching tool to explain and explore the political philosophy of Machiavelli in *The Prince*.[1]

## Michael Corleone and Niccolò Machiavelli

The character of Michael Corleone emerged out of the novel *The Godfather* in the late 1960s. In both the book and the film adaptations directed by Francis Ford Coppola, the character of Michael (played by Al Pacino in the film trilogy) at first seems like a poor choice for a Machiavellian prince. The youngest of the family's sons, he chooses to attend college and later to serve in the U.S. Marine Corps in World War II, rather than be a part of the family business. On the surface his father, Vito Corleone (played at different ages by Marlon Brando and Robert De Niro) runs an olive oil importation business, but that is only a cover for criminal activities, including gambling, bribery, and extortion. This is something in which Michael's brothers, Santino (James Caan), Tom (Robert Duvall), and Fredo (John Cazale), are willing to participate. Yet, the young Michael initially rejects these activities, telling his girlfriend Kay Adams (Diane Keaton) in the mid-1940s in *The Godfather*, "That's my family, Kay; it's not me." Michael's desire apparently is to marry Kay, settle down, and make an honest living, eschewing the power politics and dishonest behavior of his father and brothers.

This rather inauspicious start for Michael is the exact opposite of Niccolò Machiavelli's early career. To understand this difference, one needs to realize that while Michael Corleone grew up in a wealthy, powerful mafia family, Machiavelli was born in 1469 in Florence, in a disunited and weak Italy. Indeed, during Machiavelli's youth and adulthood, Italy was not one country; it was divided into several city-states. The more united foreign powers at the time (such as France, Spain, and the Holy Roman Empire) had more influence in European affairs, and over the Italian people, in the late fifteenth and early sixteenth centuries, because these nations possessed more people and more resources by being unified. This relative weakness of the Italian city-states, including his native Florentine Republic, was the backdrop of Machiavelli's political education. To better protect the interests of Italy, he wanted to acquire power in ways that young Michael did not during his privileged upbringing.[2]

At age twenty-nine in 1498, Machiavelli took the post of secretary to the second Chancery in the Florentine Republic. In this civil service position, he soon began receiving additional responsibilities, especially over foreign affairs. Machiavelli met with leaders of other countries and was sent on many diplomatic missions. It was during this period that he gained an astute understanding of politics and international affairs. All of this came to an abrupt halt, however, when the Medici family came to power in Florence in 1512 and restored it to a monarchy. The Florentine Republic suddenly was no more. This turn of events also signaled the end of Machiavelli's position of leadership and political power.[3]

In contrast, a series of shocking events in young Michael Corleone's life ultimately propelled him to greater and greater power. When another mobster, Virgil "The Turk" Sollozzo of the Tattaglia crime family, makes an attempt on his father's life, Michael starts taking matters into his own hands. Michael kills those responsible for shooting his father, and in this way he begins what becomes a meteoric rise to the top of the power structure in the mafia family. After both his first wife, Apollonia, and his brother Santino are killed by rival gangsters, Michael eventually becomes the "don," or boss, of the Corleone crime family. For decades he continues to rule over the criminal empire that his father built, first in New York and then in Reno, Nevada. Along the way, Michael navigates through many political minefields and leads the family to much financial success via illegal activities and gambling pursuits. According to *The Godfather Part III*, by the time Michael goes into retirement in 1980, the Corleone family's wealth is estimated to be in the hundreds of millions of dollars.

As for Machiavelli, his career took a turn for the worse. When the Medicis took power, they thought him to be a conspirator against the royal family, and for this he was not only fired; for a brief time he was imprisoned and tortured. After two months he was released and banished to private life. Being unemployed in his early forties, Machiavelli attempted to cull favor with the new royal family by writing *The Prince* in 1513 as a political "how-to" manual for those who govern. Machiavelli dedicated the work to Lorenzo II de' Medici, who later became the duke of Urbino, in an attempt to teach him the proper tactics that one could use to be successful in politics.[4] As Machiavelli notes in his dedicatory letter in *The Prince*, it is customary for those who wish to gain favor with a monarch to bestow a precious gift upon him or her. However, since Machiavelli had no tangible possessions of note, he wrote *The Prince* for Lorenzo, to share with him his "knowledge of the deeds of great men," which he had "acquired through a long experience of modern events and a constant study of the past" (3). The knowledge that Machiavelli espouses in *The Prince* is largely amoral. Machiavelli rarely indicated whether something was good or evil, instead advising the reader what would be effective.

Although Michael Corleone is fictional and Machiavelli was real, each one experienced power politics, one in the criminal underworld and the other on the international stage. The career of one culminated in a significant building of power, while the other had everything taken from him while still relatively young. Still, each of these men of Italian heritage lives on and has influence. In Michael Corleone's case, he is, according to the American Film Institute, the eleventh-greatest villain in motion picture history, with *The Godfather* film ranked as the second-greatest movie in American history.[5] Al Pacino's performance and the story of *The Godfather* have been alluded to in many art forms since the early 1970s, and hundreds of television programs and movies have referred to the film in the subsequent four decades.[6] As for Machiavelli, his influence has gone far beyond his immediate intended audience of Lorenzo, as people around the world still read *The Prince* a half millennium later. According to one scholar, *The Prince* is the most famous book on politics ever written.[7] Now let's look more closely at Michael Corleone in *The Godfather*, to understand the themes espoused by Machiavelli in *The Prince*.

## The Lion and the Fox

From the very beginning of his rise to power, Michael Corleone demonstrates his understanding of a key analogy from *The Prince*, that of the lion and the fox. Machiavelli explains that a great leader will know how to fight both by law and by force and that using only one method is insufficient. The two can be characterized as fighting by the methods of humans and by the methods of beasts. Machiavelli then divides the methods of fighting like beasts into the methods of the lion and of the fox: "A prince being thus obliged to know well how to act as a beast must imitate the fox and the lion, for the lion cannot protect himself from traps, and the fox cannot defend himself from wolves. One must therefore be a fox to recognize traps, and a lion to frighten wolves. Those that wish to be only lions do not understand this" (64). Machiavelli's point here is that a successful leader will exhibit both strength (the lion) and cunning (the fox) when appropriate. If one tries to strong-arm opponents when one is weak, one will lose; conversely, if one acts too craftily when one could attack with sufficient force, one is wasting resources. Thus, a great leader will be a beast in both the manner of the lion and that of the fox, depending on what is necessary.

Michael Corleone acts as the fox early on in *The Godfather*. When he visits his father in the hospital after an attack on Vito's life, Michael finds that the guards being paid to protect his father have left. After moving his father to another room, Michael encounters Enzo, a baker and family friend who has brought flowers to Vito at the hospital. Michael asks Enzo to stand at the entrance to the hospital. It is night and they are both wearing overcoats, but neither one is armed. Michael, acting like the fox, tells Enzo to get rid of the flowers and says, "Put your hand in your pocket like you have a gun." Michael does the same, and the two of them standing there are enough to scare away the hired killers, who continue driving past the hospital's entrance, rather than confront persons whom they believe to be Don Vito's armed guards.

Shortly thereafter, Michael demonstrates that he can also act like a Machiavellian lion (with a touch of the strategic fox). It becomes readily apparent that Sollozzo has bribed a police captain, McCluskey, to try to make Vito Corleone more vulnerable at the hospital. When Michael confronts the officer about this, Captain McCluskey punches Michael in the face, breaking his jaw. A few days later, other members of the Corleone family arrange for Michael to meet with Sollozzo and McCluskey, under the pretenses that Michael will patch things up with the two men. Something much more sinister is being planned by Michael, however. A revolver is strategically planted in the restroom of the restaurant where they plan to meet. Michael, who is searched by Captain McCluskey when he is picked up, is excused from the table at the restaurant to use the restroom, and when he returns, he shoots and kills both men. In this case, unlike the one involving Enzo, Michael is powerful enough, via a handgun, to use force.

There is another instance of Michael as a fox in *The Godfather Part II*. Michael is subpoenaed to testify before a U.S. Senate committee that is investigating organized crime. During his testimony, Michael denies involvement in the mafia. However, the government has Frank Pentangeli, a *caporegime* (a high-ranking member or captain) in the Corleone family who took direct criminal orders from Michael. Pentangeli is offered immunity for his criminal acts if he will testify that Michael is the don of the family business; if this happens, Michael is sure to be indicted for perjury. Pentangeli is heavily guarded by FBI agents at an army base, so Michael cannot have him killed. However, playing the fox, Michael arranges for Pentangeli's brother, who lives in Sicily, to appear at Pentangeli's Senate committee testimony. This sends a clear message to Pentangeli—that he is breaking a code of silence if he testifies, which will bring both shame and misfortune on his family. Pentangeli refuses to implicate Michael in any criminal activities before the Senate committee. Later, Michael sends his brother, Tom, to inform Pentangeli that if he commits suicide, Pentangeli's family will not be harmed. Shortly thereafter, Pentangeli slits his wrists. This is another demonstration that Michael could use cunning to accomplish his goals at a time when he did not have the power to carry out a hit on someone so well guarded as Frank Pentangeli.

## Committing All of One's Cruelties at Once

Another important Machiavellian skill that Michael Corleone exhibits is when to carry out one's actions. Early in *The Prince,* Machiavelli explains how different types of principalities need to be ruled according to how a prince acquires them or based on the makeup of the territory and the people who live there. When describing the correct course of action for those who attain power by "villainy," Machiavelli states that cruelty may be necessary "for the need of securing one's self" and ensuring that one is established as the leader, rather than for the sake of being cruel (34). As will be explored in more detail below, Machiavelli has in mind that cruelties should be committed only in the service of a greater good. He then clarifies by stating:

> In taking a state the conqueror must arrange to commit all his cruelties at once, so as not to have to recur to them every day, and so as to be able, by not making fresh changes, to reassure people and win them over by benefiting them. Whoever acts otherwise, either through timidity or bad counsels, is always obliged to stand with a knife in hand, and can never depend on his subjects, because they, owing to continually fresh injuries, are unable to depend upon him. For injuries should be done all together, so that being less tasted, they will give less offense. Benefits should be granted little by little, so that they may be better enjoyed. (35)

In other words, Machiavelli tells us that when a leader comes to power, especially if that leader comes to power by force, she or he should commit all necessary acts of cruelty at once, thereby wiping out potential enemies right away and winning the support of those who have not been harmed. Otherwise, the ruler risks being distrusted by followers, as they will never know whether they will be the next ones to be killed.

Michael Corleone follows this advice quite well in *The Godfather*. After his brother Santino died, Michael became the next logical choice to replace his father as the don. Although Vito Corleone was in semiretirement for some time in his later years, it was not until Vito died that Michael completely took over the family business. Shortly thereafter, Michael has a number of rival dons and traitors to the family killed, including *caporegime* Salvatore Tessio (played by Abe Vigoda) and his own brother-in-law, Carlo Rizzi. In all, Michael has at least seven potential enemies killed on the same day right after he takes over, in a move that Michael characterizes as follows: "Today, I settle all family business." His statement also signaled to all remaining members of the Corleone crime family that they were trusted. Machiavelli would approve of this move as a very effective way for a leader like Michael to finalize his ascension to power.

## Deception and the Need to "Keep Your Friends Close but Your Enemies Closer"

Michael Corleone deceives many people throughout the *Godfather* film trilogy. In a similar vein, throughout *The Prince*, Machiavelli stresses the importance of using deception to accomplish one's goals in politics. This is because Machiavelli sees deception as a key tool to ensure that a leader is able to be successful. After describing some traditionally laudable qualities, Machiavelli states: "It is not, therefore, necessary for a prince to have all of the above-mentioned [good] qualities, but it is very necessary to seem to have them. I would even be bold to say to possess them and always observe them is dangerous, but to appear to possess them is useful. Thus it is well to seem merciful, faithful, humane, sincere, religious, and also to be so; but you must have the mind so disposed that when it is needful to be otherwise you may be able to change to the opposite qualities" (65). Machiavelli's point is that a great ruler must at least appear to be a "good" person to win the support of the people and to have them think that he or she is a moral person. However, always following these virtues can leave a leader vulnerable to an unscrupulous enemy, so the leader must also be willing to act in less moral ways by being deceptive. Put another way, in the words of Machiavelli, one must "be able to do evil if constrained" (65).

Michael Corleone follows this advice, and he does so for reasons remarkably similar to Machiavelli's. For instance, Michael interrogates his brother-in-law Carlo for information about who tried to set him up by telling him, "Don't be afraid, Carlo. Come on, do you think I'd make my sister a widow? I'm Godfather to your son." In fact, after Carlo tells Michael what he needs to know, Michael has him killed mere minutes later.

Michael tries to deceive his enemies quite a bit in the three *Godfather* films. Michael's signature line in this regard occurs in a scene early in *The Godfather Part II*. Michael visits Frank Pentangeli at a time when Pentangeli is still acting as a *caporegime* for Michael. Michael confides in Pentangeli that he knows Hyman Roth, an old business associate of his father, tried to kill him. Pentangeli then says, "Let's hit 'em all. Let's hit 'em all now, while we got the muscle." Michael, in another example of Machiavellian fox behavior, reveals that he is playing this game at a much higher level. He replies, "My father taught me many things. . . . He taught me, keep your friends close but your enemies closer. Now, if Hyman Roth sees that I interceded in this thing, and the Rosato brothers failed him, he's gonna think his relationship with me is still good. . . . That's what I want him to think. I want him completely relaxed, and confident, in our friendship. Then I'll be able to find out who the traitor in my family was." In the film, Michael does not want to kill Roth (even though he clearly can) because he needs to keep Roth alive to find out which member of his family betrayed him. At the same time, that one line, "Keep your friends close but your enemies closer," is the ultimate example of Machiavellian deception: Michael is making someone who is his enemy think that he considers him a close confidant. All the while, however, Michael is using Roth, whom he ultimately has killed at the end of *The Godfather Part II*.

Michael is also quite deceptive with his own wife, Kay, on whose behalf he always claims to be acting. For instance, in *The Godfather*, Michael's sister Connie (played by Talia Shire) is distraught because she has figured out that Michael killed her husband, Carlo. Upon hearing Connie's allegation, Kay asks Michael if it is true, and he denies it. In *The Godfather Part II*, Kay asks Michael when the family business will be legitimate, and Michael claims that he is trying to no longer be involved in criminal activities, even though he is really making no effort in that direction.

Yet, all of this deception pales in comparison to Michael's deception when it comes to religion. Throughout the films, he pretends to be a devoutly religious Catholic while he is also committing immoral acts. One of the more notable moments in this regard occurs in *The Godfather* when Michael agrees to be godfather to Connie and Carlo's son. During the christening, the priest asks Michael a series of questions about his faith. Michael agrees that he believes in God, Jesus Christ, the Holy Ghost, and the Catholic Church. He also agrees that he renounces Satan, all of his works, and all of his pomps. But even as he is making these statements in the church, Michael's henchmen are murdering rival mafia dons and other people in cold blood. Michael continues this use of religious deception in *The Godfather Part III* when he receives papal honors for his charitable work. Kay, however, who by this time has divorced Michael, is not fooled. She tells him, "I didn't come here to see you disguised by your church. I think that was a shameful ceremony."

Returning to *The Prince*, deception with respect to one's religion is something that Machiavelli emphasizes repeatedly. When describing the need to appear to be a moral person, Machiavelli advises: "A prince must take great care that nothing goes out of his mouth which is not . . . mercy, faith, integrity, humanity, and religion. And nothing is more necessary than to seem to have this last quality, for men in general judge more by the eyes than by the hands, for everyone can see, but very few have to feel" (65–66). For Machiavelli, a ruler must appear to be religious, as this puts others at ease that the leader is a good person, allowing her or him to continue engaging in illicit activities without raising suspicion. Clearly, this same sentiment was shared by the character of Michael Corleone.

## Acting for the Greater Good: Why the Ends Justify the Means

Upon reading the preceding paragraphs, one might get the impression that both Michael Corleone and Machiavelli are cold, heartless thugs who mercilessly and sadistically advocate killing on a whim. According to their words, however, nothing could be further from the truth. Both men shun the use of deception and similar tactics simply for their own sakes. Instead, they agree that a great leader is one who acts for the greater good. For example, at one point in *The Prince*, when describing the barbarous cruelty and inhumanity of an ancient king, Agathocles the Sicilian, Machiavelli makes the following observation: "It cannot be called virtue to kill one's fellow-citizens, betray one's friends, be without faith, without pity, and without religion; by these methods one may indeed gain power but not glory" (32). Thus, contrary to popular belief, it appears that Machiavelli did have something of a moral compass. Indeed, he thought that cruelty or atrocities committed for no greater reasons were reprehensible. Thus, great leaders will not act in this way.

What, then, is the ultimate goal for Machiavelli? He states in *The Prince* that "in the actions of men, and especially of princes, from which there is no appeal, the end justifies the means" (66). This is the most succinct statement of Machiavellian philosophy, at least what he espouses in *The Prince:* that the end justifies the means. For Machiavelli, the great end is the good of the people, especially the good of the Italian people. As is clear from his statement regarding Agathocles, Machiavelli thought the overall good of the people was important. Indeed, toward the end of *The Prince,* he begs Lorenzo (his most direct intended audience) to work toward the good of the Italian people and the unification of Italy. In his last chapter, titled "Exhortation to Liberate Italy from the Barbarians," Machiavelli implores Lorenzo: "This opportunity must not, therefore, be allowed to pass, so that Italy may at length find her liberator" (98). Clearly, this greater goal of the good of the people, more specifically for Machiavelli the good of the Italian people, was the end that justified the means described above. In pursuit of such goals, a leader should encourage the people to close ranks against outsiders. It is only by acting immorally that a leader can accomplish great things for the people. As the old saying goes, if you want to make an omelet, you have to break a few eggs.

The character Michael Corleone has a similar goal. He believes (or fools himself into believing) that he commits various crimes, including murders, for the good of his family. He sees his family as the ultimate entity that he must protect. For instance, in *The Godfather,* Michael travels to Las Vegas to meet with Moe Greene (played by Alex Rocco) in an attempt to buy out Greene's share of a casino-hotel that the Corleone family partly owns. Greene proceeds to argue with Michael, refusing to sell his portion of the business, and Fredo comes to Greene's defense. After Greene leaves, Michael turns to Fredo and says, "Fredo. You're my older brother and I love you. But don't ever take sides with anyone against the family again. Ever." Michael believed that Fredo overstepped his bounds by siding with Greene, especially in public, which made Michael appear to be a weak leader and worked against the ultimate good of the family.

The emphasis on the importance of acting to protect his family exists for Michael throughout the *Godfather* trilogy. In *The Godfather Part II,* he has a heart-to-heart talk with his mother shortly before her death, in which he worries about losing his family. He wonders if by being strong for his family, he might lose it. At this point, Michael is realizing that the acts of cruelty he has committed against others, acts that he thought needed to be done to protect the family, might not be understood by his family, particularly his wife and children. Michael's concern for his family extends to *The Godfather Part III*, where he shouts in an argument with Kay, "I spent my life protecting my son. I spent my life protecting my family! . . . I did what I could Kay, to protect all of you from the horrors of this world."

Michael's protection of his family members had its limits, though. If family members betray Michael, he no longer sees them as part of the family. This was evident in his order to murder his brother-in-law Carlo after Carlo worked with a rival mafia family. He also distances himself from Fredo in *The Godfather Part II* after learning that Fredo conspired with the rival gangsters who tried to kill Michael. Michael's statement to Fredo is telling: "Fredo, you're nothing to me now. You're not a brother, you're not a friend. I don't want to know you or what you do." Fredo was no longer a member of the family in Michael's eyes, and he was thus someone whom Michael no longer felt obligated to protect. Toward the end of the second *Godfather* film, Michael has Fredo killed. Since Fredo was no longer his brother, Michael could justify killing Fredo in the name of the greater good, the good of the Corleone family. This reasoning is remarkably similar to what Machiavelli prescribed.

## The Difference between the Powerful and the People

Implicit in Machiavelli's statement cited above ("in the actions of men, and especially of princes, from which there is no appeal, the end justifies the means") is the notion that leaders should be held to different standards than average people. It is clear that Machiavelli intends the audience of *The Prince* to be leaders (recall the language from his dedicatory letter), and it is equally clear that he was not advocating that every person in society use the types of tactics he wrote of in *The Prince*.

Michael Corleone believed in this sentiment as well. In *The Godfather*, after Michael has returned to America from Sicily, he tells Kay that he would like to see her again. Kay questions Michael why he would work for his father in the family business, something a few years earlier he claimed he would never do:

MICHAEL. I'm working for my father now, Kay. He's been sick, very sick.

KAY. But you're not like him, Michael. I thought you weren't going to become a man like your father. That's what you told me.

MICHAEL. My father's no different than any other powerful man.

KAY. Hah.

MICHAEL. Any man who's responsible for other people—like a senator or a president.

KAY. You know how naïve you sound?

MICHAEL. Why?

KAY. Senators and presidents don't have men killed.

MICHAEL. Oh, who's being naïve, Kay?

In this passage, Michael demonstrates his Machiavellian belief not only that the ends justify the means, but also that this consequentialist action is something necessary for those in positions of power.

This belief of Michael's, and his differentiation between himself as leader and the rest of his family, is confirmed in an exchange with Senator Pat Geary in *The Godfather Part II*. Geary, when meeting privately with Michael, tries to extort money from Michael in exchange for allowing the Corleone family to have a Nevada gaming license. When Michael asks why he would even consider paying more than the standard license fee, Geary responds, "Because I intend to squeeze you. I don't like your kind of people. . . . The fact is that I despise your masquerade, the dishonest way you pose yourself. Yourself and your whole fucking family." Michael's response: "Senator, we're both part of the same hypocrisy. But never think it applies to my family." Michael's statement is more evidence that he understands the need for himself, as well as politicians, to be deceptive and justify the means by the ends. However, he also wants to protect his family from the sordid nature of politics, and he does not think the same rules apply to them. This fits the general tone of *The Prince*, as there is no indication that Machiavelli thinks the rules he prescribes should apply to everyone in society. Rather, like Michael Corleone, Machiavelli is constantly referring to leaders when he states what the most effective means are to reach a noble end.

## The Importance of Studying History

Throughout *The Prince*, Machiavelli emphasizes the importance of studying history to become a successful leader. Recall from his dedicatory letter that Machiavelli has "knowledge of the deeds of great men" because he has undertaken "a constant study of the past." Machiavelli confirms this later in *The Prince* when he writes, "A prudent man should always follow in the path trodden by great men and imitate those who are most excellent" (19–20). Indeed, if one reads *The Prince,* one finds numerous historical examples, especially from ancient Rome and Greece, used as evidence to prove Machiavelli's points.

Michael Corleone was also a student of history, something he alludes to throughout the *Godfather* films. For instance, at one point in *The Godfather Part II,* he says to his brother Tom, "If anything in this life is certain, if history has taught us anything, it's that you can kill anyone." In *The Godfather Part III,* Michael notes how studying history explains the violence of the mafia and its rise to power in Sicily. Throughout the three movies, Michael also tries to model his actions by those of his father, whom Michael sees as a great leader for the family.

## Why It Is Better to Be Feared Than Loved . . . But Don't Be Hated!

Of course, no complex fictional character could completely fulfill and perfectly espouse any political theory. Although Michael Corleone comes close to embodying the Machiavellian prince, he ultimately fails to follow Machiavelli's advice in one respect. Machiavelli advises in *The Prince* that "one ought to be both feared and loved, but as it is difficult for the two to go together, it is much safer to be feared than loved, if one of the two has to be wanting." Machiavelli believes this is true because "love is held by a chain of obligation which, men being selfish, is broken whenever it serves their purpose; but fear is maintained by a dread of punishment which never fails" (61). Thus, Machiavelli counsels leaders to be feared, rather than loved, because love can be fickle, whereas fear will never fade. As noted by political philosopher Leo Strauss, Machiavelli emphasizes fear over love because it promotes self-reliance for a leader: "Whether one is loved depends on others, while being feared depends on oneself."[8] Machiavelli cautions, though, that "a prince should make himself feared in such a way that if he does not gain love, he at any rate avoids hatred" (61). Indeed, being hated can cause those around a leader to rise up and rebel when they can no longer tolerate a leader's oppressive behavior.

Throughout the *Godfather* film series, Michael lives the experience of

Machiavelli's mantra that it is better to be feared than loved. Many men fear him and consistently do his bidding because of fear. Yet, Michael struggles to obtain lasting love from his family members, especially his wife, Kay. She was not one of his henchmen or a rival gangster, so Kay never feared Michael in the way many others did. From the opening of *The Godfather*, Kay is in love with Michael, and she maintains that love for many years, even as Michael becomes more and more Machiavellian. By the end of *The Godfather Part II*, however, her love has faded, and Kay confirms to Michael in an argument, "At this moment, I feel no love for you at all. I never thought that would happen, but it has." This is one of the great tragedies of the *Godfather* trilogy. All of the terrible acts that Michael commits, which he claims for years he did on behalf of his family, ultimately cost him his family. Michael and Kay eventually divorce, and Michael's relationship with his children is nothing like the relationship he and his siblings had with his father. Thus, Michael tragically proved Machiavelli's warning that love is not as lasting as fear and that being hated often spells disaster for a leader.

## Closing the Door on Machiavelli and Michael Corleone

There is no question that Niccolò Machiavelli's *The Prince* has had an influence on the modern world. It has been alleged or verified that *The Prince* was read by, and had an influence on, many world leaders, including James Madison, Napoleon Bonaparte, Abraham Lincoln, Benito Mussolini, Joseph Stalin, Winston Churchill, Richard Nixon, and Bill Clinton.[9] The influence of *The Prince* is so well-known and widespread that even the pop singer Lady Gaga has publicly advocated that President Barack Obama read it to better understand foreign relations.[10]

Regardless of one's interpretation of the book, and whether or not one agrees with Machiavelli's advice in it, there is no question that it remains an important work of political science today and that it has been relied upon by countless politicians and other leaders. Studying the character Michael Corleone in the *Godfather* trilogy can help one better understand Machiavelli's messages in *The Prince*. Both men believed that violence, cruelty, and deception were necessary to be successful in politics. Yet, to quote Michael from *The Godfather*, for each man such acts were not personal; rather, for them they were "strictly business."

## Notes

1. Kenneth L. Deutsch and Joseph R. Fornieri, *An Invitation to Political Thought* (Belmont, CA: Thomson Wadsworth, 2009), 221; *Merriam-Webster's Collegiate Dictionary*, ed. Frederick C. Mish (Springfield, MA: Merriam-Webster, 2009), 744.

2. "Italy's City-States," *The End of Europe's Middle Ages*, 1997, University of Calgary Applied History Research Group, www.ucalgary.ca/applied_history/tutor/endmiddle/c-states.html (accessed August 18, 2001).

3. Max Learner, introduction to *The Prince and Discourses*, by Niccolò Machiavelli (New York: Modern Library, 1950), xxv–xxvii, hereafter cited parenthetically in the text.

4. Niccolò Machiavelli, *The Prince*, trans. Harvey C. Mansfield (Chicago: University of Chicago Press, 1998), 3n3, 108n2.

5. "AFI's 100 Years . . . 100 Heroes & Villains," 2003, American Film Institute, www.afi.com/100Years/handv.aspx (accessed August 18, 2011); Lawrence Van Gelder, "'Citizen Kane' Wins an Election," *New York Times*, June 21, 2007, www.nytimes.com/2007/06/21/arts/21arts-005.html?ref=americanfilminstitute (accessed September 25, 2011).

6. Jenny M. Jones, *The Annotated Godfather: The Complete Screenplay with Commentary on Every Scene, Interviews, and Little-Known Facts* (New York: Black Dog & Leventhal, 2007), 248.

7. Harvey C. Mansfield, introduction to Machiavelli, *The Prince*, vii.

8. Leo Strauss, "Niccolo Machiavelli," in *History of Political Philosophy*, ed. Leo Strauss and Joseph Cropsey (Chicago: University of Chicago Press, 1987), 300.

9. See David J. Siemers, *Presidents and Political Thought* (Columbia: University of Missouri Press, 2009); Howard Zinn, *Howard Zinn on War* (New York: Seven Stories Press, 2001); Steven F. Hayward, *Churchill on Leadership: Executive Success in the Face of Adversity* (New York: Three Rivers Press, 1998).

10. Daniel Freedman, "Lady Gaga to Obama: Read Machiavelli," *Forbes*, June 28, 2011, www.forbes.com/sites/danielfreedman/2011/06/28/lady-gaga-to-obama-read-machiavelli/ (accessed August 22, 2011).

# Part 2

# THE STATE, THE INDIVIDUAL, AND POLITICAL MORALITY

# 4

# SOCIAL CONTRACT

## Rebellion and Dissent aboard *Serenity*

*Susanne E. Foster and James B. South*

The major plot of *Serenity,* the companion movie to Joss Whedon's TV series *Firefly,* pits the crew of the spaceship *Serenity* against their interplanetary government, the Alliance. River Tam (Summer Glau), a member of the crew who begins as a stowaway, was severely damaged while at an Alliance school for "gifted" individuals.[1] By the time the movie opens, River's brokenness and the Alliance's persistent attempts to find her lead the captain and crew to believe she is a threat to their safety. While attempting to discover what happened to River and why the Alliance is so desperate to recover her, the crew learn that an Alliance experiment in controlling human aggression annihilated the population of the planet Miranda and created the Reavers, a group of hyperviolent individuals.

> MAL. I know the secret now. The truth that burned up River Tam's brain and set you after her. And the rest of the 'verse is gonna know it too. 'Cause they need to.
> THE OPERATIVE. You really believe that?
> MAL. I do.
> THE OPERATIVE. You willing to die for that belief?
> MAL. I am. Of course, that ain't exactly Plan A.

In this scene, which occurs late in *Serenity,* we see Malcolm ("Mal") Reynolds (Nathan Fillion), the captain of the spaceship *Serenity,* expressing the reasons why he finds himself at odds with his interplanetary government, the Alliance. Over the course of the series *Firefly* and its sequel movie *Serenity,* the Alliance has been shown to be systematically keeping secrets from its citizens and to have policies that lead the government to sacrifice members of the community in pursuit of some greater good. By contrast, the relationship that develops between Mal and the crew of *Serenity* is one in which each individual is kept informed of the plans, and reasons for the plans, of the group, and in which those plans are never predicated on sacrificing any member of the crew for the good of the others. One especially salient feature that emerges from the interactions of the crew members is that they demand compliance with the rules that keep everyone safe while not judging one another's motives and actions as long as crew members stay within these boundaries.

At the beginning of the series, Mal and his crew are rebelling against their interplanetary government, attempting to avoid interaction with or dependence upon the Alliance. But as the series progresses, the crew of *Serenity* moves from rebellion to dissent, working to hold the Alliance accountable for its decisions and to force it to change its policies and actions. The complex story of the community that develops among the crew of *Serenity* and their changing relationship to their government can best be understood by exploring the meaning of the term *consent* within the framework of "social contract theory,"[2] both in the classical sense, expounded by John Locke, and in the development of the view found in the writings of the contemporary philosopher Stanley Cavell, who points out succinctly that "the force of the idea of a social contract is to put the advantage of a society, as it stands, in question."[3]

## Rebellion and Marginalization

The series begins a few years after a civil war between the Alliance and a rebel group called the Resistance. A member of the Resistance, Mal was present at the Battle of Serenity Valley, where the Resistance was defeated. His decision to name his ship *Serenity* and his penchant for picking battles each year on the anniversary of that defeat demonstrate his deep anger and inability to let go of the war. As captain he gathers to himself other individuals who are marginalized by or rebelling against the Alliance government. His own continuing rebellion against the Alliance is further demonstrated by his decision to make a living for himself and his crew by engaging in illegal activities, thereby depriving himself and his crew of the protection the Alliance could provide them and forcing them to hide from the threat of violence from the Alliance itself.

We contend that Mal's relationship to the Alliance consists of an attempt to withdraw consent from the social contract. Locke claimed that citizens enter into a social contract in order to protect their property and the rights that flow from it. In entering into the contract, citizens consent to be governed, that is, they give up some autonomy and freedom in exchange for a social world in which they can flourish, while being cognizant of the kinds of behavior and practices that are now off-limits to them.[4] Mal's rebellion as captain of *Serenity* may well strike us as juvenile, a mere thumbing of his nose at the government that defeated the Resistance. After all, Mal is now living a life in which he barely scrapes by, often short of fuel and parts for his ship as well as food and provisions for his crew. Moreover, he continually puts his crew at risk while engaging in illegal activities. It is worth noting that, ironically, even to the degree that Mal is able to make do in his rebellious activities, he is nonetheless parasitic upon the good functioning of the social contract. One can become an outsider only by leaving the inside intact. Furthermore, the community on board the ship presupposes the language and social customs of the wider community.[5] In short, it seems that despite his attempts at rebellion, Mal is still a member of the Alliance community to the extent that he relies on the good functioning of the Alliance to make his own living possible.

Some social-contract theorists at this point invoke Locke's term *tacit consent* to describe how it is that consent has been given when "few people have actually consented to their governments so no, or almost no, governments are actually legitimate."[6] On this interpretation, Mal's use of Alliance-backed currency and goods such as produce and Alliance-developed technology might seem analogous to Locke's example of the tourist who uses the roadways of another country and thereby agrees to abide by the laws of the state.[7] The problem for the social-contract theorist who wants to make this move is that Locke's use of the concept is restricted to aliens present within a state; he nowhere makes the claim that tacit consent provides for genuine membership in a political community. Indeed, as Cavell notes, even in the sections where Locke brings up the notion of tacit consent, "he reiterates his contention that *membership* in the polis requires *express* consent."[8] So, we are left with three questions: What is required before one can be said to have given express consent? What would be required to withdraw that consent? and What would legitimate the withdrawal?

Cavell's insight is that express consent is best understood in light of an adequate account of withdrawal of consent. In what follows, we will discuss in some detail the ways in which Mal and the other crew members seem to have withdrawn consent. But we will show, drawing on Locke's work, that they do not manage to actually withdraw consent. The crew's initial response to the Alliance does not rise above acting out in a juvenile and rebellious manner. Locke foresaw rebellious reactions such as Mal's, but he argued that they were fruitless insofar as they would fail to effect social change: "The examples of particular injustice, or oppression of here and there an unfortunate man, moves them [the mass of citizens] not." And so, Locke concludes, "Nor let anyone say, that mischief can arise from hence, as often as it shall please a busy head, or turbulent spirit, to desire the alteration of the government."[9]

Mal's crew consists of those who find themselves actively harmed by their government, or marginalized, or simply forgotten—as can happen in any society. These crew members, then, represent concretely those whom Cavell describes as subject to "specific inequalities, and lacks of freedom, and absence of fraternity."[10] So, for example, Jayne Cobb (Adam Baldwin) starts out as a member of a group of bandits threatening Mal and the crew. When Mal points out to him that he will benefit financially if he switches sides, Jayne ends up fighting against his erstwhile companions on behalf of Mal ("Out of Gas").[11] Just as Jayne was a mercenary before, he is now clearly in a kind of mercenary relationship with Mal. It is always an open question whether someone will make him a better offer and give him a financial reason to turn on Mal and his crew. So Mal's agreement with Jayne is a strictly financial one.

Inara Serra (Morena Baccarin) holds the position of a Companion, a profession akin to a legalized form of "prostitution" that involves a set of cultured, intellectual, and social functions similar to the Japanese notion of a geisha. Prior to leasing a shuttle aboard the spaceship *Serenity,* Inara walked away from her position as a rising member of the Companion House Madrassa. Although being a member of this guild afforded her a considerable amount of power, respect, and political clout, not to mention luxuries in food and clothing, it also meant she was socially compromised and constrained in a number of ways. Although we are not told the explicit reasons she has for leaving that position to take up residence with Mal and his crew, whose actions clearly lack social respectability, it is clear that by taking a position upon *Serenity* she gained a degree of autonomy and distance from the direct affiliation with her guild while still plying her trade as a Companion. Her initial agreement to become part of the *Serenity* crew is explicitly financial. She tells Mal that he cannot enter her shuttle and that her services will not be available to the crew. But during their initial negotiations, Mal calls her a "whore," attempting to assert his moral superiority, and she responds that he does not get to call her that again—as a stipulation of their agreement—and thus makes it clear that in addition to financial gain, she requires a position in which she is not being judged morally ("Out of Gas").

Kaylee Frye (Jewel Staite), in contrast, becomes a member of the crew because she has no good reason to stay on her home planet, which appears to be exceptionally poor and limited in resources and opportunities. Rather than being morally compromised in the way Inara is, Kaylee's circumstance is marginalization through poverty. She refers to her life as boring, and her agreement with Mal is to use her exceptional skills as a mechanic to keep the ship in flying condition, in return for the adventure of being part of Mal's crew ("Out of Gas"). She betters her circumstances by being able to indulge her sensuality: wearing pretty dresses, eating strawberries, and acting on an earthy sexuality. This suggests that while Kaylee is marginalized by her society, she is too naive actually to rebel.

Simon Tam (Sean Maher) and his sister River are from a well-positioned family on one of the more cosmopolitan planets in the Alliance. The family, in short, has the privilege of power and wealth. The parents have sent River to a school for gifted individuals, but it turns out that the school is really an Alliance program engaged in experimentation and exploitation of the students' gifts in order to train them for later use as Alliance operatives. She manages to get a message to her brother asking for help. Simon, although already embarked on an impressive career as a doctor, poses as an Alliance official and infiltrates the facility where River is being kept. He is able to extract her, but he and his sister are now wanted by the Alliance because River, while at the school, was accidentally given access to top-level secrets. Her knowledge of the Alliance's past misdeeds and Simon's knowledge of what was going on at the school threaten the Alliance. This act of rescuing his sister costs Simon a lot. He is unable to function openly as a physician, and it is clear he is drawn to practicing medicine. For example, in a scene in which he smuggles River into a medical facility for a series of diagnostic tests on her brain, he risks being caught in order to save a patient from the incompetence of another doctor ("Ariel"). Simon and River, then, represent those individuals in a society who are subject to gross, but isolated, injustices.

The initial moment of their joining the crew of *Serenity* is especially complex. Simon masquerades as an ordinary passenger and smuggles River on board in his luggage. When an Alliance operative follows him, his act puts the crew of *Serenity* in danger. Although the crew protects Simon and River from the Alliance, Simon now must negotiate an agreement with Mal to become part of the crew and not just a passenger. He offers his services as a doctor—services they will need because, in their dangerous and illegal work, they will be unable to obtain needed medical help openly for fear of exposure ("Serenity"). This negotiation has to be reaffirmed frequently since, as a result of the experiments performed on her, River's behavior is erratic and often puts the crew in danger.

## Building Community: Speaking in Mutuality

Our discussion of the individual crew members so far shows that the group on board the ship began as a mere collection of misfit individuals marginalized or persecuted by the Alliance. They have assembled for diverse reasons. First, they want to achieve the advantage of their common protection. Second, each believes that as a member of this particular crew, he or she can more effectively meet his or her needs for various goods and services. Third, each will now have opportunities for meaningful action, free from the prior constraints imposed by the social structures supported by the Alliance. Over the course of the series, though, it turns out that through their diverse abilities and the leadership of Mal, they begin to form a community, one that becomes superior to the political community fostered by the Alliance. The new community that develops on *Serenity* shows its superiority in four ways. Decisions are always made based on some common agreement; no one's good is sacrificed for the group; in spite of the diversity of moral perspectives among the crew, each is assured of the respect of the rest of the community; and although Mal is in a leadership role on *Serenity*, his leadership is by common consent and not absolute. In contrast to Locke, who argues that a prince is in a state of nature in relation to his subjects because there is "no common, higher appeal" between them, we believe that *Firefly* exemplifies a different model, one in which disagreements between Mal and the crew cannot be settled by a higher appeal but nonetheless can be resolved by a common appeal.[12]

The first key element in the communal understanding of the crew is their willingness to tolerate and even respect differences in goals and conceptions of the good held by the other crew members. After all, everyone is well aware that Jayne's sole motivation for being on *Serenity* is the hope of financial benefit. No one upbraids him for his motives, and the only limit Mal ever places on Jayne is that his pursuit of money cannot be at the expense of any member of the community. When, in one episode, Jayne sells out the Tams, Mal threatens to open an airlock, thus pulling Jayne out into space. Mal makes his point: "You turn on any of my crew, you turn on me. But since that's a concept you can't seem to wrap your head around, then you got no place here. You did it to me, Jayne, and that's a fact" ("Ariel").

Another example of this mutual toleration involves Mal and Inara's substantially different standards of respectability. When Inara points out that, unlike Mal's smuggling, her own career is legal, Mal responds that unlike hers, his chosen profession is not morally questionable ("Out of Gas"). Nonetheless, the two respect each other and work together. When an Alliance official questions Inara's willingness to associate with the crew of *Serenity*, Inara responds, "It's a mutually beneficial business arrangement. I rent the shuttle from Captain Reynolds, which allows me to expand my client base. The Captain finds that having a companion on board opens certain doors that might otherwise be closed to him" ("Bushwhacked"). But it is clear that the relationship develops beyond a business arrangement predicated on mere mutual toleration. When a man Inara is accompanying to a party implies that Inara is a whore and his property, Mal rushes to her defense. Inara asks Mal about his behavior: "You have a strange sense of nobility, Captain. You'll lay a man out for implying I'm a whore, but you keep calling me one to my face." And Mal responds: "I may not show respect for your job, but he didn't respect you. That's the difference, Inara. He doesn't even see you" ("Shindig"). Another element in the crew's mutual relationship is that decision making aboard the ship is always transparent and results from a discussion among them, as seen throughout the series. Even more significant, though, is that the community's plans are restricted by the need to meet the goals of all the members. When Inara points out to the captain that he is seeking jobs in areas where she cannot get work, Mal, however grudgingly, takes on jobs in a more populated area ("Trash").

An especially poignant example of the community's commitment to the good of each of the members, and one in which the other crew members are forced to act contrary to the expressed desires of Mal, the captain of the ship, occurs in "Out of Gas." When the ship's engines are crippled, knocking out life-support systems, Mal directs the others to take the shuttles away from the ship and send out distress signals. Reluctantly, they leave. He remains on board to avoid using life-support resources in either shuttle and hoping for a miracle. A passing ship spots *Serenity,* and Mal barters with its captain for the part he needs to repair the engines. Once on board, though, the pirates turn on Mal, planning to kill him and take *Serenity* as their own. Gunfire is exchanged, and Mal, though injured, acquires the part and forces the others off the ship. Bleeding profusely, he attempts the repairs and as he passes out, he manages the repair. Disobeying his orders, the shuttles return and Simon is able to save Mal's life. When Mal awakes, he challenges the others: "I call you back?" Zoë (Gina Torres), the ship's first officer and fellow soldier from his Resistance days, states that she takes full responsibility. Simon adds, "The decision saved your life," and Zoë remarks, "Won't happen again, sir." Mal's response to Zoë's "apology" is "Good," but he continues by saying, "Thanks, I'm grateful."

As "Out of Gas" shows, in contrast to a Lockean model, where there is no mutuality between prince and subject and the prince is "in a state of nature" with regard to his subjects because there is no higher authority by which to settle disputes, Mal's leadership role depends on common consent, and meaningful dissent can occur between the crew and its leader. Cavell provides resources for understanding this sort of community through his discussion of the forms of life constitutive of community. In an important passage, Cavell writes:

> We learn and teach words in certain contexts, and then we are ex-
> pected, and expect others, to be able to project them into further
> contexts. Nothing ensures that this projection will take place (in
> particular, not the grasping of universals nor the grasping of books
> of rules), just as nothing insures that we will make, and understand,
> the same projections. That on the whole we do is a matter of our
> sharing routes of interest and feeling, senses of humor and of sig-
> nificance and of fulfillment, of what is outrageous, of what is similar
> to what else, what a rebuke, what forgiveness, of when an utterance
> is an assertion, when an appeal, when an explanation—all the whirl
> of organism Wittgenstein calls "forms of life." Human speech and
> activity, sanity and community, rest on nothing more, but nothing
> less, than this. It is a vision as simple as it is difficult, and as difficult
> as it is (and because it is) terrifying.[13]

So genuine community does not require a higher authority but relies instead on a set of shared agreements in language, thought, feelings, and interests. Understood in this way, we see that despite Mal's early attempts at rebellion, which required an appeal to a higher standard, Mal is embedded in a community that is simultaneously dependent on and aversive to the broader community exemplified by the Alliance. With no higher authority to which he can appeal, Mal instead has to abandon his rebellious attitude toward the Alliance and turn to a form of expression that exists within that community and does not make an appeal to some outside source: dissent. That dissent finds expression in the companion film, *Serenity.*

### Dissent: "If you can't do somethin' smart . . . do somethin' right."

When the *Firefly* series was prematurely canceled, Joss Whedon, the show's creator, was fortunate to get funding to make a movie that could serve to wrap things up. As part of the plot of the movie, the crew finds itself in a bar pursuing payment for a completed job. A subliminal message on a telescreen triggers River's Alliance conditioning and she violently attacks everyone around her. Just before the attack, she whispers the word "Miranda." Miranda turns out to be the name of a terraformed planet that the Alliance claimed had been rendered uninhabitable through some natural event. In order to find the cause of River's violent behavior, in hopes of curing her, the crew sets out on a dangerous journey to discover what really happened on the planet. This time, not only must the crew dodge the Alliance, but they must pass through Reaver territory. Reavers are humans who have become vicious cannibals, supposedly driven mad by spending too much time in deep space, away from human communities ("Bushwhacked").[14]

When *Serenity* arrives at Miranda, the crew discovers that there has been no natural catastrophe. Instead, the inhabitants are dead, but without apparent cause. Eventually they find a recording made by an Alliance scientist revealing that the government released a chemical, called "The Pax," onto the planet in hopes of making the population "better." But rather than simply removing excess aggression, the chemical destroyed all motivation in virtually all the planet's inhabitants. They simply stopped and thus died. A minute fraction of the population had the opposite reaction. Their aggressive tendencies were tremendously magnified. The release of the chemical, it turns out, was the true origin of the Reavers.

The carelessness with which the Alliance acted on Miranda, and the resulting slaughter, is consistent with its routine attitude toward its citizens. In seeking out River Tam, Alliance operatives exterminated anyone they believed to have talked to her, and in attempting to prevent the crew from releasing the information they have acquired about Miranda, the Alliance indiscriminately destroys any community that they believe might harbor Mal and his crew.

In the final part of the movie, we see Mal and his crew risk their own lives to try to get the news of what really happened at Miranda out to the public. Mal still desires to bring down the Alliance, but he does not simply run away, as in his earlier rebellion from it. Instead, he is trying to do something with revolutionary potential. He demonstrates his commitment to the community governed by the Alliance by showing how the government has become corrupt. Locke, in his account of social-contract theory, made it clear that he thought people would be willing to put up with significant harms from government simply because that course was easier than rebellion. He claims that, "til the mischief be grown general, and the ill designs of the rulers become visible, or their attempts sensible to the greater part, the people . . . are not likely to stir."[15] But the actions of Mal and the crew in reaction to their discovery on Miranda are aimed at making the "ill designs of the rulers become visible." To maim and exterminate human beings in an experiment to improve human nature certainly qualifies as an "ill design." The crew's development of a community that involves mutual respect and tolerance is a model of the social contract that now stands in stark contrast to the Alliance.

Cavell reminds us, "It is a very poorly kept secret that men and their societies are not perfect," but we are always in community despite imperfections because we share language, customs, and the like. "To speak for oneself politically is to speak for the others with whom you consent to association, and it is to consent to be spoken for by them . . . as someone in mutuality speaks for you, i.e., speaks your mind."[16] As Mal expresses his newfound reasons for taking on the Alliance: "Someone has to speak for them." At no point in the series are Mal and his crew able to break free of the larger community they struggle against. In addition to the goods and services for which they must barter, their own smaller community presupposes the language and customs of the interplanetary government. And at no point is Mal content with his stance toward the Alliance. The bigger question, then, is, How does one respond when one cannot assent to the words and actions of one's community? Cavell writes, "Dissent is not the undoing of consent but a dispute about its content, a dispute within it over whether a present arrangement is faithful to it."[17] At the end of *Serenity*, we see Mal expressing that dissent: "You all got on this boat for different reasons, but you all come to the same place. So now I'm asking more of you than I have before. Maybe all. Sure as I know anything I know this, they will try again. Maybe on another world, maybe on this very ground swept clean. A year from now, ten, they'll swing back to the belief that they can make people . . . better. And I do not hold to that. So no more running" (*Serenity*). And once he broadcasts the truth, regaining his voice within the community, dissenting from the lies and actions of the Alliance, he lets go his rebellious anger and need to isolate himself. We see Mal and the crew of *Serenity* continuing their association, but now in a vastly different relationship to the Alliance.

## Notes

1. Simon Tam, River's brother, had rescued her from the Alliance and put her in stasis. While she was in this condition, he smuggled her on board in his luggage. We discuss this incident in some detail later in the chapter.

2. For another treatment of social-contract theory and *Firefly*, with different emphases, see the helpful and interesting essay by Joseph Foy, "The State of Nature and Social Contracts on Spaceship Serenity," in *Joss Whedon and Philosophy*, ed. Dean Kowalski and Evan Kreider (Lexington: University of Kentucky Press, 2012), 39–54. Foy makes good use of Hobbes in showing that the further one gets from civilization, the closer one is to a Hobbesian state of nature. In addition, Foy notes the way in which *Firefly* is indebted to traditional narratives of the Old West.

3. Stanley Cavell, *The Claim of Reason* (Oxford: Oxford University Press, 1979), 23.

4. John Locke, *Second Treatise on Government*, in *Locke's Two Treatises of Government*, ed. Peter Laslett, 2nd ed. (Cambridge: Cambridge University Press, 1970), sec. 222, p. 430.

5. This is a continual theme in the writings of Stanley Cavell. A clear statement of his view can be found in his *Must We Mean What We Say?* (Cambridge: Cambridge University Press, 1969), 52.

6. Alex Tuckness, "Locke's Political Philosophy," in *Stanford Encyclopedia of Philosophy*, http://plato.stanford.edu/entries/locke-political/.

7. Locke, *Second Treatise*, secs. 119–22.

8. Cavell, *Claim of Reason*, 24 (emphasis in the original).

9. Locke, *Second Treatise*, sec. 230, p. 436.

10. Cavell, *Claim of Reason*, 24.

11. Episode names are given parenthetically in the text.

12. Stanley Cavell, *Pursuits of Happiness* (Cambridge, MA: Harvard University Press, 1981), 18–182.

13. Cavell, *Must We Mean What We Say?* 52.

14. Foy, in his "The State of Nature," takes the Reavers to represent humans in the Hobbesian state of nature and does an interesting job of comparing their brutality with the brutality of the Alliance.

15. Locke, *Second Treatise,* sec. 230, pp. 435–36.

16. Cavell, *Claim of Reason,* 27.

17. Ibid.

# 5

# DWIGHT SCHRUTE AND SERVILE AMBITION

## Tacitus and Rousseau on the Lackey Politics of *The Office*

*Matthew D. Mendham*

Much of the brilliance of the first few seasons of NBC's comedy *The Office* was derived, quite simply, from pathology. Leading the maladjustment was Regional Manager Michael Scott, whose frequent missteps resulted from a highly insecure and narcissistic personality. This made him capable of every sort of adolescent nuisance and cowardly pandering. Yet without fail, he displayed a boundless capacity to deceive himself into believing his employees felt all the love and admiration for him that he so desperately needed. Further analysis of Michael we will leave to trained psychologists and turn to our main topic here: the more politically minded Dwight Schrute, particularly as he appears in the early seasons of the program.[1] For him life is about power and authority, even heroism and weaponry. The leading salesman of Dunder Mifflin, he brings an unrivaled level of discipline and organization to his work. He also brings peculiar habits derived from his Amish heritage and his old-fashioned beet farm. Yet, while these traits make him quirky, there is another factor that makes him—amid many unsavory characters—the most despised person in the office. This is his basic approach to social interaction. In normally functioning societies, various influences, including affection, friendship, politeness, professionalism, and convictions about innate human dignity, have always been indispensable in making interactions tolerable. But with rare exceptions, Dwight does not concern himself whatsoever with any of these gentle buffers. Rather, he relates above all through the prism of power, both in striving to attain power and in respecting those—and only those—who have it. Take, for instance, his monologue shortly after he was assumed to be inheriting the Regional Manager position from Michael: "How is the new boss? *Tough.* Do people respect him? They have to. Do they *like* him? Irrelevant. They do not. And I hate them back."[2] Dwight thus displays many of the faults that great political observers have noticed about a certain unprincipled kind of ambition, including a degrading submissiveness toward superiors and a harsh dismissiveness toward peers and inferiors. Or, to use a phrase that has become well known recently, Dwight's typical approach to social interaction is "kissing up, kicking down."

With the exception of a handful of well-adjusted characters, *The Office* can be seen as a sort of cage-match of personal and social pathology. Insofar as the show has been crafted with psychological insight and realism, it stands to reason that the dysfunctions it puts on display would often parallel—albeit on a more frivolous level—forms of corruption that have been criticized by leading political theorists. To my knowledge, the best frameworks for understanding Schrute's pathologies of power can be derived from Marcus Cornelius Tacitus (c. 55–117 CE) and Jean-Jacques Rousseau (1712–1778). Tacitus is often viewed as the greatest of the ancient Roman historians; he starkly analyzed the brutality, paranoia, and decadence of imperial Rome, which followed the collapse of the republic. Rousseau is commonly recognized as one of the greatest political theorists, although he remains controversial for his radical republicanism and his scathing criticisms of the inequality, luxury, and oppression of Europe in the time of the Enlightenment. The task of this chapter is to show that the imperial palaces of the first-century Roman Empire, as well as the aristocratic courts of eighteenth-century France, reveal certain patterns of behavior that are clearly echoed in the office parks of twenty-first-century America.

Although in the next section I will introduce the crucial political teachings of Tacitus and Rousseau and will interweave the observations of various political thinkers throughout our discussion, it may be useful to begin with some philosophical claims that particularly evoke Schrute. Most commonly, a person who is ambitious and preoccupied with power is a feisty, stubborn type—one who likes to give orders but chafes at following them and thus strives to minimize the frequency and degradingness of submission to others. Rousseau often praised vigorous, republican societies exemplifying this sort of proud independence and love of liberty. He thus faulted the great majority of modern people for being willing to degrade themselves in order to gain the comforts and securities offered by the modern commercial and political system. Such people are "busy, restless, ambitious, detesting freedom in others and not wanting any for themselves, provided that they . . . dominate the will of others—they torment themselves their whole life long by doing what is loathsome to them; they omit nothing servile in order to command."[3] Rousseau mentions that this last phrase—to "omit nothing servile in order to command"—comes from Tacitus's discussion of Otho. Otho was a Roman general who usurped the throne to become emperor and reigned four months before being overthrown himself. For Rousseau, this phrase shows that "Tacitus knew the human heart. . . . Few men have healthy enough hearts to be able to love liberty: All wish to command, and at that price none fear to obey. A little upstart gives himself a hundred masters in order to acquire ten valets."[4] It is somewhat counterintuitive and paradoxical that a person obsessed with power and domination would so eagerly embrace abasement and subordination. Tacitus and Rousseau were also surprised by the many people in their times who were desperate to taste great power and wealth and at that price eagerly endured the degradation of being treated like "lackeys"—servants of particularly low standing and respectability.[5] This paradox might capture much of what is complex and intriguing about Dwight Schrute. His fawning, flattering service to Michael, alongside his rough treatment of his co-employees, is traceable to his ambition being so "servile"—that is, "slavish," both in the degrading things he is willing to endure and in his narrowly selfish and calculating outlook.[6]

## *Dwide Schrude* and the Origins of Servile Ambition

We know that Dwight craves power, and we know that he behaves in a "servile" (that is, slavish) manner toward his superiors. If anything, he may go beyond Rousseau's observations, in that he often seems to positively delight in being servile, at least in relation to Michael. According to our political theorists, the rise and preponderance of this sort of character results from a corrupt social system. After outlining the political theories of ambition in Tacitus and Rousseau, I will suggest that the sources of ambition in Schrute seem to be of a more distinctive, personal nature.

For Tacitus, looking at his contemporaries and the recent past in comparison with the greatness of the earlier Romans, the explanation was fairly straightforward. For most of their history, the early Romans were politically free—citizens of a republic, not subjects of a monarchy. They also had the firm and public-minded sort of character that was required to maintain that freedom and was reinforced by the exercise of that freedom. By contrast, under the absolute power of the emperors, strength and open disagreement in service of the common good gave way to cowardice and fawning in order to placate a single man. Under the early republican system, competitive drives such as ambition were restrained by an equal system of laws and expressed themselves in the pursuit of excellence in political speech, political service, and military victory. Under the imperial system, competitive drives could only encourage mediocrity, treachery, and dishonest flattery of the powerful.[7]

For Rousseau, the rise of destructive forms of ambition is more complex, being closely linked with his overall political and historical theories. At one level, Rousseau seems close to Tacitus in finding certain healthy forms of ambition to flourish in virtuous republics and other, destructive forms of ambition to prevail in corrupt societies. However, at another level, Rousseau seems to suggest that society itself is the problem, since it was only with the rise of society that humans came to develop a range of highly destructive, competitive passions, including ambition as well as greed, envy, and contempt. Instead of having a natural and healthy self-love (*amour de soi*) based simply on personal well-being, humans become consumed by a vain self-love (*amour-propre*) and are even willing to neglect or subvert their substantive well-being, so long as they can drag someone else down and thus increase their own comparative status in the eyes of society. Especially in his early *Discourse on Inequality*, Rousseau presents this as the universal tale of civilized humanity. The heroes in this account are not Spartan or Roman citizens but the "savages" of the most primitive times and conditions:

> Savage man and civilized man differ so much in their inmost heart and inclinations that what constitutes the supreme happiness of the one would reduce the other to despair. The first breathes nothing but repose and freedom, and wants only to live and to remain idle, and even the Stoic's *ataraxia* [tranquility] does not approximate his profound indifference to everything else. By contrast, the Citizen, forever active, sweats, scurries, constantly agonizes in search of ever more strenuous occupations. . . . This, indeed, is the genuine cause of all these differences: the Savage lives within himself; sociable man, always outside himself, is capable of living only in the opinion of

others and, so to speak, derives the sentiment of his own existence solely from their judgment.[8]

From this perspective, the opportunism and obsession with status that we find in Schrute is simply a clear picture of social and civilized humanity, from Sparta to Scranton.[9]

This being said, at least as Rousseau's political thought came to be fully expressed, his main problem does not seem to be with society or civilization as such. In his practical models for politics, he does not think we can return to the simplicity and freedom of the savage, but he does wish to recreate some of their integrity at a more complex level. He believes that citizens of a few small communities, isolated from the corruptive charms of the modern world, might be able to satisfy their competitive passions not by struggling against their compatriots for wealth and status, but by striving with them for civic honor and glory. In this way they would find their greatness by identifying themselves with a free and virtuous state, in comparison with the slavish and base states all around them. Thus *amour-propre* is elevated and redirected through a deeply inculcated patriotism.[10] The true citizen is unlike the savage in having extensive *amour-propre* but like him in not having a kind of *amour-propre* that naturally leads to conflicts of interest with his neighbors. Another major problem Rousseau wished to avoid was common to virtually all societies—the abuse of political and legal authority, which forces people to submit themselves to the arbitrary wills of powerful individuals. A virtuous community can avoid this fate only if it universally and directly takes up the duties of governing itself, passing laws that apply uniformly to everyone, in service of the common good alone. In submitting to such laws, a citizen can thus "nevertheless only obey himself and remain as free as before."[11] Again, the true citizen is unlike the savage in needing to obey, but he is like the savage in remaining free of all dependence upon, or subjection to, any particular individuals and their wills.

We can see that Rousseau rejects not civilization so much as *modern* civilization, and modern civilization is found lacking in comparison with both the simple savage and the true republican citizen. He thought these destructive social passions such as greed and envy were reaching their most acute expressions in the sort of open, individualistic, commercial, and "enlightened" societies that were fairly new in his times but have continued to expand and reinforce themselves since then. Whereas many, including Rousseau's predecessor Montesquieu, had viewed England's commercial economy and balanced, representative government as the most free and admirable model the world had to offer, Rousseau would have none of that. Since these new societies undermined economic independence and made people increasingly dependent on others, humans' destructive social tendencies would reach their most calculating heights. Greed and inevitable conflicts of interest would stratify economic life, frivolous fashions would pass for cultural excellence, and a narrow elite would supplant every sort of direct political activity. Instead of honor found in public service and patriotism, we have "the passions of petty self-interest, concentrated together with egoism in all hearts" by inept institutions in which genius never had any share."[12] Thus Rousseau offered scathing criticism of any society driven by greed and comparative status, often entailing a great willingness of individuals to humiliate themselves in order to subordinate others. Whereas the earliest savage had neither knowledge nor opportunity for such ambition, and the true citizen seeks superiority through the community alone, the modern finds his identity only through the eyes of others. Even the most faithful and self-abasing ally secretly aspires to betray and surpass his superiors and would carry out such wishes if only given the assurance of success.[13]

While many would argue, with some justification, that modern liberal societies have proved more resilient and less monolithically corrupt than Rousseau anticipated, there is much in his portrayal that rings alarmingly true. And while Schrute seems to embody much of the fawning and cal- culating ambition portrayed by Rousseau and Tacitus, his character does not completely fit these models as far as the *causes* of his servility are con- cerned. For one thing, Schrute does not seem to be a result of domination by, or dependence upon, superiors, as Tacitus and Rousseau both found. The needy Michael is stunningly weak as a personality and a leader. Better- adjusted characters, such as Jim Halpert and Ryan "the Temp" Howard, are more than capable of making the excuses necessary to distance themselves from Michael's psychological vortex. Second, Dwight does not seem to fit Rousseau's account of corruption by peers, whether through imitation or through competition. Dwight has nothing but contempt for their profes- sional skills and feels no need to earn their confidence or approval in his quest for dominance. However, he does come closer to Rousseau's analysis in desperately needing to feel superiority over his peers in his own mind and in needing to have that confirmed by the existing (albeit pathetic) leader.

Dwight's servile ambition therefore seems to result more from internal and personal factors than from broader sociopolitical forces. The program does not attempt to fully explain Dwight's origins—after all, how can such a person really be explained? But we do find several important reminiscences of his upbringing in the Schrute household.[14] These are often described by Dwight in a charmed, even wistful manner. For instance, "I remember every hot summer morning, dad driving us all over to Rocky Glenn's swimming hole near Factoryville. We would splash away until 10 a.m., and then work the beet fields until well after midnight."[15] He also mentions love for his father in describing the origins of his name: "My father's name was Dwight Schrute. My grandfather's name was Dwight Schrute. His father's name: *Dwide Schrude*. Amish."[16] Although Dwight does not seem to have been raised in a full-fledged Amish manner, there are Amish elements of his upbringing that, at least to most outsiders, might be judged negatively. In explaining his decision to shun Andy Bernard for three years (following the wall-punching incident), Dwight coolly observes: "I was shunned from the age of four until my sixth birthday . . . for not saving the excess oil from a can of tuna."[17] In all of Dwight's recollections of his homespun upbringing, we find a great deal of the sorts of austerity that were common in scarcity-driven, traditional societies—a vigorous work ethic, shame about waste, and respect for elders. But such factors don't seem to go far in explaining his rough treatment of his peers, his lust for power, or the peculiar neediness of his submission to Michael. Many people who have emerged from regimented upbringings and incompetent workplaces have maintained their senses of personal dignity and social respect. Although we may never know the reasons, we shall see that Dwight ended up going another way.

## "To Intimidate My Subordinates": Schrutian Authority

Before we discuss Dwight's characteristically fawning services to Michael, we might turn, briefly, to those rare moments when authority has been vested in Dwight, allowing him to experience his deeper fantasies of power—at least partially. Here I will comment on his stern responses to social disorder in general, his many opportunities to exercise petty authority, and his fleeting moments of supreme command as Regional Manager of the Scranton branch. Our philosophical guides will then help us understand the stark contrast between his treatment of superiors, on the one hand, and of peers and inferiors, on the other hand.

Schrute's approach to any question of violent action—of fear, weaponry, survival skills, and heroism—is unmistakably boyish. Upon supposedly taking over the Scranton branch, he names Jack Bauer as his ideal choice for his "number two"; in explaining true citizenship to Jim, he cites Han Solo. He is thrilled about the fireworks he received from his uncle. Nunchucks, throwing stars, spudguns, and blowguns are featured prominently in his at-work arsenal (not to mention several grown-up survival knives). He is always easy to convince about a major security threat, as when Jim sends him alleged top-secret correspondence from the CIA. It is this pattern of paranoia—of compulsively exaggerating levels of danger—that makes him systematically overreact to perceived threats or disorder. Thus, although he has various tendencies that are downright fascist, in the early seasons we are focusing upon, he remains an essentially comic figure and (mostly) harmless.[18] Thus, also, even when his convictions at least partially overlap with mainstream and reasonable views—for instance, one shouldn't smoke marijuana at work—his crackdowns as "volunteer sheriff's deputy" are patently disproportionate. He goes so far as to overrule Michael in this case, although the manager's authority normally holds great sway for Dwight. He sternly rebuffs Michael's various attempts to escape the drug testing: "It has to be official, and it *has* to be urine. . . . That is the law according to the rules." Even in "Dwight's Speech," during his moment of greatest anxiety, we find him ultimately rallying as he communes with the authoritarian ethos of his (lightly revised) Benito Mussolini speech.[19]

Stern overreach is also inevitable when Schrute is delegated any sort of partial authority. This occurs far more often than it should, since Michael is constitutionally incapable of making a decision that might be unpopular with his employees. Beginning very early in his documented career, it has been Dwight alone who has been willing to fill that gap, whatever unpopularity may come. Authorized to select a new and cheaper health care plan, he "slashed benefits to the bone," saving the company "a fortune." This was partly due to his sense of the basic frivolousness of health care, since it did not exist "in the wild" and he himself had never been sick, having a "perfect immune system." Dwight's response to the ensuing office revolt—a series of aggressive invasions of privacy—might not stand among the great profiles in leadership. Lacking charisma and a sense of proportion, he also inspires quitting rather than excellence both in his exotic initiation of Ryan at the beet farm and in his drill-sergeant approach to the "Beach Games." In another instance, Dwight is faced with a severe case of negligence that is apparently the fault of the notorious slacker Creed Bratton, and then he confronts Creed's (manufactured) evidence against one Debbie Brown. When Creed insists that there is "no time" to hear Debbie's plea of innocence and that "someone has to be held accountable," Dwight agrees. It is "time to put this dog down," since "mercy is for girl babies." Here it is probably Jim Halpert who provides the best analysis of Dwight's lesser forays into authority. As Dwight wields an oversized dry-erase board and vindictively pronounces that it will be Jim who will need to work on the coming Saturday, Jim finds the display "so sad," as "the smallest amount of power I've ever seen go to someone's head."[20]

We might only beg for mercy, then, when a Schrute attains the heights of authority. Without ever being given official word from Corporate, in two cases Dwight is told by Michael that he will be promoted to Regional Manager. The first one is "The Coup." Reversing his normal subservience to Michael, Dwight allows Angela to prod him into thinking that Michael's bumbling ways—particularly, getting caught by Jan Levinson during "Movie Monday"—are going to get the entire branch fired and that only Dwight can save the branch. After much internal turmoil, Dwight stages a secret meeting with Jan and makes his bold proposal to her.[21] Jan, in turn, secretly informs Michael of the treachery, and Michael gets his revenge by telling Dwight that Corporate seems to be reversing their job positions, all the while emphasizing Dwight's unflinching loyalty and honesty. During his hour or so of presumed authority, Dwight's new regime seems ominous. He announces to the crew: "I just want to say, to the few of you who will remain under my employ, that I intend to lead you into the black with *ferocity!*"

Dwight's second pseudo-promotion occurs in "The Job." He is then voluntarily granted the position by Michael, since the latter is fully self-assured of earning a promotion to Corporate but his desperate attempts to find a replacement other than Dwight have come to nothing. Here one might grant that Schrute's reign had some strengths. With the institution of "Schrutebucks," he came to use some carrots alongside his many sticks (and looming axes). And his seminar on nitrogen and the origins of paper might, indeed, have been an improvement over Michael's many meetings, which—as the new boss announced—"wasted an enormous amount of the group's time and patience with non-work related ethnic celebrations and parades of soft-minded dogoodedness." However, after Michael's delusions of Corporate promotion vanish, he resumes his former authority and asks Dwight why his office has been painted black. Dwight can then only sheepishly reply: "To intimidate my subordinates."[22]

More generally, Dwight's approach to subordinates is the inverse of Michael's. In staging "The Coup," Dwight's leading proposal to Jan for reforming the branch is to "get rid of waste—which is half the people there."

By contrast, Michael chides Donald Trump's iconic "You're *fired!*"; his own catchphrase would be, "You're *hired,* and you can work here as long as you want."[23] In this connection, Michael invokes Machiavelli's famous question of whether it is better for a prince to be loved or feared. But he offers a solution quite overlooked by the Florentine: "Easy: both. I want people to be afraid of how much they love me."[24] While Michael's management style leaves almost everything to be desired, Dwight's is apparently even worse. Even as a co-employee, Dwight's manner of relating does not earn the affection or even respect of his peers. When he is announced for any leadership position, everyone—except for the like-minded and allied Angela—is filled with dread and disgust.[25] There are many reasons for this, but perhaps the most important one is that although Dwight typically shows immense devotion and respect for Michael, he is almost always stern and full of contempt for everyone else. This follows a pattern observed by Tacitus and Rousseau—that when people have ambition but not substantive morals, they relate to others only with a view to benefiting themselves. Accordingly, such people treat the wealthy and strong with servile flattery but the poor and weak harshly as tools.[26] For instance, upon receiving much-needed advice on a Valentine's gift, Dwight immediately tells Pam, "Okay, shut up." And expecting a *Washington Post*–caliber reporter to respond to his press release about the "product recall," he only pretends to offer a drink to the *Scranton Times* reporter, before slamming the door in his face.[27]

Another philosophical implication of servile ambition is that a person can seem to faithfully adore his leader, and yet when their power relations are overturned, the adoration can turn instantly to jubilant scorn.[28] Without going quite that far, we can see some of this in "The Coup." When Michael tells Dwight he should inform "the troops" about his new position, Dwight casually brushes him aside: "When I'm ready, Mike." But above all, what Michael could not forgive was Dwight's failure to maintain his usual praise of the manager's Sebring convertible—declaring it instead "a ridiculous choice for this climate."[29] This drew Michael's hoax to an abrupt end, bringing Dwight to new depths of humiliation in begging forgiveness from the man who was now revealed as supreme after all.

## "Assistant (to the) Regional Manager": The Soul of a Lackey

Given the results of his abortive attempts at leadership, then, his colleagues might be grateful that Dwight normally operates near the middle of the hierarchy. Apart from the few exceptions discussed above, Dwight relates to Michael with preeminent obedience and dedication. Adding to the humiliation is the fact that, for all his efforts, he normally receives only mockery and derision from Michael. On the other hand, one factor weighing in favor of Dwight as a moral figure is that he seems to have a genuine admiration for Michael and to desire true friendship with him. Thus, if the essentially servile character is self-abasement and fawning solely to advance one's own standing, then perhaps Dwight does not embody the purest sort of servility.

Dwight's subservience to Michael knows few bounds, and I will not attempt to document it fully. In general, if there is a request that seems too frivolous (like picking up Michael after he burns his foot on a Foreman Grill), too demeaning (like rubbing butter on that foot), or too disgusting (like smelling Michael's breath before a cocktail party), Dwight alone will accept the charge.[30] And he does so with zeal. If Michael is lonely and depressed that his employees have inadequately celebrated his birthday and fears that only his mother will buy him a present, Dwight is there: "I probably care more than she does."[31] When Michael and Dwight arrive at CFO David Wallace's house for a cocktail party among the company's major players, Dwight observes that Michael is dressed "exactly like the servants." He eagerly accepts Michael's demand that they change shirts and even expresses relief, without any regard to his own appearance at the party: "That would have been embarrassing. Crisis averted."[32] These are the sorts of incidents that lead Jim to describe Dwight as having a "dog-like obedience to authority."[33] Despite his higher ambitions, Dwight often seems quite satisfied to be Michael's lackey. But one need not have Rousseau's level of outrage against constraint and subordination to be able to recognize that it is natural and proper to feel indignation when one's human worth or distinctive merit is consistently overlooked or insulted.[34]

Meanwhile, for all Dwight's efforts, Michael is almost always cold in return. Much of the scorn for Dwight is summarized in Michael's early script for "Threat Level Midnight," in which a character originally named Dwight is chided throughout as "such an idiot," "the worst assistant ever," and "disgusting." In reality, Dwight is not particularly unintelligent, incompetent, or unhygienic; it also doesn't seem to be his servility that provokes Michael's contempt. Rather, just as Dwight is drawn to authority and dominance, Michael is drawn to popularity and physical attractiveness—the status-markers of the adolescent world. And by adolescent standards, Dwight is plainly a "nerd." Unfortunately for Michael, the cooler youngsters in the office pay little attention to their lonely, forty-something boss. Pam rebuffs his somewhat guarded romantic overtures, while Ryan and Jim make an art form of resisting his social invitations through feeble excuses.[35] The result is a partial love triangle, with Dwight and Michael giving much love but receiving none from the ones they long for.

But occasionally Dwight's heartache cuts deeper still, for two reasons. First, it is not merely out of ambition that he obeys Michael and craves his attention. Amazing though it may seem, Dwight offers several expressions of disinterested praise of Michael, often when he is beyond Michael's earshot. Michael did, after all, post the greatest sales numbers in the company's history, and Dwight freely admits that he will never match them.[36] Dwight also longs for friendship and a sort of fatherly approval from Michael.[37] A second cause of heartache is that even though Dwight will undergo any breach of social dignity on behalf of Michael, he does have broader moral principles, which are not as easily suppressed. In "Drug Testing," Michael believes he might fail a forthcoming drug test due to inadvertent drug use at an Alicia Keys concert. When his various pretexts for avoiding the test are foiled—mostly by the vigilant but oblivious Dwight—Michael demands a cup of urine from his most obedient and clean-living employee. After real resistance, Dwight succumbs, but he remains highly distressed. He even resigns as volunteer sheriff's deputy, having broken his oath. Again, it is Jim who is the mouthpiece of truth: "Why does he do the things that he does for Michael? I just don't get it. What is he getting out of that relationship?"[38] Though sad for Dwight, the episode reflects upon him somewhat well. Servile ambition is worth understanding, in part, because it motivates a large share of participation in totalitarian regimes and atrocious acts. In this respect, the level of moral integrity that Dwight displays in resisting a fairly minor breach of justice may suggest that his servility is by no means the most sinister kind.

## "I Really 'Schruted' It": The Unbridled Servility of Andy Bernard

If Schrute's combination of servility and ambition is staggering yet ultimately in tension with other moral standards, Bernard's may be pure and boundless. In contrast to Dwight, with his country-bred industriousness and self-reliance, Andy is characterized by privilege and entitlement. He schemes to climb the corporate ladder not through any objective professional achievements, but through "face time with the boss" and machinations to subvert his chief rival—Dwight himself. His origins and ethos are more straightforward than Dwight's. He often mentions his graduation from Cornell University, where he was admitted partly as a legacy and partly through a last-minute a cappella performance to the admissions office. He graduated from there in four years but "never studied once" and was "drunk the whole time." His peculiar work ethic might also be inferred from his claim "Every success I've ever had at my job or with the lady-folk has come from my ability to—slowly and painfully—*wear someone down.*"[39]

Andy's overbearing personality and groundless self-promotion were fully on display while he was working with Jim (as well as Karen Filippelli) at Dunder Mifflin Stamford. But his pathologies shift into higher gear upon his arrival at the Scranton branch, since apparently Michael presents himself as a perfect target for servile flattery, while Dwight presents himself as a grave obstacle to achieving domination. Andy vows to be "the number two guy" at Scranton within six weeks, through tactics such as "name repetition, personality mirroring, and never breaking off a handshake."[40] While I take these to be commonplaces of current pop psychology, it may be worth noting a parallel in Tacitus's account of the ways Gaius Caligula was able to ingratiate himself with the emperor Tiberius, who had become morbidly suspicious, murderous, and perverse in his old age. According to Tacitus, "Gaius concealed a monstrous personality beneath a deceitful veneer of moderation. . . . Whatever Tiberius' mood for the day seemed to be, he would adopt the same, using language little different from his."[41] While Andy is far more frivolous than monstrous, he does have a hidden, wrathful side. But early on, he seemed a perfect fit for his boss, since he could tirelessly ape, praise, and apparently delight in Michael's standard, adolescent antics. As a pampered, perpetual adolescent himself, Andy might even have been sincere in channeling Michael's humor in "Lazy Scranton" and "Night at the Roxbury."[42]

As viewers know, Andy's aggressive pursuit of "face time with the boss" eventually exasperated Michael and led to the Ivy Leaguer's fall from grace. But his scheming initially found much success in a fine sequence of episodes, "Traveling Salesmen" and "The Return." As the sales team is set to go out in pairs, and Andy is given the first choice of a partner, he turns to the obvious flattery, served as irony: "Hmmm, well. . . . Let me think about this for a minute. Oh, I don't know: Michael Scott, Ph. D.! Doctor of *Sales.*" As Andy and Michael walk across the parking lot, Michael throws Dwight a bag of dirty laundry (the latter's punishment for his attempted coup). Here Andy lays on the servility, offering as a favor what Dwight has only consented to do under duress: "You know if you want your laundry done right. . . . I used to work at Abercrombie. So . . . *pretty* good folder." While we cannot rehearse the many insults and allegations Andy hurls against Dwight, one exchange nicely captures Andy's brazen manipulations as well as Michael's cluelessness. Immediately following a sales meeting that was botched by Andy's attempts to brag about himself or praise Michael rather than relate to their client, Andy makes another attempt in Michael's car:

> ANDY. I . . . I'm so sorry, man. I really screwed that up.
> MICHAEL. Ah, no. Don't worry about it.
> ANDY. I really "Schruted" it.
> MICHAEL. What?
> ANDY. "Schruted" it. It's just this thing that people say around your
>   office all the time. Like, when you screw something up in a really
>   irreversible way, you "Schruted" it. I don't know where it comes
>   from though. Do you think it comes from "Dwight Schrute"?
> MICHAEL. I don't know. Who knows how words are formed.

Displaying another characteristic of servile ambition, Andy is even willing to violate laws in order to advance his personal standing—in this case, by breaking into Dwight's car. There he finds the (apparent) evidence he needs to frame Dwight and get him fired.[43]

Andy's next character developments are of Roman proportions. Tacitus is in agreement with the leading tradition of ancient Roman historians that the pivotal factor in republican Rome's moral and political decline was the loss of all serious external rivals with the final destruction of Carthage. Then, says Tacitus, "When once we had brought the world to our feet and exterminated every rival state or king, we were left free to covet wealth without fear." The "old ingrained human passion for power" could then burst into strife between patricians and plebeians, and a series of civil wars brought down the republic.[44] Paralleling this, we find that Andy's tiresome frat-boy ingratiation can only be fully unleashed once his great rival, Dwight, has been removed. Soon thereafter, Jim "Big Tuna" Halpert is under siege whenever at his desk, and Michael hides behind doorways to find some moments when Andy isn't "being in my face and annoying the bejesus out of me."[45] Just before Andy's fateful explosion of frustration, Michael is coming to realize the oversized role Dwight has long played in the office, not only in sales but in daily tasks that Michael has long thought the cleaning crew was doing, such as watering the plants and arranging Michael's desk toys "in a very pleasing way." When Michael then discovers that Andy's evidence against Dwight was wrongly applied, he displays some rare maturity in sincerely apologizing to Dwight and asking him to return to his old job.

Thus it seems that Bernard outdoes Schrute in servile ambition, since in Andy it is unqualified by moral scruple, cultural tradition, or personal affection. Michael himself comes to realize something of this after bringing Dwight back: "It takes a big man to admit his mistake and that's what I did. The important thing is I learned something. I don't want somebody sucking up to me because they think I'm going to help their career. I want them sucking up to me because they genuinely love me."[46] Michael's embrace of servility remains, but he recognizes here that Dwight has real admiration, respect, and loyalty for him—it is not a purely instrumental relationship. To this we might add that, for all the servility, paranoia, authoritarianism, and sheer nerdiness that can be found in Dwight, there are real elements of moral greatness in him as well. He is uniquely undaunted by "The Fire," and he prevents Roy's nasty attempted assault against Jim. What is more, when Jim then attempts to offer gifts in order to show his gratitude, Dwight persistently refuses: "I saw someone breaking the law, and I intervened. . . . Citizens do not accept prizes for being citizens."[47]

To conclude, we might be grateful that Dwight's pathologies and vices have prevented him from wielding real power for long. To a large extent, he embodies what might be seen as the two leading elements of servile ambition—a willingness to endure profound degradation in order to advance oneself and a tendency to treat people solely according to their instrumental worth and hence their social power and status. But he also has a certain love of the law and of the public good, which Tacitus and Rousseau would see as essential to a citizen's character in a flourishing republic. They would also say that these republican virtues—which Tacitus links with "the old integrity of character" and Rousseau with the "old ruggedness"[48]—tend to flourish in more simple, independent, rustic environments. There is much in Dwight Schrute that seems as outdated as his '87 TransAm, his outhouse, and his sixty-acre working beet farm. Time will tell whether his republican virtues will pass in the same way. But whether they combine it with older and higher virtues, as Dwight does, or serve it pure and unmixed, as Andy does, characters driven by servile ambition will continue to be found. And people who care about sustaining a just liberty should know a few things about such characters' tactics and motives, employed from ancient Rome and early modern France to current-day Scranton. These high-minded friends of liberty might even, from time to time, come to recognize—and hopefully resist—a bit of Schrutian servility within their own motivational patterns as well.

## Notes

1. I focus on Dwight during the first four, and especially the first three, seasons of *The Office*. After that, he is deeply affected by his breakup with Angela Martin; I would say he goes "over the edge," and his character becomes far more morbid, violent, sensualistic, and calloused. In addition, I agree with other observers that the overall quality of the show declined markedly after this point. Therefore, focusing on the earlier version of the character—whom we might call "Vintage Schrute"—seems more appropriate for a brief chapter. Descriptions and quotations from *The Office* come from the DVDs for seasons 1–4 (New York: National Broadcasting Corporation and Universal Studios, 2005–2008). I have also benefited from consulting unofficial transcriptions at www.officequotes.net.

2. "The Job," season 3, episodes 24–25, deleted scenes.

3. Rousseau, *Reveries of the Solitary Walker*, trans. Charles E. Butterworth (Indianapolis: Hackett, 1992), book 6, p. 84.

4. Rousseau, *Letters Written from the Mountain*, in *Letter to Beaumont, Letters Written From the Mountain, and Related Writings*, trans. Christopher Kelly and Judith R. Bush (Hanover, NH: University Press of New England, 2001), book 8, p. 261n. The Tacitus quote may be found in *The Histories*, trans. H. H. Fyfe, rev. D. S. Levene (New York: Oxford University Press, 1997), 1.36, p. 24.

5. Alexis de Tocqueville clarifies that among aristocratic peoples, many higher ranks of servants display "a sort of servile honor" and are capable of many elevated virtues, including a taste for etiquette, pride in ancestry, and complete dedication without the feeling of abasement.

> But it was almost never so in the inferior ranks of the domestic class. One conceives that whoever occupies the last step in a hierarchy of valets is base indeed.
>
> The French had created a very definite word for this last of the servants of aristocracy. They called him lackey.
>
> The word lackey served as an extreme term, when all others were lacking, to represent human baseness; under the old monarchy when one wanted to paint a vile and degraded being in a moment, one said of him that he had the *soul of a lackey* [*l' âme d'un laquais*].

*Democracy in America*, trans. Harvey Mansfield and Delba Winthrop (Chicago: University of Chicago Press, 2000), vol. 2, part 3, chap. 5, p. 547; French version in *De la démocratie en Amérique*, preface by André Jardin (Paris: Gallimard, 1986), 2:248.

6. In his excellent discussion of the meanings of words related to "freedom," C. S. Lewis clarifies that the connotations of our current word *servile* are not what they were in the ancient world. Whereas we now mean "an abject, submissive man who cringes and flatters," in the ancient world, "the true servile character is cheeky, shrewd, cunning, up to every trick, always with an eye to the main chance, determined 'to look after number one.'... Absence of disinterestedness, lack of generosity, is the hall-mark of the servile." *Studies in Words* (1960; Cambridge: Cambridge University Press, 2000), 112; see also 22–23. Cf. Tacitus, *Histories* 1.90.

7. See Daniel Kapust, "Between Contumacy and Obsequiousness: Tacitus on Moral Freedom and the Historian's Task," *European Journal of Political Theory* 8, no. 3 (2009): 293–311; and Dean Hammer, *Roman Political Thought and the Modern Theoretical Imagination* (Norman: University of Oklahoma Press, 2008), chap. 4.

8. Rousseau, *Discourse on the Origin and Foundations of Inequality among Men*, in *The Discourses and Other Early Political Writings*, trans. Victor Gourevitch (Cambridge: Cambridge University Press, 1997), part 2, pp. 186–87.

9. For general discussions supporting much of this and the next two paragraphs, see Arthur Melzer, *The Natural Goodness of Man: On the System of Rousseau's Thought* (Chicago: University of Chicago Press, 1990), chaps. 3–5; Laurence D. Cooper, *Rousseau, Nature, and the Problem of the Good Life* (University Park: Pennsylvania State University Press, 1999), chaps. 1–2; Matthew D. Mendham, "Gentle Savages and Fierce Citizens against Civilization: Unraveling Rousseau's Paradoxes," *American Journal of Political Science* 55, no. 1 (2011): 170–87; and Mendham, "Enlightened Gentleness as Soft Indifference: Rousseau's Critique of Cultural Modernization," *History of Political Thought* 31, no. 4 (2010): 605–37.

10. See esp. Rousseau, *Discourse on Political Economy*, in *The Social Contract and Other Later Political Writings*, trans. Victor Gourevitch (Cambridge: Cambridge University Press, 1997), 15–16, 20–21.

11. Rousseau, *The Social Contract*, in *Social Contract and Other Writings*, sec. 1.6, pp. 49–50.

12. Rousseau, *Considerations on the Government of Poland*, in *Social Contract and Other Writings*, chap. 2, p. 180.

13. See *Discourse on Inequality*, note 9, pp. 197–99.

14. A useful point of comparison here is Michael, who, delusions aside, had a rather unhappy childhood. Notably, he seems to have been highly affected by his parents' divorce, followed by a tear- and urine-soaked outburst at his mother's remarriage—"I *hate* you!" "Phyllis's Wedding," season 3, episode 16.

15. An outtake from "Drug Testing," in season 2, bloopers.

16. "Drug Testing," season 2, episode 20. He is quite proud of these origins, mentioning them as a key possible talking point in asking an attractive saleswoman out

on a date. "Hot Girl," season 1, episode 6. Apparently Dwight also has some Catholic heritage. "The Carpet," season 2, episode 14, deleted scenes.

17. "Safety Training," season 3, episode 20. For the peculiar Schrute wedding traditions—they are "a *bleak* affair"—see "Phyllis's Wedding," season 3, episode 16.

18. For a helpful discussion of paranoia, aggression, conventionalism, and other factors commonly associated with authoritarianism, see John Levi Martin, "*The Authoritarian Personality*, 50 Years Later: What Lessons Are There for Political Psychology?" *Political Psychology* 22, no. 1 (2001): 1–26.

19. For Jack Bauer, "The Job," season 3, episodes 24–25; for Han Solo and the Schrutian arsenal, "The Negotiation," season 3, episode 19; and "Survivor Man," season 4, episode 11; for the fireworks, "The Client," season 2, episode 7. For the CIA correspondence, "A Benihana Christmas," season 3, episodes 10–11; for the urine test, "Drug Testing," season 2, episode 20. See also Dwight's reflections on "this heinous culprit" and praying "to Thor himself," near the end of the bloopers of season 2. For Mussolini, "Dwight's Speech," season 2, episode 17.

20. "Health Care," season 1, episode 3; "The Initiation," season 3, episode 5; "Beach Games," season 3, episode 23; on Debbie Brown, "Product Recall," season 3, episode 21; on the dry-erase episode, "Basketball," season 1, episode 5. When Dwight is authorized to take care of Angela's cats, he stringently applies his farmer's ethic of utility—"Cats do not provide milk, wool, or meat. . . . Sometimes the right thing to do is to put it out of its misery." By euthanizing the beloved Sprinkles, he ruins his relationship with Angela and apparently his own brittle psyche as well. "Fun Run," season 4, episodes 1–2. After his breakup with Angela, Dwight loses his earlier harmlessness, becoming a genuine psychopath. A key change may be found in his plans to deal with the security guards in "Branch Wars," season 4, episode 10, an episode immediately following two key breakup episodes.

21. This scene reveals another reason that Dwight's ambition is unlikely to take him very far—he is quite uncouth. This comes out especially when he is around social elites, such as Jan Levinson and David Wallace, who are accustomed to a high level of professional gentility. See the devouring of the waffles during the interview with Jan ("The Coup," season 3, episode 3) and the prodding of David and his wife during their corporate party about the size, cost, and structural soundness of their house ("Cocktails," season 3, episode 18).

22. "The Coup," season 3, episode 3; "The Job," season 3, episodes 24–25. In "The Job," while painting the manager's office black with Andy, Dwight quotes Dante's inscription of the gates of hell: "Abandon all hope, ye who enter here!" Cf. Dante, *Inferno* 3.9, including the more recent translation by Robert Hollander and Jean Hollander (New York: Doubleday, 2000).

23. "The Alliance," season 1, episode 4.

24. "The Fight," season 2, episode 6. Cf. Machiavelli, *The Prince*, trans. Harvey Mansfield (Chicago: University of Chicago Press, 1998), chap. 17. While not related to

leadership style, the only direct mention of Machiavelli in the show is by Dwight. Praising the ruthlessness of a version of white elephant gift swaps, Dwight reflects: "Yankee Swap is like *Machiavelli* meets . . . . . . Christmas." "Christmas Party," season 2, episode 10.

25. Even for Machiavelli, a leader must appeal to fear but must avoid hatred (for evident wickedness) and contempt (for exposed weakness). See *The Prince*, chaps. 17 and 19. But Cicero would add the counterpoint that one must above all earn the affection and confidence of the people, rather than play upon their fears. See *On Obligations*, trans. P. G. Walsh (New York: Oxford University Press, 2008), 2.23–29. While Machiavelli and Cicero are often taken to represent diametrically opposed alternatives regarding politics and power, Schrute fails by both standards.

26. Tacitus observes of Curtius Rufus, a man of low birth but high achievements, that he was "morosely sycophantic towards his superiors, arrogant towards his inferiors, and difficult with his peers." *Annals*, trans. J. C. Yardley (New York: Oxford University Press, 2008), 11.21, p. 226. For Rousseau, many consequences follow once humans become interdependent and develop a host of unnatural needs: "[One] must constantly try to interest [others] in his fate and to make them really or apparently find their own profit in working for his: which makes him knavish and artful with some [i.e., those stronger than him], imperious and harsh with the rest [i.e., those weaker than him], and places him under the necessity of deceiving all those he needs if he cannot get them to fear him and does not find it in his interest to make himself useful to them." *Discourse on Inequality*, part 2, pp. 170–71. For Rousseau's model of proper relations amid (limited) dependence and (moderate) inequality, see especially *The Social Contract*, book 2, chap. 11.

27. "Valentine's Day," season 2, episode 16; "Product Recall," season 3, episode 21. Consider also Dwight's response to Angela's claim, "We can make a difference here," after "the coup" appears successful.

28. For these quick reversals, see Tacitus, e.g. *Histories*, 1.32, 1.45, 3.64, 3.85, 4.11. The point is nicely illustrated in Fénelon's *Telemachus*, another work that had a major impact on Rousseau. It portrays a fictional encounter of a virtuous but long-disgraced citizen, Hegesippus, who carries out the king's orders to exile Protesilaus, a corrupt but long-favored executive of the king. "At these words all the pride and arrogance of the favorite [Protesilaus] fell in a moment. . . . He throws himself at the feet of Hegesippus, trembling, faltering, weeping, and embraces his knees, though a little before he would hardly have deigned to take the least notice of him. All those who but lately offered him the incense of fulsome flattery, seeing him irrevocably undone, insulted him without pity." *Telemachus, Son of Ulysses*, trans. Patrick Riley (Cambridge: Cambridge University Press, 1994), book 11, p. 188; see also book 14, p. 243.

29. "The Coup," season 3, episode 3. Notice also Dwight's satisfied grin after he is required to bounce Michael from reentering Phyllis's wedding: "I'm sorry, it gives me no pleasure." "Phyllis's Wedding," season 3, episode 16. Although Ryan was never internally servile toward Michael during his years when his job required him to serve as a lackey, a similar reversal occurs—with some vengeance mixed in—when Ryan returns to Scranton

as Michael's boss and insists that Michael leave a meeting and get him a glass of water. See "Dunder Mifflin Infinity," season 4, episodes 3–4, deleted scenes.

30. "The Injury," season 2, episode 12; and "Cocktails," season 3, episode 18, with an apparently honest verdict on Michael's breath: "Good not great."

31. "Michael's Birthday," season 2, episode 19. Michael gives an immortal reply, pointing to a James Dean poster: "You're making it worse. I bet Luke Perry's friends don't treat him like this."

32. "Cocktails," season 3, episode 18.

33. "Halloween," season 2, episode 5.

34. A theme running through the early books of the *Confessions* is Rousseau's bitterness at his harsh treatment by various masters and their inability to recognize his merits. See, for instance, *Confessions*, trans. Angela Scholar (New York: Oxford University Press, 2000), book 1, p. 31; book 3, p. 90 ("What, still a lackey?"); book 6, p. 262. For Rousseau's model of proper treatment of servants—to have "enough respect for the dignity of man albeit in servitude to put him only to tasks that do not abase him" and never to have them "serve merely as an instrument of others"—see *Julie, or the New Heloise*, trans. Philip Stewart and Jean Vaché (Hanover, NH: University Press of New England, 1997), part 4, letter 10, esp. p. 386; and part 5, letter 2, esp. p. 439. Rousseau's teaching on human dignity had a major impact on modern thought by transforming Immanuel Kant's views of the matter and becoming a central element of Kant's ethics. See Allen Wood, *Kant's Ethical Thought* (Cambridge: Cambridge University Press, 1999), 5–9.

35. This excuse-making tradition reaches its maturity with Ryan's response, upon being invited by Michael to Benihana's for lunch: "I'm not feeling so well. I've got a ton of work to do here. MSG allergy, peanut allergy, I just ate there last night." He holds up his Blackberry's list of excuses to Jim, who has thus been left defenseless against Michael's invitation. "A Benihana Christmas," season 3, episodes 10–11. See also Ryan's ambivalence and embarrassment about Michael before and after the speech in "Business School," season 3, episode 17, as well as in Ryan's car during "The Fire," season 2, episode 4. Michael's open disrespect for the unpopular and unattractive becomes especially destructive at the "Job Fair," season 4, episode 17.

36. Sales numbers in "The Coup," season 3, episode 3, deleted scenes. Also, when Michael initiates a paper sales competition, Dwight exclaims with sincere delight, "Michael is gonna wipe the floor with us!" "The Carpet," season 2, episode 14. And he considers it hilarious and absurd that Michael once had a position so lowly as a bottle capper in a factory. "The Convention," season 3, episode 3, deleted scenes. However, this should be interpreted in view of the fact that Dwight seems to be prone to disinterested admiration—even worship—of authority figures who have achieved anything manly. Captain Jack inspires Dwight's awe for having served in the navy during the Persian Gulf War ("Booze Cruise," season 3, episode 11, deleted scenes), and Josh the Stamford Regional Manager becomes a guru for having served in the Coast Guard and worked on a kibbutz ("The Convention," season 3, episode 2, including deleted scenes).

37. See, in particular, the conversation between Michael and Dwight as they are finally convinced that their branch will be closing and their jobs will be lost. "Branch Closing," season 3, episode 7.

38. "Drug Testing," season 2, episode 20.

39. For Andy and Cornell, "Launch Party," season 4, episodes 5–6; and especially his introduction in "Gay Witch Hunt," season 3, episode 1. He is, of course, not just any legacy at Cornell: "A lot of people were like, 'Oh, you just got into Cornell because your dad donated a building.'" "Branch Wars," season 4, episode 10. For wearing someone down, "Traveling Salesman," season 3, episode 13.

40. "The Merger," season 3, episode 8. To a similar list, Andy adds "positive reinforcement through nods and smiles" just before his entrance to the anger management program. "The Return," season 3, episode 14.

41. Tacitus, *Annals* 6.20, p. 195; on Caligula's ambition, see also 6.45, p. 210. For Plato, flattery and slavishness are thus rightly condemned because they accustom people to accept insults from the vulgar for the sake of money. The "spirited" part of the soul is thus distorted—instead of being like a proud, strong lion, it becomes like a ridiculous ape. *Republic*, trans. G. M. A. Grube, rev. C. D. C. Reeve (Indianapolis: Hackett, 1992), 8.590b.

42. "The Merger," season 3, episode 8.

43. "Traveling Salesmen," season 3, episode 13.

44. Tacitus, *Histories*, 2.38, p. 80. See also Sallust, *Catiline's War*, in *Catiline's War, The Jugurthine War, Histories*, trans. A. J. Woodman (London: Penguin, 2008), secs. 9–16; Augustine, *The City of God*, trans. R. W. Dyson (Cambridge: Cambridge University Press, 1998), 2.18, 3.21; cf. the contention of Scipio against destroying Carthage, in Plutarch, *Cato the Elder*, in *Roman Lives*, trans. Robin Waterfield (New York: Oxford University Press, 1999), sec. 27. The Roman narrative of decline resulting from prosperity and grandeur also seems to play a role in the "meteoric rise"—and fall—of Ryan Howard (see especially "Night Out," season 4, episode 15).

45. Michael also laments, "I don't understand how someone could have so little self-awareness." "The Return," season 3, episode 14. Placed in the mouth of Michael, the claim has delicious irony. Apparently, just as Andy has outdone Dwight in servility, he is now outdoing Michael in narcissism and lack of genuine empathy.

46. "The Return," season 3, episode 14. Andy confirms this hypothesis later on: "Let me be clear. There's only one thing that's important to me, and it's not friendship. It's dominance." "Women's Appreciation," season 3, episode 21, deleted scenes.

47. "The Fire," season 2, episode 4; and Roy's violence in "The Negotiation," season 3, episode 19.

48. Tacitus, *Annals* 1.4, p. 5; see also 3.26, p. 108; Rousseau, *Letter to d'Alembert on the Theatre*, trans. Allan Bloom (Ithaca, NY: Cornell University Press, 1960), 112; see also 111–13. For positive models of robust, primitive freedom in Tacitus, see *Annals* 3.25–28; *Agricola*, secs. 13, 15–16, 30; *Germany*, e.g., secs. 7, 11, 21, 37, 44.

*Agricola* and *Germany* are in a combined edition, trans. A. R. Birley (New York: Oxford University Press, 1999). And for Rousseau's positive models, *Discourse on Inequality,* esp. part 1; and *Essay on the Origin of Languages,* in *The Discourses and Other Early Political Writings,* esp. chap. 9. Note also Rousseau's extensive citations of *Agricola* in *Social Contract,* 3.9, pp. 105–6n.

# 6

# WHO WATCHES THE WATCHMEN?

## Kant, Mill, and Political Morality in the Shadow of Manhattan

*S. Evan Kreider*

*Watchmen* is arguably the most revolutionary graphic novel ever written. It showed a generation of readers that a so-called super-hero comic book could engage a sophisticated adult audience and deal with complex moral and political issues. At the heart of the text is a classic quandary: is it ever morally acceptable to sacrifice the interests of a few for the greater good of the many?

*Watchmen* presents a not-so-alternate version of the 1980s in which the world stands on the brink of a massive nuclear war. Adrian Veidt, otherwise known as the hero Ozymandias ("The World's Smartest Man"), has carried out a plan to save the world and to unite the people of all its nations by faking an alien invasion, killing millions of innocent people in the process. Once the other heroes discover this, Adrian persuades them to stay silent, so as not to destroy the utopia that he has created; or rather, he persuades all but one of the heroes. Rorschach, the most brutal and least sane member of the group of heroes—really more a vigilante than a hero—refuses to cooperate. In his mind, Adrian is a murderer, and justice demands that he be held accountable, regardless of the consequences. He makes it clear that he will tell anyone who will listen to him about Adrian's actions, even if the world dies by nuclear fire as a result. Finally, Dr. Manhattan, a man of almost godlike power over space, time, and matter itself, and the only truly superpowered member of the group, steps in and kills Rorschach to prevent him from pursuing a course of action that will likely lead to the destruction of all human life. However, this resolution is not as simple as Dr. Manhattan siding with Adrian and vindicating his decision. When Adrian asks him: "I did the right thing, didn't I? It all worked out in the end," Dr. Manhattan responds: "'In the end'? *Nothing* ends, Adrian. Nothing *ever* ends."[1]

The authors of *Watchmen* refuse to give us a simple answer to the difficult issues that underlie this story. Instead, they present a variety of views, each delivered through a character that is flawed but merits sympathy in his own right. In this chapter, we will explore the three aforementioned characters and the values that each represents.

## Rorschach: Deontology and Absolutism

After the rest of the heroes agree to remain silent about Adrian's extreme solution to the world's problems, Rorschach is the sole hero to break ranks. Rorschach decides to remain true to his value system, even though it could lead to the death of every person on earth, himself included. This value system can be characterized as deontological in that it is based on principles requiring that we determine the morality of our actions independently of their consequences. It is also absolutist in that it does not allow for any exceptions or compromise. The definitive example of a deontological and absolutist thinker in the history of moral philosophy is the eighteenth-century German philosopher Immanuel Kant.

According to Kant, the essence of morality can be captured by a principle that he refers to as the Categorical Imperative. Kant states that this principle can be given several different formulations, the first of which is "Act only according to that maxim whereby you can at the same time will that it should become a universal law."[2] The basic idea behind this rather technical-sounding statement is fairly simple: for an action to be morally permissible, it must be something that everyone could do without becoming self-defeating or self-contradictory.

For example, imagine that I need a loan to pay my mortgage and avoid losing my home, but I know that I will not be able to pay back that loan. Since I know that the bank won't give me the loan unless I promise to re-pay it, I consider making a false promise, wondering if perhaps the severe circumstances might justify such behavior. Kant's first formulation tells me that such a false promise would be morally permissible only if it could be universalized—that is, "What if everyone in similar circumstances did the same thing?" The answer is fairly obvious. If everyone made false promises to repay loans, no bank would ever consider giving loans in the first place; in other words, such behavior would actually defeat its own purpose.

There are a couple of important things to note about this. Despite how it might sound at first, this formulation is not an appeal to consequences but, rather, to logical consistency. Kant is not asking us to consider whether a world in which people make false promises is a good or bad world. Rather, he is asking us to consider whether there is a logically possible world in which people make false promises to get loans. There is no such world, of course, for if everyone made false promises, there would be no loans to get. To put it another way, Kant is telling me that I cannot decide that a certain course of action is rational for me in my circumstances unless I can conceive of a world in which everyone in the same circumstances could ("could" in the sense of "logically possibly") do the same thing. Morality requires rational, logical consistency: if it's okay for me, then it must also be okay for you under the same morally relevant circumstances. The consideration of good or bad consequences is, according to Kant, extraneous and irrelevant. This kind of nonconsequentialism is called "deontology" because it derives from the Greek *deon,* meaning "that which is required." Thus, as a deontological thinker, Kant believes there are certain things that morality requires of us (specifically, logical consistency), prior to and independent of any consideration of consequences.

Another important implication of this process is that morality does not allow us to make exceptions for ourselves. "But I really need that loan," I might be tempted to tell myself. "I'm not saying everyone should do this all the time, but isn't it okay for me, just this once?" Kant makes it clear that this sort of reasoning simply isn't moral reasoning. Precisely what it means to say that an action is morally permissible is to say that it is permissible not just for me but for anyone in the same circumstances. Making exceptions for oneself to rules that others ought to follow is the very definition of immoral behavior. In this regard, Kant subscribes to what is known as moral absolutism: there are moral rules that apply to everyone, and exceptions are never permissible.

Rorschach shows Kantian-style moral reasoning at the climax of the text. He refuses to deceive the world by helping to cover up Adrian's actions, regardless of the potentially catastrophic consequences of revealing Adrian's scheme. After the other heroes agree to keep Adrian's secret, Rorschach simply responds, "Joking, of course," and begins to walk away. When Night Owl, another of the heroes and the individual closest to being a friend of

Rorschach, says, "Rorschach, wait! Where are you going? This is too big to be hard-assed about! We have to compromise," Rorschach replies "No. Not even in the face of Armageddon. Never compromise" (12:20). In Rorschach's mind, there are moral absolutes, and they must be observed. Regardless of his reasoning, Adrian has murdered millions of innocent people, and an evil act such as that can never be justified by a greater good. Rorschach anticipates this earlier in the text, when he ponders to himself: "Is it futile? Soon there will be war. Millions will burn. Millions will perish in sickness and misery. Why does one death matter against so many? Because there is good and there is evil, and evil must be punished. Even in the face of Armageddon I shall not compromise in this" (1:24).

Rorschach also serves as an example of Kant's second formulation of the Categorical Imperative: "Act in such a way that you treat humanity, whether in your own person or in the person of another, always at the same time as an end and never simply as a means."[3] Sometimes called the "respect for persons" formulation, this phrasing of the Categorical Imperative asks us to recognize and respect the intrinsic value of humanity. According to Kant, what gives humans a special kind of value and dignity above all other earthly creatures is our capacity for reason and autonomy—that is, the ability to think and to choose for ourselves.

One especially important implication of this principle concerns Kant's views on punishment. We show respect for people's rationality and autonomy by holding them responsible for their behavior. In the case of crimes, we hold criminals responsible for their behavior by punishing them for it, not because we hope to deter further crime, or because we hope to rehabilitate the criminal, but simply as a matter of justice; that is, simply because they deserve it. Furthermore, in order to hold criminals fully responsible for their crimes, we must punish them proportionately—the punishment must fit the crime, or "an eye for an eye." Thus, Kant supports the death penalty for the crime of murder. When someone takes a life, the only truly proportionate punishment is death. Whether or not the death penalty has good or bad consequences for society (for example, whether or not it has a deterrence effect) is irrelevant to Kant. The criminal simply deserves to die, and we actually demonstrate our respect of the criminal as a rational, autonomous human being by putting him to death for his crimes.

Rorschach clearly endorses Kant's view of retribution, including the use of the death penalty. "There is good and there is evil, and evil must be punished . . . but there are so many deserving of retribution and there is so little time" (1:24). Rorschach has no problem administering the appropriate penalty to those who deserve it, as he demonstrates throughout the text. Perhaps the most important example is the one Rorschach discusses during his "origin story," as he relates it to the prison psychiatrist while he is temporarily incarcerated, about midway through the text. As he tells it, Rorschach had been investigating the disappearance of a young girl, only to discover that she had been killed brutally and most likely abused beforehand as well. It was this moment when he truly became Rorschach, when he saw the true evil of which humans are capable and saw that it was his responsibility to punish that evil appropriately—which in this case he does by chaining the murderer to his stove and setting his house on fire, allowing him to burn to death—a punishment arguably as brutal as the crime that he committed (6:18–26).

Furthermore, Rorschach clearly thinks of such punishment as a sign of respect for the criminals. He admits that earlier in his career as a crime-fighter, he has not shown them such respect. "Soft on scum. Too young to know any better. Molly-coddled them. Let them live" (6:14). By failing to punish the criminals appropriately, he was treating them with kid gloves, as though they were mere children, incapable of understanding or controlling their own actions. By punishing them as they deserve, he is no longer "molly-coddling" them but is treating them the way they deserve to be treated, as rational, free, adult human beings, who truly are capable of evil acts.

By now, the reader can be forgiven for any concerns about Kantianism. After all, although Rorschach is a fascinating character, he's not exactly a moral exemplar of any sort. His behavior throughout *Watchmen* is extremely brutal, to say the least, and there are certainly some concerns about his sanity as well. If that is the case, then can we also infer that there is something immoral and possibly even psychotic about Kant's moral theory? To Kant's credit, the answer is no. Although it is true that Rorschach's behavior bears some of the marks of Kant's moral theory, Rorschach goes wrong precisely because he does not fully instantiate Kant's views. Specifically, he actually fails to observe fully either formulation of the Categorical Imperative.

First, Rorschach's vigilantism cannot be universalized and thus fails to meet one of the tests required by the first formulation of the Categorical Imperative. Taking the law into one's own hands and punishing people (especially by way of the death penalty) according to one's own standards of right and wrong would be self-defeating if everyone did it. After all, there are plenty of folks on both sides of the law who consider Rorschach a murderer, presumably deserving of death himself! So if everyone killed everyone who one personally thought deserved to die, there wouldn't be anyone left to punish those who do deserve punishment, thus defeating the purpose of pursuing such punishment in the first place.

Second, Rorschach does not fully respect the rationality and autonomy of other people, as required by the second formulation of the Categorical Imperative. Unlike Kant, Rorschach does not believe that there are real, objective values in the universe. Instead, Rorschach embraces a kind of nihilism that is closer to some existentialist thinkers than to any Kantian. "Existence is random. Has no pattern save what we imagine after staring at it for too long. No meaning save what we choose to impose," Rorschach says. "Was reborn then, free to scrawl own design on this morally blank world" (6:26). Since Rorschach believes there is no reason, purpose, or value to existence (much less to people), he believes that gives him the right to create his own values and impose them on the world. Not only can this not be universalized (it's logically impossible for all of us to impose our own values on everyone else); it is completely disrespectful of everyone else.

As a result, we see that Rorschach's moral shortcomings are not the result of his Kantianism, but rather of his failure to embrace Kant's moral system completely and consistently. As much as we might admire and respect some aspects of Rorschach's moral conviction, we certainly can't view him as the hero of the piece in any final sense. Fortunately, the authors of *Watchmen* present us with a variety of other characters who might fill that role for us. In particular, Ozymandias seems to represent the diametric opposite of Rorschach's views, so perhaps after careful examination, he might qualify as a true moral exemplar.

## Ozymandias: Consequences and Exceptions

Adrian (aka "Ozymandias") takes a very different approach to these issues than Rorschach. Specifically, he can be characterized as a consequentialist rather than a deontologist. Furthermore, the kind of consequentialism he seems to endorse also differs from Rorschach's thinking in that it is not absolutist moral thinking: it allows for occasional exceptions to supposedly common-sense moral guidelines.

According to consequentialism, right and wrong are determined by the consequences of our actions. In the simplest terms, consequentialism states that an action is right if it has good consequences and an action is wrong if it has bad consequences. Of course, this seemingly simple idea becomes much more complicated once we start talking about specific consequentialist theories, of which there are many. Adrian's approach to moral issues appears to demonstrate a particular brand of consequentialism known as utilitarianism.

The basic idea behind utilitarianism is "the principle of utility." Simply put, the principle of utility states that we ought to promote the greatest good for the greatest number. In essence, the principle of utility tells us that we ought to consider the consequences of our actions not just for ourselves but for all of those who are affected by them. Then we are to calculate all the potential benefits and harms that could result to each of those affected by our actions, and finally, we are to choose the course of action that leads to the greatest good consequences for the greatest number. Different utilitarians have different ideas about what exactly counts as a benefit or harm in the morally relevant sense and different ideas about how exactly we go about calculating this greatest good and greatest number, but the sorts of things Adrian has in mind are fairly straightforward: he believes that he has an obligation to save humanity from a nuclear war, thereby preventing death, destruction, pain, suffering, and possibly even the extinction of the human race.

Furthermore, different utilitarians have different ideas about how exactly to apply the principle of utility to our actions. The earliest utilitarians were known as "act utilitarians." The act utilitarians believed that each and every individual action needs to be judged based on the specific consequences that result from it. For example, if you were to ask an act utilitarian whether or not lying is morally permissible, his response would be "It depends." If the lie in question leads to overall bad consequences—say a lie that ruins a personal relationship, or one that gets someone fired from her job—then that particular lie is morally wrong. However, if the lie in question leads to good consequences—perhaps by making someone feel better about herself or smoothing over an awkward social situation (a "white lie"), or even by saving someone's life (e.g., a lie that deceives a crazed ax murderer about the whereabouts of his victim)—then that particular lie would be morally permissible. Having said that, most act utilitarians would be happy to admit that lying usually doesn't promote the greatest good, and so under normal circumstances, we should probably avoid lying. That general guideline is not absolute and will have plenty of exceptions for the morally reflective person.

Adrian certainly seems to demonstrate a kind of act utilitarian thinking.

In *Watchmen,* the world is hurtling toward a nuclear war between the United States and the Soviet Union and their respective allies. If this happens, billions will die, either from the war itself or from the fallout from it. Adrian believes that the only way to prevent loss of life on this scale is to give the earth's nations a common, external enemy, and so he hatches a plan to fake an alien invasion. Unfortunately, in order to make this invasion convincing, and in order to make sure that no one finds out that the invasion is a fraud, millions of innocent people must die. The text provides several examples of Adrian acting toward this greater good in an act utilitarian manner, at least at first glance.

At the very beginning of *Watchmen,* we discover that the Comedian (Edward Blake, another of the costumed "heroes"—a nihilist who thinks that life is meaningless and therefore "just a big joke") has been brutally murdered. Later, we learn that the Comedian accidentally stumbled upon Adrian's plan. Although he took no joy in it, Adrian realized that he would have to kill the Comedian to keep his plan a secret. "Blake understood, too. He knew my plan would succeed, though its scale terrified him. That's why he told nobody. It was too big to discuss . . . but he understood. At the end, he understood" (11:25).

One of the things the Comedian had discovered was an island where Adrian had a team of people working to create the "alien" creature that Adrian would use in his fake invasion. Once the work is complete, Adrian puts his team on a boat, supposedly headed home—and then blows up the boat, killing them all (10:18).

Once it is time to carry out his plan, Adrian goes to his Antarctic retreat. After a long monologue in which he attempts to justify his extreme measures to save the world, he poisons all of his servants, so that they too might never reveal his plan. "Do you comprehend the triumph to which you have contributed, the secret glory that it affords? Do you understand my shame at so inadequate a reward?" (11:11).

All of these examples pale in comparison to the culmination of the plan itself, in which Adrian teleports his "alien" into the heart of New York City, the resulting explosion of which kills millions. Shortly thereafter, Adrian sees news reports that seem to vindicate his plan: the world powers put aside their differences, stop the "nuclear clock," and agree to work together for the safety of Earth against the supposedly alien enemy. "I did it!" Adrian shouts—perhaps not catching the double meaning of his own words (12:19).

Once again, the reader may be forgiven for thinking that something has gone seriously wrong here. Since there is something intuitively wrong about Adrian's actions, does that imply that consequentialist thinking is incorrect? Not necessarily. There are a couple of ways the consequentialist might respond to our moral discomfort.

First, it might simply be that Adrian is using the wrong kind of consequentialist thinking. There are many different consequentialist theories other than utilitarianism; furthermore, there are many different varieties of utilitarianism. For example, in addition to act utilitarianism, there is a form of utilitarianism known as rule utilitarianism. Some utilitarians abandoned act utilitarianism after considering several obvious objections to it. First, it completely omits any conception of individual rights or justice, seemingly allowing us to sacrifice the interests (and even lives) of the few in order to benefit the many, and there is something extremely counterintuitive about abandoning such core moral and political concepts as rights and justice. Moreover, critics claim that act utilitarianism falls prey to the so-called calculation objection. This objection comes in many forms, but the short of it is that it is impossible to calculate accurately all of the potential consequences of every possible action that any of us might do. Worse, there is something "self-defeating" (in Kant's terms) about act utilitarianism: we'd have to spend so much time calculating the consequences of our actions that we'd never have time to actually do anything! As a result, thinking about the greatest good for the greatest number that might result from each and every possible action guarantees that we won't do any good at all, much less the greatest good.

To correct for these perceived problems with act utilitarianism without abandoning utilitarianism altogether, rule utilitarianism argued that we can simplify our consequentialist reasoning by acting according to general rules of behavior rather than calculating the consequences of each and every action. For example, instead of thinking, "Should I murder this person? Would that bring about the greatest good?" every time we meet someone, the rule utilitarian would have us ask ourselves "In general, would a rule that allows murder be for the greatest good? Or would a rule against murder better promote the greater good?" Clearly, as a general policy, a rule against murder better promotes the greater good than a rule that allows murder. Thus, the rule utilitarian would say that we ought to adopt a general rule against murder and simply follow it. By taking this approach, the rule utilitarian avoids the calculation objection.

A definitive example of a utilitarian thinker is John Stuart Mill, the author of *Utilitarianism*. Mill is also a strong supporter of individual rights, which he defends in his work *On Liberty*. For Mill, the most important rules of society are those that protect its members from others: "The only purpose for which power can be rightfully exercised over any member of a civilized community, against his will, is to prevent harm to others."[4] However, Mill makes it clear that this is not a separate (much less deontological) principle but rather a derivative of the principle of utility: "I regard utility as the ultimate appeal on all ethical questions; but it must be utility in the largest sense, grounded on the permanent interests of man as a progressive being."[5] Essentially, Mill argues that the best way to bring about the greatest good for the greatest number is to structure society around a set of rules that protect people's rights.[6]

Mill spends a great deal of time discussing which specific rights society needs in order to promote the greatest good for the greatest number. Some of the specific ones he discusses may be debatable, but no champion of individual rights (much less Mill) would disagree that at a bare minimum, innocent people ought to have the right not to be murdered. A society that does not protect its members from murder is as far from the greatest good for the greatest number as one could get—in fact, it's not clear there could even be such a society at all (very quickly, there would be no one left . . . ). Thus, the right to be protected against murder can be conceived of as a rule that promotes the greatest good for the greatest number, and Adrian has clearly violated that rule in a big way.

There is also another way someone might criticize Adrian's thinking without abandoning consequentialism—indeed, without necessarily even abandoning act utilitarianism. Specifically, an act utilitarian might agree in principle that sometimes extreme measures are required to prevent something even worse from happening but argue that Adrian simply didn't go about calculating the consequences of his action carefully enough. In particular, his solution to the threat of nuclear war rests on keeping his scheme a secret indefinitely, and that's just not very likely. As we've already seen, the Comedian came across Adrian's plan quite by accident, and there's no reason to think that someone else might not do the same. Furthermore, Adrian was assuming that he would be able to persuade the rest of the heroes to keep his secret, and that clearly failed with Rorschach. Adrian might counter that he could always kill them as well. Perhaps that would be possible for most of the heroes—after all, he did kill the Comedian, and he allowed Dr. Manhattan to kill Rorschach—but killing Dr. Manhattan would certainly present a much, much greater challenge. In fact, we see the failure of Adrian's calculation with regard to this precisely: Adrian created a chamber to destroy Dr. Manhattan, but it failed, and even Adrian himself admitted he wasn't sure in the first place whether it would work (12:14). Finally, we see on the very last page of the text that his plan is likely to come to light, as Rorschach's journal, which Rorschach mailed just before leaving for the Antarctic, does indeed find its way to the press. The implication is that Adrian's plan will be revealed, and the murder of millions of innocent people will have accomplished no good (12:32).

As a result, it seems that Adrian's problem isn't so much his consequentialism as the fact that he's a rather poor consequentialist. In that regard, he's not unlike Rorschach, who was guilty of comparable errors as a deontologist. Thus, all we have so far is a critique of two wrong ways to think about things, but surely the text of *Watchmen* provides us some clue about the right way to think. To that end, let us now turn our attention to Dr. Manhattan—arguably the true "hero" of the piece.

## Dr. Manhattan: The Value of Life and Compromise

Although it might seem so from the above examples, consequentialism and deontology are not necessarily incompatible. Indeed, some philosophers would argue that an adequate theory of right and wrong has to combine elements of both. This seems to be the approach of Dr. Manhattan. His own views rest on a deontological principle concerning the value of human life, but he also uses consequentialist thinking in order to calculate the best way to preserve life.

During a pivotal section of the text shortly before the climax of the story, Dr. Manhattan teleports his recently ex-girlfriend Laurie Juspechyk, also known as the hero "Silk Spectre," to his retreat on Mars so that they can debate his possible intervention in Adrian's plan. Dr. Manhattan (who views the world through the lenses of physics more than those of ordinary human life) begins the debate by claiming that life has no intrinsic value. At first, he does not see any value in the lives of ordinary people, but only because he is thinking in strict consequentialist terms. "Humanity is about to become extinct," Laurie says. "Doesn't that bother you? All those people dead . . ." "All that pain and conflict done with?" he replies. "All that needless suffering over at last? No . . . No, that doesn't bother me. All those generations of struggle, what purpose did they ever achieve? All that effort, and what did it ever lead to?" (9:10). At first, Dr. Manhattan seems to be taking a utilitarian approach and arguing that the suffering of human life outweighs its benefits; thus the "greatest good" might actually be extinction.

However, he soon changes his mind, once he sees that the value of human life isn't something to be determined by its benefits. Rather, life has intrinsic value as a "thermodynamic miracle," that is, an event

> with odds against so astronomical they're effectively impossible, like oxygen spontaneously becoming gold. I long to observe such a thing. And yet, in each human coupling, a thousand million sperm vie for a single egg. Multiply those odds by countless generations, against the odds of your ancestors being alive; meeting; siring this precise son; that exact daughter . . . until your mother loves a man she has every reason to hate, and of that union, of the thousand million children competing for fertilization, it was you, only you, that emerged. To distill so specific a form from that chaos of improbability, like turning air to gold . . . that is the crowning unlikelihood. The thermodynamic miracle. (9:26–27)

Of course, this is true not only of Laurie, but of anyone. Each life is a miracle of physics and statistics, making each life precious beyond measure. From this, Dr. Manhattan finally concludes that each life does have an intrinsic value that deserves to be preserved, whether or not that life leads to particularly good consequences for the world or even itself.

Once he establishes this deontological principle of the intrinsic value of human life, Dr. Manhattan is willing to engage in consequentialist thinking about how to best preserve life. Toward the very end of the text, when the heroes are coming to the conclusion that they must keep Adrian's secret, Dr. Manhattan concurs. "Logically, I'm afraid he's right. Exposing this plot, we destroy any chance of peace, dooming earth to worse destruction. On Mars, you [Laurie] demonstrated life's value. If we would preserve life here, we must remain silent" (12:20). The value of life—and the obligation to preserve it that this value entails—outweighs the value of other moral considerations such as truth-telling.

Furthermore, in such an extreme circumstance, that also means that the value of many lives may outweigh the value of a single one, in typical consequentialist fashion. Dr. Manhattan confronts Rorschach before he can leave and inform the world about Adrian's plot. "You know I can't let you do that," Dr. Manhattan tells Rorschach. "Of course," Rorschach replies. "Must protect Veidt's new utopia. One more body amongst foundations makes little difference. Well, what are you waiting for? Do it" (12:23–24). And Dr. Manhattan does. He certainly takes no pleasure in it, and would prefer not to do so, but if life has value, then in such circumstances, Dr. Manhattan must think about the preservation of life, even if it requires the sacrifice of one.

## Who Watches? The Political Implications of *Watchmen*

The implications of the competing moral views depicted in *Watchmen* are far-reaching. These views give us guidelines for not only personal behavior, but also political organization. In particular, the text serves as an endorsement of the principles behind modern rights-based democracies, seen as a reasonable compromise of deontology and consequentialism. In other words, the careful line that Dr. Manhattan walks between the extremes of Adrian and Rorschach is precisely that line around which rights-based democracies are built.

One implication of the text concerns the idea of the importance of transparency in a rights-based democracy. After all, a democracy is supposed to be government by the people. Of course, we elect representatives to make some decisions for us, and we hope that they are informed enough to make good decisions on our behalf, even at times when they can't let everyone know exactly what they're doing, such as during a time of war. They are still supposed to be our representatives, ruling on our behalf, according to the will of the people. As such, we expect a certain degree (a fairly large degree, actually) of transparency, so that we the people can decide whether they are doing their jobs the way they are supposed to do them. We may not need to know every little detail in every situation, but at no time do we agree that our government may act in complete secrecy or even deception—to do so is to act as tyrants, not as representatives.

Of course, Adrian demonstrates exactly these dangers. His tragic flaw is the oldest of them all—hubris. He believes that he is smarter than everyone else—and perhaps he is. However, he thinks that his intelligence gives him and him alone the right to make decisions on everyone else's behalf. He consults no one—not the people at large, not their elected representatives, not the other heroes, and not even Dr. Manhattan (the only other person on earth at least as smart as Adrian). This hubris is precisely how he is led down the tragic path that ends in the death of millions and, as the end of the text suggests, the revelation of his plan to the world, making it all for naught.

Another and even more central political implication of the text concerns the way in which modern rights-based democracies strive to find the appropriate balance between the rights of the individual and the greater good of the larger citizenry. For example, the American Constitution does this in part through the Bill of Rights. These rights protect the individual from society—whether that be another individual, the government, or, as Tocqueville (and later Mill, quoting Tocqueville) put it, "the tyranny of the majority." At the same time, limits are placed on individual rights when the right of individual action is outweighed by the significant threats it might pose to society.

A clear example of this is freedom of expression. The first amendment protects the right of individuals to express their opinions, whether moral, political, religious, or otherwise, regardless of how unpopular those opinions might be. At the same time, this right does not grant individuals free reign to say whatever they want in any manner, at any time, in any place. There are occasions when the expression of opinion goes beyond mere expression and constitutes a serious harm or threat of harm to others, such as revealing military secrets to the enemy during a time of war, or even just yelling "Fire!" in a crowded movie theater. By granting such rights but also clearly delineating their limits, we do our best to find that line between the deontological sovereignty of the individual over himself and the consequentialist greater good of society at large.

It's not difficult to imagine on which side of the line our various heroes would fall. Adrian, concerned only with the greater good (and in a far too simplistic manner) would be likely to ignore individual rights such as free speech altogether—after all, the story he has invented to save the world is little more than propaganda, and he kills everyone involved in his scheme who might be tempted to tell anyone about it. Rorschach clearly favors individual rights such as free speech, without thought of the consequences, no matter how severe—he demonstrates this by his determination to tell the world about Adrian's plot. Arguably, Dr. Manhattan is the one who most closely resembles the compromise between the rights of the individual and the greater good of society—he was convinced by Laurie of the value of the individual but is also willing to intervene in extreme circumstances, as he does when he kills Rorschach. This certainly suggests that Dr. Manhattan is the closest thing to a true hero in the text, given that he most closely embodies the moral compromise between deontology and consequentialism on which modern rights-based democracies are built, as endorsed by *Watchmen*.

## The Shadow of Manhattan

*Watchmen* is truly a complex tale of competing values and difficult dilemmas. Both Adrian and Rorschach are interesting characters who evoke sympathy; indeed, both are honorable men in their own ways. As such, they provide excellent examples of some of the most important philosophical theories of right and wrong. However, they are also obviously flawed heroes, and as a result, they show us the potential flaws of their philosophical viewpoints, as well as how those viewpoints can be misused. Although the authors of *Watchmen* provide no easy answers, there is certainly a suggestion that if anyone is the true hero of the piece, it may be Dr. Manhattan. If that is correct, then truly, "we are all of us living in the shadow of Manhattan" (4:32)—and perhaps that's not such a bad place to be.

## Notes

1. Alan Moore and Dave Gibbons, *Watchmen* (New York: DC Comics, 1987), issue 12, page 27, hereafter cited parenthetically in the format 12:27 (issue: page number).

2. Immanuel Kant, *Grounding for the Metaphysics of Morals,* trans. James W. Ellington (1785; Indianapolis: Hackett, 1994), 421.

3. Ibid., 429.

4. John Stuart Mill, *On Liberty* (1859), ed. Elizabeth Rapaport (Indianapolis: Hackett, 1978), 9.

5. Ibid., 10.

6. Unfortunately, there's no single quote that makes this general claim as explicit as we'd like for a chapter such as this. However, Mill devotes most of *On Liberty* to arguing for several specific individual rights (e.g., free speech) on the grounds that each best contributes to the greatest good. From these multiple specific arguments, Mill implies the more general argument that a society based on individual rights best promotes the greatest good.

**Part 3**

# THE LIMITATIONS AND POSSIBILITIES OF POLITICAL LIFE

# 7

# *Avatar*, Marx, and the Alienation of Labor

*Mark C. E. Peterson*

Have you ever had a lousy job? A job that sucked the life out of you, ground you down, made you feel like a cog in the impersonal machinery of paying rent and staying fed? Philosophically speaking, Karl Marx remains the expert on what makes a lousy job lousy. It's an experience common to everyone, and it drew Marx's attention in the 1840s as he watched industrialization, with its social and psychological fallout, roll out across Europe. The issue is just as important for us today, and yet it is easier to find Marxist political philosophy in recent movies than in recent politics. For example: consider James Cameron's 2009 sci-fi blockbuster *Avatar*.[1]

Cameron's film follows the adventure—the pilgrimage—of Jake Sully, a crippled and discarded fragment of industrial-corporate society. Jake knows all about lousy, and his story embodies everything Marx had to say about a world in which economic relations have replaced social ones. Jake's world is run by corporations, corporations so big that they have taken over the functions of government; corporations that dictate not only the economic and political realities of life, but the social and cultural ones as well. These social and cultural realities determine what counts as happy, what counts as successful, and what counts as meaningful; Jake's life is a failure on all three. We can imagine him discharged from the military, crippled in the line of duty, soured and curdled by his experience. Alienated from his culture, from his fellow humans, and even from himself, Jake goes to work for the gargantuan RDA Corporation. He is flown to a distant mining colony on a moon called Pandora. His job: take part in a scientific study of the indigenous, humanoid population called the Na'vi. Pandora's atmosphere is toxic to humans, so, in order to initiate relations with the Na'vi, the corporation developed biological robots, or "avatars," by merging Na'vi and human DNA. These artificial bodies are designed, ostensibly, to facilitate anthropological studies, but their real mission is to expedite the exploitation of Pandora's most important natural resource: a mineral—and metaphorical sledgehammer—called *unobtainium*. The avatars look and function like Na'vi but are engineered to contain the consciousness of a remote human operator, so that their human "drivers" can move around on Pandora as if they were Na'vi themselves. Jake lands the job because his identical twin brother Tommy, a PhD certified genius under contract to the corporation, was killed. Avatars, genetically tailored to a single driver, are expensive. Hiring Jake, an uneducated former Marine grunt, is simply more cost-effective than growing a brand new avatar for someone else.[2]

Once he arrives on Pandora and gets plugged into his avatar, Jake's adventure begins in earnest: working as a security escort, he goes into the field to study the Na'vi and is nearly killed; he is rescued by Neytiri, daughter of the local Na'vi chieftain, adopted by the tribe, taught their customs, integrated into the spiritual-neural network that permeates everything on Pandora—the network that the Na'vi identify as "Eywa," their mother goddess—and, of course, inevitably, he falls in love. In the course of learning to operate his avatar, Jake, whose human body was broken and crushed into a wheelchair, regains full use of his physical functions. Back on his feet again, physically and psychologically, he comes to see himself and his culture from the Na'vi point of view. Along with his mobility, Jake's avatar restores the human experiences his human life has denied him. Recovering his humanity, so to speak, he seizes control of his avatar and leads the Na'vi—and Pandora itself—in a rebellion against the human occupation. At the end of the movie, Jake's consciousness is transferred permanently into his avatar. Leaving his human body behind, Jake becomes a Na'vi. As Jake saves the Na'vi from the invading and alien human beings, the Na'vi save Jake from his own alienated humanity.

And here's the punch line: Jake overcomes his alienation by becoming an alien.

Now, is Cameron simply making a terrible pun, or is something else going on here? The answer is, Both. *Avatar* the movie provides an excellent example of Marx's philosophical account of what makes a lousy job lousy, or, to use Marx's technical jargon, what creates estranged or alienated labor.[3]

We'll begin with a quick tour of Marx's core ideas and then, like the RDA Corporation itself, mine the movie to expose just how these themes move around, like tectonic plates, underneath the topography of the plot and characters. Exploring the Marxist themes in *Avatar* reveals not only the relevance of Marx today, but how Jake's journey is our own.[4]

Marx watched alienation spread across Europe during the early and middle 1800s as capitalism, in the form of industrial assembly lines, shoved the guilds and artisans to the margins of economic power. Highly skilled, individual workers were less efficient. They couldn't compete. They got run over. They were replaced by assembly line workers. Marx noticed that the key to this new mode of production was in the way it changed the relationship between workers and the products they produce. On the surface this looks like a small change, but it is the trigger, the butterfly's wing, the first domino in a cascade that affects the entire economic and psychological structure of work. Once this relationship has been altered, alienation is the natural consequence—and from here it spreads. Having become alienated from what we produce, we next become alienated from our own labor, then from ourselves, and finally even from our fellow, equally alienated, workers. Cameron's dystopian future is simply nineteenth-century Europe writ large, so we can count on *Avatar* to provide useful examples of all four flavors of alienation.

## Estrangement from the Object of Labor

Let's spend a few moments working through the changed relationship between workers and the objects they produce: this is the core, underlying cause of alienation. What does it mean exactly to say that industrial production changed this relationship in a way that causes alienation? Think about building a horse-drawn carriage. Teaching a person to build an entire horse-drawn carriage takes years of dedicated, time-consuming, and expensive training. An assembly line reduces the job to one repetitive task per worker—such as attaching the wheels. Industrial capitalism changed the worker's job from making a whole carriage to making only the wheels, then to making only the spokes and sprockets, and finally to making—money: earning wages. Marx suggests that making money is not as personally satisfying as making things. Industrial production takes the objects produced away from the worker and replaces them with wages.

In fact, you become a slave to the object you make, because making that object is the source of the wages that keep you alive. Marx put it this way: "The worker becomes a servant of his object, first, in that he receives an *object of labor,* i.e., in that he receives *work,* and, secondly, in that he receives *means of subsistence.* This enables him to exist, first as a worker; and second, as a *physical subject.* The height of this servitude is that it is only as a *worker* that he can maintain himself as a *physical subject* and that it is only as a *physical subject* that he is a worker." In simpler language, jobs that turn you into a wage-slave, a servant of your own productions, satisfy you only as a wage earner, not as a human being—and that's what it means to be estranged or alienated from the products of your labor. How many people have said, "This job is sucking the life out of me?" Marx thinks we should take that idea seriously.[5]

What was true of assembly lines, or mining, in nineteenth-century England is no different from corporate, white-collar, assembly lines today. We still call our jobs "the salt mines," paper pushing, or the grist mill. Nothing we "make" belongs to us; everything we make we make on behalf of "the company" or "the boss." Even in professions like medicine, industrial production techniques have begun to change the relationship between doctor and patient. The healthy patient is no longer something produced by the physician; patients are now a product of the medical-insurance-health-care industry. Education too is threatened by industrial production techniques, turning schools into assembly lines and teachers into wage slaves. Extended three hundred years into the future, we can find this situation played out in Cameron's movie in one particularly clear example. Jake, with some disgust, describes the mercenaries who were serving as a security force for mining operations on Pandora. Like him, most had been in the military back on Earth; but back on Earth, Jake tells us, they were fighting for freedom. On Pandora they were only fighting for the money. Here too wages had replaced the personally satisfying object of their labor.

In order to get a clearer idea of what Marx has in mind, it might be useful to consider what a nonalienating job looks like. Here's a non-sci-fi example: my friend Brian installed tile in my bathroom. I could call him a "professional tile-installer" or even a "handyman," but these labels hardly scratch the surface. In reality, Brian is a highly skilled artisan who loves what he does. Think about his relationship to the things he makes, such as my bathroom. I paid him for his labor, and the bathroom is in my house, but I am under no illusions about whose bathroom it is: it is Brian's bathroom. If he dropped by, he'd probably say, "Let me have a look and see how my work is holding up." It remains *his* work even though, legally, it belongs to me. Even I think of it as "Brian's work." Brian's relationship to the objects he produces is quite different from the relationship an industrial assembly-line worker has to his or her work. What's the difference? Marx suggests that, in a perfectly practical sense, we always put ourselves into our work, whatever it is. The only question is, What do we get back in return? Brian gets a lot back; but on an assembly line, when you put yourself into your work, you don't get anything back—except the wages you earn. The industrial economy itself is structured in such a way that whatever you make is taken away from you. Whatever you make belongs to the company's owners. This is true whether you're working on an assembly line, in an office, or guarding giant bulldozers on a distant off-world mining colony.

Estrangement from the objects you produce is stage one.

Once you find yourself in this situation, alienated from the objects you produce because of the way the economic system has structured your relationship to what you produce, alienation creeps into every part of your life.

## Estrangement from the Labor Itself

What's next? The worker becomes estranged from her or his own labor. Marx writes:

Till now we have been considering the estrangement, the alienation of the worker only in one of its aspects, i.e., *the* worker's *relationship to the products of his labor.* But the estrangement is manifested not only in the result but in the *act of production,* within the *producing activity,* itself. How could the worker come to face the product of his activity as a stranger, were it not that in the very act of production he was estranging himself from himself? The product is after all but the summary of the activity, of production. If then the product of labor is alienation, production itself must be active alienation, the alienation of activity, the activity of alienation. In the estrangement of the object of labor is merely summarized the estrangement, the alienation, in the activity of labor itself.[6]

In simpler language, once you have sold your labor, even your labor does not belong to you. Your boss owns it. This is stage two.

The best example from the film is when Sigourney Weaver's character,

Dr. Grace Augustine, scientific director of the avatar program, insists that "her" work—anthropological and biological studies of the Na'vi and Pandora—belongs to her rather than to the corporation. She continually acts as if her scientific investigations were independent from and more important than the company's economic motives. She is clearly in denial about who owns what. The corporate executive on-site, Parker Selfridge, is operating under no such delusions. Grace is rudely awakened to the truth when Selfridge explains that the local Na'vi clan lives atop one of the richest deposits of unobtainium and that, regardless of their value to science, he would be sending in the company's security forces to drive them away—and blow the place up. When she objects that she still has work to do collecting (invaluable!) scientific data, he reminds her that the corporation owns her work and that she works for the corporation. She protests. He locks her up. End of discussion.

## Estrangement from Self and from Species-Being

The third kind of alienation is the one people usually notice first. Marx calls this alienation from yourself, from your own human nature. We'll turn to Marx and *Avatar* in a moment, but there is a quick and easy litmus test for this experience in your own life. Ask yourself this question: "When you're at work, is that who you *really* are?" You might stop and take a quick inventory: you have an idiotic and vindictive boss, overly entitled customers, and you have to constantly fake a friendly smile in order to avoid being fired. If this describes your job even remotely, then the answer is easy: "Nope, that's not who I really am. I can't be me at work."

Welcome to stage three.

Once again, if we take this common experience seriously, we can throw some light into the existential wasteland of the past hundred years. Think about this: most people in industrialized countries work eight hours a day, five days a week. If you subtract another eight hours for sleep, then most people get to live their "real" lives for only about eight hours a day. Plus weekends. Unless you work overtime. And if alienation is bad nowadays, imagine what it was like when Marx was writing in the nineteenth century. In those days industrial workers put in ten-hour days, six days a week. If you take out time for sleep, then typical industrial workers might have been able to live their "real" lives for only a few hours a day. Every hour on the job is an hour being "someone else." Alarmingly, if a lousy job prevents you from being "the real you" when you're at work, then who or what *are* you? Everyone with an alienating job knows the answer. You're part of the machinery. You're another brick in the wall.[7]

Marx takes it a step further:

> First, the fact that labor is *external* to the worker, i.e., it does not belong to his intrinsic nature; that in his work, therefore, he does not affirm himself but denies himself, does not feel content but unhappy, does not develop freely his physical and mental energy but mortifies his body and ruins his mind. The worker therefore only feels himself outside his work, and in his work feels outside himself. He feels at home when he is not working, and when he is working he does not feel at home. His labor is therefore not voluntary, but coerced; it is *forced labor.* It is therefore not the satisfaction of a need; it is merely a *means* to satisfy needs external to it. Its alien character emerges clearly in the fact that as soon as no physical or other compulsion exists, labor is shunned like the plague. External labor, labor in which man alienates himself, is a labor of self-sacrifice, of mortification. Lastly, the external character of labor for the worker appears in the fact that it is not his own, but someone else's, that it does not belong to him, that in it he belongs, not to himself, but to another.[8]

That original, seemingly simple change in the relationship between worker and object eventually distorts even your personal identity. If your job ever made you feel like a stranger in your own life, this explanation accounts for it. It certainly accounts for Jake's state of mind as he rolls off the transport onto Pandora.

Marx notes that when you cannot be your "self" at work, even more than your personal identity is put at risk: your humanity is. We hear this all the time. People chained to alienating jobs regularly complain that they aren't treated as human beings. The job alienates them not only from themselves as individuals, but from themselves as human beings. Marx describes this experience as alienation from one's own "species-being." At first glance, jargon like this looks irritatingly obscure, but jargon is simply shorthand for more complex ideas. The original German term, *Gattungswesen*, might be better translated as one's "essential" or "inherent" nature as a human being. Marx writes that estranged labor "estranges from man his own body, as well as external nature and his spiritual aspect, his human aspect." Tying this back to the beginning, once you find yourself in a relationship that produces alienation, and the dominoes start to fall, you inexorably wind up alienated from your own human nature. If you've ever had a truly lousy job, you know exactly what he's talking about.[9]

The principal administrator on Pandora, Selfridge, and the head of corporate security, Colonel Quaritch, have both clearly lost their humanity; they have confused their personal identities with their identities as employees of the corporation. Like many people in positions of power, they have been positively reinforced for this confusion. This is evident in Selfridge, who despite being a good "company man," seems to struggle for a moment or two with his decision to "pull the trigger" and send Quaritch in to exterminate the Na'vi. His corporate identity prevails, however, and he gives the order to go. Colonel Quaritch, the perfect soldier whose sole identity is defined by the company that hires him, has become his title; the human being who might have felt compassion and prevented him from slaughtering the Na'vi is long gone. When the scientists try to appeal to this humanity, their arguments fall on deaf ears. Deafness to human compassion is one of the symptoms of an alienated personal identity.

And here we run head first into the front end of Cameron's terrible pun. What's the difference between the business executive who straps on the tailored business suit of his or her work-related identity and Jake, who straps on a genetically tailored avatar? It's that Jake, by becoming a nonhuman, regains his humanity, while Selfridge and Quaritch, by exploiting aliens, lose their humanity. For Jake, alienation from his human life is literally what restores his human life. For the company men, their alienation from human life has cost them their humanity.

Again, compare this to a nonalienating job. In nonalienating jobs people are able to be who they *really* are: the list often includes people in religious professions, teachers, doctors, lots of small-business owners, and my friend Brian, the tile guy. These workers, no matter how long their working day, get to be who they are twenty-four hours a day. In nonalienating jobs, your life still belongs to you. In alienating ones, it doesn't. For Brian, his labor is the activity by which he makes things (bathrooms), but in a perfectly concrete and practical way, his work with tile is actually what it means to *be* Brian. Put more simply, when your activity is owned by someone else, so are you. What becomes clear as the film proceeds is that Jake will not allow his activity to be owned by someone else.[10]

We have one more piece of alienation to consider.

## Estrangement from Other Humans

Alienation's most toxic effect is found in Marx's final observation: the capitalist economic system (the system that changed the relationship between workers and the objects they produce) alienates us not only from what we make, from our activity as workers, and from ourselves as human beings, but also from other, equally alienated, workers—from the very people with whom we have the most in common. This is stage four.

How does alienation poison my relationships with other workers? After a while, feeling alienated becomes normal, ambient, and invisible. You stop paying attention to it. When you get home, rather than face the uncomfortable process of shifting gears back to your real identity (when you are no longer pretending to be Clark Kent) and admitting to yourself that the job is literally preventing you from living your own life, you numb your brain with television or the Internet or beer until you fall asleep. Alienation seeps into your identity, and once alienation becomes a normal part of human life, anyone who is *not* alienated from her or his job will not seem to be "normal." In fact, if being human means being an alienated assembly-line worker, and for many people it does, then anyone who is not alienated will not look "human" at all. Such a person will not act in the way a *properly* alienated human is supposed to act.

Example: Were you ever hired for a lousy job and at some point early on, you decided to do a "good job" anyway? Did you try to make lemonade out of lemons? Did you try to enjoy yourself and find a crumb of cheerful, personal satisfaction despite the soul-crushing lousiness? Probably. And did you discover that this approach made your fellow workers angry? Probably. Here's the reason: from their point of view—as human beings already alienated from what they make, from their own work, and from their own essential human nature—you look like an irritating newbie, like some weird creature too stupid to see how lousy the job is. There must be something fundamentally wrong with you since, from their point of view, there must be something wrong with anyone who enjoys his or her work. Worse, if you try to treat them as human beings, they will resent it. Treating them as anything but estranged will remind them that they're estranged: from what they make, from their work, and—worst of all—from their own lives. People do not like to be reminded that they have lousy lives.

Have you run into that?

Once people are sufficiently estranged from each other, each person views every other person "in accordance with the standard" of estrangement. People who are not alienated from their work don't share in the defining, alienated, identity. To workers whose identity consists in being alienated from other workers, nonalienated workers are, therefore, not identifiable as "real" workers at all. In extreme cases, they are barely identifiable as "real" human beings. Marx expressed it this way: "The estrangement of man, and in fact every relationship in which man [stands] to himself, is realized and expressed only in the relationship in which a man stands to other men. Hence within the relationship of estranged labor each man views the other in accordance with the standard and the relationship in which he finds himself as a worker."[11]

This particularly pervasive aspect of alienation appears in *Avatar* in the way Selfridge and Quaritch treat the science team. The scientists are untrustworthy, from the company's point of view, specifically because they don't seem to be estranged: the scientists are engaged in and love their jobs; scientists don't simply *do* science, they *are* scientists; they might be in denial about who really owns them, but this is a good mistake to make—from their point of view, their identity continues to be determined by their own interests and by their own actions. They *are* their work in a way that makes Selfridge and Quaritch suspicious. They are not cogs in the corporate machinery. Dr. Augustine's most important personal payoff is not financial, but rather her personally fulfilling investigations and discoveries about the Na'vi. Estranged workers don't act that way, and so Quaritch asks Jake to spy on them.

One final counterexample: have you ever had a nonalienating job and tried to explain it to people who have alienating jobs? It can be dangerous. When you do, someone will usually scoff and, incredulity dripping from her or his lips, say, "Why don't you get a *real* job?" You've heard it if you're an artist or a musician or a teacher—or if your work satisfies you in ways that inoculate you from alienation. Following Marx's observation almost to the letter, alienated workers measure everyone in accordance with the standard of estrangement. If you're not alienated, then there's something wrong with you. In fact, let's follow this thread for a moment. Here are some consequences of accepting the logic of alienation. In a culture of alienation, (1) all work creates alienation, and therefore, if you are not alienated, you must not be working; (2) work that does not create alienation cannot be "real" work; (3) people who are not alienated, therefore, must not be "real" people; and finally, (4) the only way to be accepted by your fellow alienated workers is to be an alienated worker too. From this, alienated, point of view, a happy nonalienated life is not possible; therefore, if you happen to be happily nonalienated, you must be crazy. This explains why, from the point of view of the RDA Corporation executives, the scientists don't seem to be doing anything "serious" at all.[12]

This concludes our look into Marx's sketch of estranged labor. Examining the way a new economic system—in this case, nineteenth-century capitalism—changes the relation between a worker and what she or he produces, Marx noticed that the industrial worker (unlike a skilled artisan) becomes alienated from the objects he or she produces. The alienation created by this changed relationship then takes root in the work itself, in our essential identity as human beings, and in our relationships to other workers. Since our economic system, like the one Marx criticized and the one Jake Sully lives in, is grounded in the same alienating relationships, we are subject to the same trap. This is why most sensible people, once aware of the predicament, simply throw their hands in the air or crawl under a rock—but not Jake Sully. This is precisely where Jake's salvation begins.

## Solution to Alienation

Jake arrives on Pandora fully estranged by his immersion in the social-economic system. He's been alienated from everything he makes, from his activity as a worker, from his own soul, and from everyone he works with. His life is lousy, because, in a word, he's been thoroughly alienated; everything in his life has worked to make him a stranger in his life. Even though his circumstances are extreme, Jake faces the same dilemma confronted by anyone in an alienating life: How do I escape? It's a dilemma because in order to crawl out of an alienated life, you have to find a way to live a nonalienated life, something seemingly impossible when the economic system, the system that keeps you alive, reinforces the very circumstances that create your alienation. What to do? There is one obvious solution. If everything about being human is alienating—and for Jake, it is—then, in order to stop being alienated, you have to *stop being human.*

But before we follow Jake into the alien life that saves him from the alienation of being an alienated human being, let's take a moment and consider the *wrong* way to resolve alienation, especially since becoming an alien is, technically, not an option available to most of us. Yet.

In real life, people cope with alienation using a catalog of wrong-headed solutions, all of which fail because they treat the symptoms (the lousy pay, lousy hours, or lousy boss) instead of the cause (the dysfunctional relationship our economic system creates between workers and the objects they produce). Most people begin to engage their alienation by asking for a raise—on the assumption that more money will take care of the problem. This is a bit like asking for more candy to distract yourself from a toothache caused by too much candy—but it's a normal and human reaction. Marx is blistering on this subject: "An enforced *increase of wages,"* he states, "(disregarding all other difficulties, including the fact that it would only be by force, too, that such an increase, being an anomaly, could be maintained) would therefore be nothing but better *payment for the slave,* and would not win either for the worker or for labor their human status and dignity." You can put the slave in a nicer house, buy the slave a nicer car, or a personal jet—but nothing really changes. A slave with better pay, better hours, or a better boss, remains a slave. Marx's observation from 1844 is played out explicitly in the movie. The RDA Corporation's head of security on Pandora, Colonel Quaritch, promises Jake that if he spies on the scientific personnel, the company will get him "new legs" and deliver him from his wheelchair. New legs are no different from a corner office or a company car, and the scene illustrates the difficulty of escaping from a worldview in which alienation is the norm. Most sensible people in that position would have accepted the offer, but this promise, this Faustian deal, to heal Jake's estrangement from his own, nonfunctioning body requires that Jake go back to work for the very system that broke him in the first place.[13] Jake has other plans.

But why do people make this mistake? Why do they treat the symptoms of alienation rather than the cause? Because it's trickier than it looks. Marx suggests that *"Political economy conceals the estrangement inherent in the nature of labor by not considering the* direct *[unmittelbare] relationship between the* worker (labor) *and production"*—it masks the alienation it creates, like a disease that hides behind a lot of easily treatable symptoms. So long as you focus on anything other than the immediate, and dysfunctional, relationship between yourself and the things you make, you'll never get around to noticing the estrangement and its viral consequences. People raised inside the economic system often don't believe it is possible to find a nonalienating and personally satisfying job that does not depend on good wages, easy hours, or a decent boss. Most people don't seem to believe it's possible to find happiness, in other words, outside of the economic system—and in our case that means an economic system that creates alienation. This might be one reason why it is easier to find alienation in movies about aliens than it is in real life. Seeing things on the Big Screen is easier, and more believable, than seeing them in our own lives.[14]

So what's the correct solution?

The Marxist answer is to address the real cause: change the dysfunctional relationship between the worker and the object he or she produces. Unfortunately, changing this relationship is difficult, even after the alienation is no longer hidden from view. People take lousy, alienating jobs not because they want to, but out of necessity. Our lives often depend on entering into that initial, alienating relationship and turning ourselves into wage slaves. Our society, like Jake's, is held in place by an economic model that creates and then depends upon estranged labor. Marx's solution, and Jake's, is to replace an economic system that creates alienated labor with a system that doesn't; in other words, with a system in which personal satisfaction, rather than wages, is the ground of our relationship to what we produce. Economic systems, once well established, are famously unwilling to bend. Marx suggests that to avoid alienation like this, only a revolution (literally, turning things around) can do the trick—exactly what we see in the film.[15]

Jake's revolution begins by wresting control of his avatar away from the corporation and, in this way, regaining control of his own identity. He then rallies the indigenous population to throw out the capitalist, alienation-creating, human colonizers. In the end, the Na'vi transfer his consciousness permanently into his avatar; his human body is sacrificed to his new alien, but nonalienated, identity. Not only metaphorically but literally, Jake overcomes the estrangement and alienation of his human life by becoming an alien: at first in surrogate form and in the end really.

From here, the rest of our analysis is easy. Once Jake moves into and takes control of his avatar, he establishes a new, nonalienated relationship to the things he makes. Consequently, (1) Jake is no longer alienated from what he makes. What he makes now belongs to him, and once this fundamental relationship is restored, the other three aspects of alienation evaporate. (2) His work once again belongs to him rather than to the corporation and his activity becomes an expression of his own existence, of himself. That "work" is to rally the Na'vi and fight off the corporate humans who have brought alienation to Pandora. Jake becomes this liberating activity, not only metaphorically but really. (3) By moving into an "alien" body, Jake ironically recovers his true humanity. No longer alienated from himself, even though he has become an alien, Jake becomes what he would have been all along but for the snare of alienation. Finally, (4) Jake is no longer alienated from others: in fact, like every other living thing on Pandora, he is literally plugged into the all-encompassing neural network that is Pandora itself: Eywa.

By changing the relationship in which he stands to his work, Jake finds himself no longer estranged from what he makes, from his labor, from himself, or from others. He is no longer a stranger in his own life. What was required? Jake had to let go of a set of culturally imposed economic relationships that prevented him from overcoming his alienation. Think of how many stories follow this model—one in which human beings recover their humanity only when exposed to aliens, aboriginal peoples, and so forth, and are thus put into conflict with their own alienating culture. The aliens, as often happens in stories like this, turn out to be more human than human beings. You should be able to see Marx's discussion of alienation in all such stories now.

## Bringing Alienation Back to Earth

The idea of overcoming alienation by becoming an alien—metaphorically rather than literally, perhaps—is interesting, at least, but what does this movie, or Marx, have to do with you? You'll need to consider two questions: (1) Do you live in a culture that tends to create the conditions of alienation? (Quick, can you be who you really are at work?) And (2) if you do, how do you avoid becoming alienated yourself? Do you have to leave your life on Earth behind in order to get over your alienation from your job, yourself, your fellow humans? Switching sci-fi metaphors, do you have to become a *Stranger in a Strange Land* to move beyond your estrangement?[16] The answer, it seems, is yes.

Marx's eventual solution to this quandary—spelled out across the volumes of his later work—is roughly the same solution Jake reaches: Jake plugs into Eywa, literally, and discovers that his relationships, now social rather than economic, are no longer alienating. Back on Earth, we need to ground our lives in a web of social relationships that are not merely economic ones—so long as by "economic" we mean the kind of system that puts us into a dysfunctional relationship with the objects we produce.

Fortunately, we do not need to leave the Earth to do as much.

## Notes

1. Karl Marx, *Economic and Philosophic Manuscripts of 1844,* ed. Dirk J. Struik, trans. Martin Milligan (New York: International, 1964), 106–19, cited hereafter as

"Struik." Variations in translations are from Struik's revisions of Milligan (from the edition published by Progress Publishers, Moscow, 1969, at www.marxists.org [accessed June 2, 2011]) and my own. Marx's discussion of alienation is found in "The Economic and Philosophic Manuscripts of 1844" and to a lesser extent in his "Grundrisse," unpublished manuscripts in which the young Marx began to work out the dialectical analysis of political economy that he explores in *Capital*. Although these texts thus do not provide a fully argued philosophical account, Marx's essay "Estranged Labor" contains a constellation of illuminating insights into how an economics-based culture can condition the identity of nations and workers. Among Marx scholars, questions remain regarding whether these unpublished early notebooks are the "real" Marx. As the reader should be aware, questions like this held profound and, during the Soviet era, lethal importance. For a succinct account of these scholastic and ideological divisions, see the preface to John McGuire's *Marx's Paris Writings: An Analysis* (New York: Harper & Row, 1973).

2. *Avatar* is the term generally used to describe the incarnation of a Hindu deity in human form. It contains the etymological root *ava-* "down" attached to *tarati* "(he) crosses over." The biomechanical avatar in Cameron's movie is precisely what makes it possible for Jake Sully to "cross over" from an alienated to a nonalienated life—by becoming an alien.

3. The German for estrangement is *Entfremdung;* for alienation, *Entäusserung.* R. G. Peffer, in his *Marxism, Morality, and Social Justice* (Princeton, NJ: Princeton University Press, 1990), 50–55, does a nice job of distinguishing the three bits of German that go into understanding alienation: *vergegenständlichung, entäusserung,* and *entfremdung.*

4. It is important to be on your guard when reading anything that claims to explicate complex philosophical themes in popular culture; to be on the lookout for what Nobel Prize–winning physicist Murray Gell-Mann calls "quantum flapdoodle," his criticism of the way New Age mysticism has inappropriately appropriated the language of modern quantum physics. The use of sexy, often impenetrable, jargon can make any article look important even when it means nothing at all. The same thing happens in political science and philosophy, so watch your back. Cf. Murray Gell-Mann, *The Quark and the Jaguar: Adventures in the Simple and the Complex* (New York: Owl Books, 2002), chap. 12, "Quantum Mechanics and Flapdoodle," 167.

5. Struik, 109.

6. Struik, 110.

7. Estimates from the Weeks Report, prepared by Joseph Weeks as part of the census of 1880, suggest average work weeks of more than sixty hours. This form of alienation is illuminated with lucid and terrible clarity in Pink Floyd's 1979 album *The Wall* and Fritz Lang's classic film *Metropolis.*

8. Struik, 110–11.

9. Struik, 114. For the etymologically minded, check the component parts of this term: *Gattung* and *Wesen.* Like a lot of Marx's technical vocabulary, this term is frightening at first but, once you crack it open, it turns into an Easter egg.

10. Kurt Vonnegut once summed it up this way: "To be is to do—Socrates. To do is to be—Sartre. Do Be Do Be Do—Sinatra."

11. Struik, 114–15.

12. The best discussion of the effects of alienating labor on society can be found in Josef Pieper's *Leisure, the Basis of Culture,* trans. Alexander Dru (London: Faber and Faber, 1952). It has an introduction by T. S. Eliot.

13. Struik, 117–18. This is something to consider next time your boss promises you a raise. It is impossible, in this context, not to think of Kenny Dobbins, one of the people interviewed in Eric Schlosser's *Fast Food Nation* (New York: Harper Perennial, 2005). Mr. Dobbins is a tragic example of how a "good employee" can be worked to death—and not notice until it's too late.

14. Struik, 109–10.

15. Marx's discussion of a revolution in consciousness and political culture goes beyond the scope of this chapter. See, in particular, Marx and Engels's *The Communist Manifesto.*

16. See Robert Heinlein's influential 1962 Hugo Award–winning novel *Stranger in a Strange Land* (New York: Putnam, 1991) about a human raised by Martians.

**8**

# Nietzschean Narratives of Hero and Herd in Walt Disney / Pixar's *The Incredibles*

*C. Heike Schotten*

BOB [to wide-eyed, expectant child]. Well, what are *you* waiting for?
CHILD. I don't know! Something *amazing,* I guess.
BOB [sighing]. Me, too, kid.

—*The Incredibles*

And to ask it once more: today—is greatness *possible?*
—Friedrich Nietzsche, *Beyond Good and Evil,* §212

In the penultimate scene of Pixar / Walt Disney's animated film *The Incredibles,* ten-year-old superhero Dash Parr is about to run a sprint race in his elementary school's track meet. As the race begins, his parents buoyantly cheer him on. "Run, Dash, run!!" they yell excitedly—and, glancing up at them, young Dash propels himself within seconds to the front of the pack. Alarmed at their son's swift ascent into first place, however, his parents suddenly reverse course, yelling "Pull back! Pull back!" Following their cues, Dash drifts to the back of the pack of racers. This causes his parents to change directives yet again, his father yelling audibly, "Don't give *up!* Make it close!" Speeding up for the last time, Dash eventually finishes second in a race that, without his parents' interventions, he could easily have won. Flushed with pleasure if not exertion, Dash turns wide-eyed to his family in the stands, smiles tentatively, and gives them the thumbs-up.[1]

As anyone who has seen *The Incredibles* knows, the reason for Dash's parents' mixed messages is not their failure to understand the point of a race, but rather their desire to limit their son's success to within a "normal" level of achievement. For running is Dash's superpower. Dash is not simply faster than a speeding bullet—he runs so fast he can escape video detection and, like Christ himself, can traverse water without sinking due to his astounding speed. Obviously, Dash is worlds beyond any elementary school track meet and could easily crush any competitor in any race, even an Olympic marathon. Indeed, were he truly to run as fast as he could, the race would be over before it even got started.

Dash's dilemma in this scene—and its compromise resolution enforced by his parents' mixed messages from the stands—can be read as an allegory of Nietzsche's critique of modern doctrines of equality. Dash is a kind of genius—he is an extraordinary boy, so extraordinary that he is, in fact, *superhuman*, and the superheroes of *The Incredibles* can be read as literalizations of Nietzsche's notion of greatness or superiority.[2] Like the higher man of Nietzsche's philosophy, Dash cannot be given free rein to express his greatness, because to do so would ruin things for everybody else. His incredible speed would ruin the track meet for other children, who could no longer look forward to competing, as well as for other parents, who could no longer nourish beliefs in their children's talents. Indeed, Dash's prowess would ruin the sport of competitive racing for every other runner in the world. Moreover, rather than celebrate his achievements, the school might deal with Dash's greatness through exclusionary limitations—by, for example, putting a ceiling on the number of wins allowed each runner or capping the maximum speed at which competitors can run. Such consequences, according to Nietzsche, are the predictable if undeserved fate of anyone who is truly exceptional. As he explains in *Beyond Good and Evil*:

> The highest and strongest drives, when they break out passionately and drive the individual far above the average and the flats of the herd conscience, wreck the self-confidence of the community, its faith in itself, and it is as if its spine snapped. Hence just these drives are branded and slandered most. High and independent spirituality, the will to stand alone, even a powerful reason are experienced as dangers; everything that elevates an individual above the herd

and intimidates the neighbor is henceforth called *evil*; and the fair, modest, submissive, conforming mentality, the *mediocrity* of desires attains moral designations and honors. (§201)

Were Dash truly to run the race as fast as he could, he would violate the norms and presuppositions of social life, which include, among others, notions of equality, fairness, inclusion, and "normal" ten-year-old behavior. According to Nietzsche, the good of the community and the enhancement of the higher type are at odds with each other. Given this conflict, society typically chooses its own self-preservation over recognition and honor of the exceptional person's greatness. The result? Mediocrity is rewarded and greatness demonized, punished, even sacrificed for the "common good." Nietzsche does not disguise his contempt for this decision calculus: "'The general welfare' is no ideal, no goal, no remotely intelligible concept, but only an emetic." He continues, "What is fair for one *cannot* by any means for that reason alone be fair for others," and "the demand of one morality for all is detrimental for the higher men." This is the case because some people are just better than others; or, in his words, because "there is an order of rank between man and man" (*BGE*, §228).

Dash's dilemma is the basic plot premise of *The Incredibles*: faced with a caste of superpowerful heroes, society would rather eliminate them than honor their greatness. Nietzsche calls this sort of resentfulness *slave morality*. A slave morality is any ethical, religious, or political code that vilifies greatness. It is articulated in a tone of resentment, by and on behalf of the majority of people—in Nietzsche's view, the many, the mediocre, all those who are *not* great—and advocates the restriction, limitation, or diminution of the rare, powerful few. In subtly advocating for the rights of superheroes to live their lives as superior and exceptional beings, then, *The Incredibles* offers a Nietzschean critique of equality and takes a rather Nietzschean position with regard to greatness. In what follows, I discuss two versions of slave morality that arise in the film—the lawsuits against the supers and the villain Syndrome's evil plot—and conclude by arguing that *The Incredibles* ultimately falls prey to the slave morality it seems to critique.[3]

## Superheroism, Suburbia, and Slave Morality

The film opens by introducing us to Mr. Incredible and his troubles, which begin (not accidentally, as we'll see) on his wedding day.[4] On his way to the chapel, Mr. Incredible is alerted to the unfolding of a crime, which he nimbly foils. However, yet more criminal activity is afoot elsewhere in the city, demanding Mr. Incredible's attention and threatening to prevent him from getting to the church on time. At this important moment of conflict, we meet Buddy, aka Incrediboy, Mr. Incredible's "biggest fan" (and soon to become his biggest enemy). Buddy's annoying, intrusive, tag-along presence as aspiring sidekick disrupts Mr. Incredible's heroics, allows villain Bomb Voyage to escape, and wreaks altogether new havoc for Mr. Incredible to salvage. Nevertheless, Mr. Incredible does indeed make it to the church just barely in time to pronounce his wedding vows. In these brief opening scenes, the greatness of Mr. Incredible is established (through his initial, successful crime-fighting activity) and the seeds are planted for what will emerge as the two major threats to his superheroism: the vengefulness of the weak, on the one hand, and the demands of marriage and family, on the other. As it turns out, many of the people Mr. Incredible saves on his wedding day later become litigants in lawsuits against him, while Buddy, burned by Mr. Incredible's rejection, begins nursing a resentful grudge that develops into a murderous revenge, ominously transforming him into Mr. Incredible's arch-nemesis, Syndrome. Meanwhile, complaining about his lateness, Mr. Incredible's fiancée (a superheroine herself) says to him, "I love you, but if we're gonna make this work, you've gotta be *more* than Mr. Incredible. You know that. Don't you?" His evasion of the question with an "I do" to the priest rather than to her makes it clear he is seeking to evade the conflict between heroism and family that his fiancée foresees. Regardless, the two threats to greatness have been established: the vengefulness of the weak and the enervating demands of married life.[5] Both are Nietzschean themes: the first is Nietzsche's critique of slave morality; the second, his critique of marriage and the great man's association with women.[6]

We next meet our protagonists fifteen years later. No longer Mr. Incredible, Bob now works for an insurance company; Helen, formerly Elastigirl, seems happy to care for their children and endlessly vacuum their sprawling suburban home. The Parrs have been relegated to this nostalgically 1950s existence because of a series of lawsuits against Mr. Incredible for saving people who "didn't want to be saved." Relayed to the viewer in newsreel form (harking back to an even earlier, prewar period in U.S. history), footage shows newspaper headlines and front-page photos of protesters holding signs saying "Hang Up the Cape," "Stop Hiding behind the Mask," and "Go Save Yourself." One photo shows an angry crowd burning Mr. Incredible in effigy. In response to this public protest, the government institutes a Superhero Relocation Program, providing "amnesty" to all supers in exchange for their retirement into a life of anonymity.[7] As a politician says on television about the superheroes, "It is time for their *secret* identity [i.e., their nonsuper identity] to be their *only* identity. Time for them to join us, or go away."

The ludicrousness of these lawsuits is played for comedy, and the film's literalization of Nietzschean greatness as superheroic saving of the innocent is meant to highlight the absurdity of the many's resentment of greatness. After all, how could anyone *resent* being saved from death? But that is precisely what the litigants allege. Although the superheroes' exceptional powers seem to legitimate their intrusion into the daily lives of ordinary people, apparently these ordinary people don't want this intrusion and actively reject it. Moreover, many of the newspaper headlines invoke security, asking if the public would be safer without superheroic interventions, suggesting that the superheroes' greatness is a danger to public welfare. Finally, the relocation of the supers does not necessarily alleviate public fear. As the announcer says, "Where are they now? They are living among us. Average citizens, average heroes." Further bolstering the 1950s feel of this part of the film, McCarthyist anxieties echo in the newsreel reporter's words: like Communists and homosexuals, former superheroes walk among "average citizens" undetected, an invisible threat to the community at large.[8] In short, the superheroes' superiority threatens the safety of "average citizens" who no longer want or need their greatness. The government thus takes action to *dis*empower the supers and render them just like everybody else. This is the film's depiction of what Nietzsche calls the "common war on all that is rare, strange, privileged, the higher man" (*BGE*, §212), waged by "the herd animal with its profound mediocrity, timidity, and boredom with itself" (*GS*, §352).

Meanwhile, dissatisfaction, conflict, and ennui pervade the Parrs' suburban idyll.[9] Bob must daily conform his enormously powerful, beefy body to the stifling contours of his now-normal life: he hunches over a disproportionately tiny desk at work and stuffs himself into the cramped space of his compact car twice daily for a mind-numbing commute.[10] He tries, ineffectively, to sublimate his superheroic penchant for saving people into helping policyholders successfully navigate his insurance company's bureaucracy, an activity for which he is ultimately fired. Meanwhile, Dash is getting into trouble at school because he has been forbidden to go out for sports. Promising to "slow up" and "only be the best by a *tiny* bit!" Dash complains:

DASH. You always say, "Do your best." But you don't really mean it.
Why can't I do the best that I can do?

HELEN. Right now, honey, the world just wants us to fit in, and to fit
  in, we just gotta be like everybody else.
DASH. Dad always said our powers were nothing to be ashamed of.
  Our powers made us special.
HELEN. *Everyone's* special, Dash.
DASH. Which is another way of saying no one is.

Dash's discontent indicates that he understands the driving force behind
the lawsuits and forced retirements, even though all of it happened before
he was born. He knows that being prevented from playing sports means
quashing his superiority, prowess, and skill. It means sacrificing his individual achievements to shore up the mediocrity and self-pity of everyone
else. And it means disguising that sacrifice with the saccharine platitude that
*everybody* is "special." Like his father, however, Dash knows that special, in
its true sense, means "better." As Bob complains regarding Dash's impending
fourth-grade graduation ceremony, "It's psychotic! They keep creating new
ways to celebrate mediocrity. But if someone is genuinely exceptional . . ."
Bob doesn't complete this sentence, but he and Dash know its conclusion:
if someone is genuinely exceptional, he must be cut down to size and made
mediocre in order to "fit in" and "be like everybody else."

The male half of the Parr family is miserable in its mediocrity; both
Dash and his father feel (rightly, in Nietzsche's view) punished by the restrictions on their activity. By contrast, the female half of the family either
longs for normality—teenage Violet wails, "We *act* normal, mom. I wanna
*be* normal!"—or else rigorously enforces it: it is Helen who forbids Dash to
play sports, while she reprimands Bob for reprising the glory days when he
returns late from "bowling," spotting rubble on his coat lapel as if it were
lipstick on his collar. Helen's anxious disapproval makes clear that Bob's
antics—just like his son's—have the potential to give them all away. For the
men of the family, superheroics are the only viable outlet for their super
powers. For the women of the family, however, superheroics pose a threat
to the happiness, normality, and long-term stability of the family unit.[11]

## Syndrome, Slavishness, and the Will to Power

While the bland social conformism of the herd dictates that the Incredibles
live their lives in hiding, as "normal" people, the bitter and vengeful Buddy
seeks not simply to normalize Mr. Incredible but to *punish* and eventually

*displace* him. This, too, is in keeping with Nietzsche's critique of slave morality, which also has a *psychological* dimension: Nietzsche finds the longing for equality to be resentful, dishonest, and vengeful. Slave moralities, he claims, are formulated by weak people who punish strength in order to compensate for their own weakness, which they reinterpret as a kind of virtue. Strength and greatness, by contrast, they interpret as injury, attack, and injustice—as wrongs that must be redressed. Slave morality, then, effects a fundamental reversal of natural hierarchy the only way it can—through deceit. The weak triumph over the strong by lying—by reinterpreting strength as *harm*.

Syndrome exemplifies these psychological dysfunctions. His transformation from the awkward, copycat, unsuper kid Buddy into the vengeful, fully-grown, arch-nemesis Syndrome is instigated by Mr. Incredible's rejection of young Buddy's proffered crime-fighting companionship. Buddy refuses to accept the fact that he is *not* super; he experiences Mr. Incredible's rebuff as an unforgivable personal rejection (rather than, say, as a necessity of the very greatness and independence that he so admires in his hero).[12] Buddy thus proceeds to produce *himself* as a superhero named Syndrome by constructing machines that function as superpowers.[13] Although Buddy does not lie his weakness into merit (as Nietzsche argues slavish types do [*GM*, 1:14]), choosing instead to *imitate* his hero ("I'll give them heroics. I'll give them the most spectacular heroics anyone's ever seen!") to the point at which he will surpass him (as he says to Mr. Incredible, "I'll be a bigger hero than you *ever* were!"). Nevertheless, the point of carrying out his vendetta against Mr. Incredible is the same as that of the slave: to *reverse* the relationship between them so that he, Buddy, is the strong and powerful one and Mr. Incredible is the weakling begging for favors. And Buddy accomplishes this reversal through lies—by blaming Mr. Incredible for his own inadequacy, manufacturing fake superpowers, and secretly assassinating all the other superheroes so that he, Syndrome, can claim to be the world's *only* hero.[14] Mr. Incredible's incredulous response to this plan is eminently Nietzschean: "You killed off *real* heroes so that you could . . . *pretend* to be one?!" This is precisely Syndrome's revenge.

Unfazed, however, Syndrome insists: "Oh I'm real. Real enough to defeat *you!* And I did it without your *precious gifts,* your oh-so-special powers." In other words, Syndrome is saying that he has changed the rules of the game. Greatness is no longer inborn, as the supers may believe (as Helen tells Vi, "You have more power than you realize. . . . It's in your blood"), but rather manufacturable and possible to mandate. This belief that anyone can do anything is, Nietzsche thinks, a hallmark of democratic and egalitarian ages that do not recognize natural distinctions or orders of rank: "The individual becomes convinced that he can do just about everything and *can manage almost any role,* and everybody experiments with himself, improvises, makes new experiments, enjoys his experiments; and all nature ceases and becomes art" (*GS,* §356). This tampering with nature is one more effect of the generalized disregard for greatness that Nietzsche believes characterizes modern egalitarianisms. Syndrome's plan, then, is actually strangely democratic insofar as it seeks to dismantle, through his own initiative and artifice, the natural schema according to which some people are super and others are not. Its "evil" is precisely its *refusal* of natural superiority; in Nietzsche's words: "Today nobody has the courage any longer for privileges, for masters' rights, for a sense of respect for oneself and one's peers—for a *pathos of distance.* Our politics is sick from this lack of courage. The aristocratic outlook was undermined from the deepest underworld through the lie of the equality of souls" (*A,* §43).

Syndrome's nefarious plan culminates in an unexpected twist that is nevertheless in keeping with his denaturing of greatness and the film's overall critique of egalitarianism: "And when I'm old and I've had my fun, I'll sell my inventions so that everyone can be a superhero. *Everyone* can be super! And when everyone's super . . . no one will be [evil laughter]." In a clear echo of Dash's earlier lament, Syndrome makes explicit the ominous threat to greatness lurking behind the democratic imperative and reveals that even the aspiration to equality is itself a longing for domination or, as Nietzsche would say, a *will to power.* As Syndrome's dreams of becoming the world's only superhero make clear, the desire to denature and democratize greatness is actually a drive toward mastery and domination. Syndrome's mantra is that only *he* will be super, and after him nobody will be. Nietzsche's point is that this is the aspiration of all slave moralities, even those that pretend to argue for the common good. Syndrome's plot is the culmination and logical consequence of civil society's legalized resentment and containment of the supers; his will to power is the ugly underside of the more banal containment of herd morality. In determining who can and cannot be super, Syndrome (or the law or society or the common man) determines that it or *he* shall rule.[15]

Ultimately, Syndrome's plot fails and ends up resuscitating the superheroes to their former greatness. This proves that the weak are essentially so and cannot do otherwise. When they attempt to assume the guises and behavior of the strong, they can only imitate, never *be* authentically. Ironically, this is also what puts the citizenry back on the side of the supers. Far from successfully conquering the world, Syndrome's artifice is foiled by the natural forthrightness of the supers' true superiority.

## *The Incredibles'* Concession to the Herd

These concluding scenes reveal *The Incredibles'* unwitting investment in normality, however—an investment that is far from Nietzschean. Caving to conventionality, the film retreats from its critique of equality and refuses to follow Nietzsche's views to their conclusion, instead taking refuge in the familiar comforts of care and community. For, however great the Incredible family is, they remain committed to using their greatness to preserve the "common good" and "public safety" that threatened their very existence in the first place. They remain, in other words, superheroes in the conventional sense: their powers serve the common good (rather than their own) and aim at preserving the human race (rather than leaving it to destroy itself if it must). In Nietzschean terms, we might say that the Incredibles' superpowers are hyperbolizations of herd instinct.[16] The "greatness" they represent is not really the greatness of which Nietzsche speaks, a greatness he believes to be at odds with the common good because it is and must be, effectively, self-serving.[17] *The Incredibles* simply ignores these difficulties by reconciling individual greatness with the welfare of all in the figure of the superhero who uses his or her greatness to serve humanity.

The film also departs from Nietzsche's teachings in its reconciliation of superiority and domesticity. Confronted with the possible death of his wife and children, Bob confesses what he has failed to understand up to this point; namely, "I've been a lousy father. Blind to what I have. So obsessed with being undervalued that I undervalued all of you." Bemoaning his desire for a superheroic life as a selfishness that detracted from what is truly important, Bob tells Helen and the kids: "*You* are my greatest adventure. And I almost missed it." In other words, the man who used to revel in a solitary life of superheroic activity now understands the daily travails of homework and housekeeping to be his "greatest adventure." Dash, too, is returned to the familial fold: after they escape from Syndrome's clutches (an adventure Dash calls "the greatest vacation ever"), he concludes with the heartwarming admission, "I love our family." The restraints that formerly chafed both father and son and made them miserable are now perceived lovingly and as essential to their happiness (perhaps in part because their recent crime-fighting adventure fulfilled long-repressed superheroic desires). It remains to be seen, however, how long this contentment can last.

Ultimately, although *The Incredibles* seems initially to defend the existence and prerogative of superior types, by the end of the film we discover that these are permissible only to the degree to which they are reconcilable with the demands of the weak, the many, the neighbor, the herd—and the household. This seeming contradiction evidences a crucial question that goes both unasked and unanswered throughout the film: why do the supers mix with humanity (or women)—much less care about their welfare—at all?[18] For reasons unknown, the supers care what humanity thinks about them and long for their acceptance. From a Nietzschean perspective, such a need for recognition from one's inferiors is incomprehensible and suggests that *The Incredibles* is actually a snapshot of the nobility's overall decline.[19] While Mr. Incredible's insistence that he works alone is an entirely appropriate and necessary characterization of his activity, throughout the film we see this resolve crumble in the face of an adoring and bratty child fan, an ungrateful civil society, a nagging wife, and demanding children. That Bob should have pity for human vulnerability or that Dash might be excited to come in second at his elementary school's track meet, however, otherwise defy comprehension. *The Incredibles* ignores this unlikely reconciliation of greatness with herd morality, playing to its audience's own longings for normality and a neat narrative conclusion without conflict. Rolling the family, community, and superheroics into one big happy ending, *The Incredibles* ultimately teaches a very un-Nietzschean lesson: that the purpose of greatness is to serve the weak and the many rather than the happiness and enhancement of the superior few.

## Notes

1. Brad Bird, director, *The Incredibles,* 2004, scene 30. All quotations from *The Incredibles* are taken from the complete script published online at the Internet Movie Script Database, www.imsdb.com/scripts/Incredibles,-The.html. No emphases are specified in the script; however, I have added them when I believe they reflect the delivery of the character and help specify the lines' meaning (thus I have italicized "up" in this quotation because I believe it accurately reflects Craig T. Nelson's delivery of this line in the film and helps clarify Bob Parr's investment in his child's success). Works by Nietzsche will be cited in text in parentheses by work and aphorism, according to the following abbreviations: *GS* for *The Gay Science: La gaya scienza,* trans. Walter Kaufmann (New York: Vintage, 1974); *BGE* for *Beyond Good and Evil: Prelude to a*

*Philosophy of the Future,* trans. Walter Kaufmann (New York: Vintage, 1966); *GM* for *On the Genealogy of Morals: A Polemic,* trans. Walter Kaufmann (New York: Vintage, 1967); *A* for *Antichrist(ian),* in *The Portable Nietzsche,* trans. and ed. Walter Kaufmann (New York: Penguin, 1968).

2. Nietzsche sometimes even talks about a kind of "super" man (*Übermensch* in German—the prefix *über* meaning "over" or "beyond" or, in some translations, "super," and *Mensch* meaning "man" or "human"). This *Übermensch* is a sketchy figure whom Nietzsche discusses primarily in his most literary text, *Thus Spoke Zarathustra.* While some commentators see the *Übermensch* as a crucial figure in Nietzsche's overall philosophy, they disagree about who this person is and what exactly he signifies (as witnessed in part by the different choices of translation; e.g., "overman" versus "superman"). For the purposes of this chapter, I am leaving the controversies surrounding Nietzsche's notion of the *Übermensch* aside and restricting my discussion to a more generalized notion of "greatness" or "superiority," a notion that may or may not (exclusively) characterize the *Übermensch.*

3. But first, a few caveats. (1) It is difficult to pinpoint exactly what Nietzsche means by greatness—both because he is evasive about the details and because scholars have different plausible interpretations of his writings. Some view Nietzschean greatness as an individualized ethic of self-mastery (e.g., artistic creativity, cultivation of one's own virtues, or a psychological self-overcoming), while others view it as a more political orientation toward mastery over others (e.g., the Nietzschean great man as lawgiver and/or destroyer of the existing order). All of these interpretations are credible and none is definitive (they may even be harmonious to some extent). (2) Another question is how far to take Nietzsche's statements about the "order of rank" between man and man. Sometimes he seems to suggest that there are essentially two basic types of human beings: the few strong, masterful ones and the many weak, slavish ones. There is ample textual evidence to suggest Nietzsche believes this and, particularly in the *Antichrist(ian),* one of his very last books, he explicitly advocates an aristocratic social hierarchy as the only healthy political arrangement because it is sensitive to this natural hierarchy (§57—although here he specifies that there are three types of human beings, ranked nevertheless). Commentators, however, have *many* different views about the kind of politics Nietzsche ultimately endorsed (or can be interpreted to endorse today); they also disagree about whether Nietzsche believes the designations "strong and weak" or "master and slave" are intractable essences or designations that are subject to change. Luckily, we don't have to take decisive positions on either of these issues for the purposes of understanding Nietzsche's critique of slave morality or its allegorization in *The Incredibles.* The important, more general, and largely uncontroversial points here are these: (1) Nietzsche is no believer in natural equality when it comes to human beings; (2) he generally celebrates the "higher man" and his greatness; and (3) he believes this type to be rare and laments the generalized underappreciation of greatness that he believed rampant in the Europe of his day.

4. Although the film's very opening scene introduces us to *three* protagonist superheroes—Mr. Incredible, Elastigirl, and Frozone—all of whom are being interviewed about their superheroic lives, the most time is devoted to Mr. Incredible, who is established here and in the very next scene as the truly main character of the film, a primariness reflected in the film's title and family patronym, which subsumes each family member's individual powers into an undifferentiated Incredible-ness and clearly establishes Frozone as a sidekick or supporting character.

5. That Mr. Incredible recognizes these impending threats, however unconsciously, is attested to by the fact that he rebuffs the help of both Buddy and his fiancée in these opening scenes with the same words: "I work alone."

6. Nietzsche's views about women—if they are taken into consideration at all (many readers dismiss them as inconsequential or too ridiculous to take seriously)—are a source of much controversy among scholars. I myself believe they are worth taking seriously (especially since he says so very much about women, gender, sexuality, and marriage in so many of his books), that they are consistent with one another, and, most importantly, that they are essential to his overall philosophical project. More of my views about these matters may be found in my book, *Nietzsche's Revolution: Décadence, Politics, and Sexuality* (New York: Palgrave, 2009). For now, a few quotes from Nietzsche will suffice—and should serve to remind us that if Nietzsche considers women to be obstacles to greatness, the consequence is that only men can be great. Regarding marriage—for any man, not just a higher one, Nietzsche says it is "a hindrance and calamity on his path to the optimum" (*GM*, 3:7). Regarding association with women, Nietzsche says in *The Gay Science*, §59, in 1885: "When a man stands in the midst of his own noise, in the midst of his own surf of plans and projects, then he is apt also to see quiet, magical beings gliding past him and to long for their happiness and seclusion: *women*. He almost thinks that this better self dwells there among the women, and that in these quiet regions even the loudest surf turns into deathly quiet, and life itself into a dream about life. Yet! Yet! Noble enthusiast, even on the most beautiful sailboat there is a lot of noise, and unfortunately much small and petty noise. The magic and most powerful effect of women is, in philosophical language, action at a distance, *actio in distans;* but this requires first of all and above all—*distance.*"

In 1888, in Nietzsche's very last work, *The Case of Wagner*, trans. Walter Kaufmann (New York: Vintage, 1967), he says: "Translated into reality: the danger for artists, for geniuses—and who else is the 'Wandering Jew'?—is woman: adoring women confront them with corruption. Hardly any of them have character enough not to be corrupted—or 'redeemed'—when they find themselves treated like gods: soon they condescend to the level of the women.—Man is a coward, confronted with the Eternal-Feminine—and the females know it.—In many cases of feminine love, perhaps including the most famous ones above all, love is merely a more refined form of parasitism, a form of nestling down in another soul, sometimes even in the flesh of another—alas, always decidedly at the expense of 'the host!'" (§3).

7. The front-page photo illustrating this new amnesty policy shows construction workers taking down a large public statue of three superheroes, a possible allusion to the removal of the statue of Saddam Hussein by U.S. troops in Baghdad in 2003 (*The Incredibles* was released in theaters in 2004). As the headlines surrounding this image suggest, the people will be "safer without" the supers and the "public" will be "safe again," just as, it was argued, the Iraqi people—and the United States—would be safer without Hussein in power.

8. Indeed, the Parrs' relocation to suburbia and their faithful reproduction of the 2.5 child ideal not only mirror the actual historical movement of white American families to the suburbs and the dramatic rise of U.S. birthrates in this era, but also underscore the fact that the Parrs' superness is, indeed, a real threat to the social order, a threat that must be normalized.

9. Given the nostalgic chronology of the film's allusions, "fifteen years later" would situate the Parrs in the middle to late 1960s, a time of increasing dissatisfaction with the American Dream and widespread social rebellion against its white, middle-class, patriarchal norms. So it is no surprise that the Parrs are unhappy.

10. Bob's size literalizes his superness, and the dramatic physical disjuncture between his body and his surroundings symbolizes his discomfort and dissatisfaction with life as an "average citizen." As his very body makes clear, Bob is *not*, in fact, average: his overwhelming strength is impossible to ignore; it is extremely difficult to hide (he damages his car merely by gripping it too tightly and saws through Dash's plate at dinner by cutting a piece of meat); and it is a fact about him that is not going to change, regardless of social outcry.

11. These familiarly gendered roles reveal the latent sexism of the film and resonate with Nietzsche's overt sexism, revealing how little has changed in the more than one hundred years since his death. Although *The Incredibles* was billed as a feminist film and received accolades for the ostensible equality between the two married partners, the film nevertheless presents women as naturally inclined toward love, marriage, children, and domesticity. Although she may have once been Elastigirl, fiercely unwilling to "settle down" and "leave the saving of the world to the men," Helen nevertheless seems to experience no conflict whatsoever in having exchanged superheroism for vacuuming, changing diapers, and picking up the kids from school. Moreover, the familiar tropes of woman as guardian of hearth and home who must reignite her husband's wandering interest and boredom with the humdrum reality of domesticity show that "superness" is not only a literalization of Nietzschean greatness but also a stand-in for heterosexual male infidelity and midlife crisis behavior. The film only uneasily resolves these by threatening Bob with the death of his wife and children—more on this in the conclusion.

12. Says Nietzsche: "Every sufferer instinctively seeks a cause for his suffering—in short, some living thing upon which he can, on some pretext or other, vent his affects, actually or in effigy: for the venting of his affects represents the greatest attempt on the part of the suffering to win relief, *anaesthesia*—the narcotic he cannot help desiring to

deaden pain of any kind. This alone, I surmise, constitutes the actually physiological cause of *ressentiment* [resentment], vengefulness, and the like: a desire to *deaden pain by means of affects* . . . 'Someone or other must be to blame for my feeling ill'—this kind of reasoning is common to all the sick, and is indeed held the more firmly the more the real cause of their feeling ill, the physiological cause, remains hidden" (*GM*, 3:15).

13. Buddy is engaged in this project from the very beginning—when we first meet him, he is showing off his new rocket boots to Mr. Incredible, who is unimpressed and, once again, tries to shake Buddy off. Recoiling from this rejection, adamant about his own greatness, and subtly denigrating Mr. Incredible even while hoping for praise and recognition from him, Buddy wails, "This is because I don't have powers, isn't it? Well not every superhero has powers, you know. You *can* be super without them. I invented these. I can fly. Can *you* fly?" As Nietzsche says, "The slave's eye is not favorable to the virtues of the powerful: he is skeptical and suspicious, *subtly* suspicious, of all the 'good' that is honored there—he would like to persuade himself that even their happiness is not genuine" (*BGE*, §260).

14. In Nietzsche's terms, "the man of *ressentiment* [resentment] is neither upright nor naïve nor honest and straightforward with himself. His soul *squints;* his spirit loves hiding places, secret paths and back doors, everything covert entices him as *his* world, *his* security, *his* refreshment; he understands how to keep silent, how not to forget, how to wait" (*GM*, 1:10).

15. As Nietzsche says about Christians: "These weak people—some day or other *they* too intend to be the strong, there is no doubt of that, some day *their* 'kingdom' too shall come—they term it 'the kingdom of God'" (*GM*, 1:15). For Nietzsche, Christianity is the slave morality par excellence, and its will to power is manifest in its longing for the day when wrongdoers will be punished and the virtuous rewarded. On this day, as the saying goes, the last shall be first and the first shall be last. In Nietzschean terms, this means that the great shall be enslaved and the slaves shall rule. Notably, Nietzsche argues that Christianity's triumphant overturning of natural hierarchy has been secularized in the movements for democracy and equality ("the *democratic* movement is the heir of the Christian movement" [*BGE*, §202]) and declares, "To us the democratic movement is not only a form of the decay of political organization but a form of the decay, namely the diminution, of man, making him mediocre and lowering his value" (*BGE*, §203).

16. Nietzsche says: "Whether I contemplate men with benevolence or with an evil eye, I always find them concerned with a single task, all of them and every one of them in particular: to do what is good for the preservation of the human race. . . . this instinct constitutes *the essence* of our species, our herd" (*GS*, §1).

17. Indeed, Nietzsche cites approvingly the "egoism" of the higher man and consistently argues that condemnation of selfishness is yet one more way in which the herd limits and forbids greatness. For example: "At the risk of displeasing innocent ears I propose: egoism belongs to the nature of a noble soul—I mean that unshakable faith that to a being such as 'we are' other beings must be subordinate by nature and have to

sacrifice themselves. The noble soul accepts this fact of its egoism without any question mark, also without any feeling that it might contain hardness, constraint, or caprice, rather as something that may be founded in the primordial law of things: if it sought a name for this fact it would say, 'it is justice itself'" (*BGE*, §265; cf. *GS*, §328, *GM*, 1:2).

18. Mr. Incredible, at least, professes ambivalence about his role as humanity's savior. In his television interview at the beginning of the film, he laments with some irritation, "No matter how many times you save the world, it always manages to get back in jeopardy again. Sometimes I just want it to *stay saved*, you know? For a little bit. I feel like the maid. 'I just cleaned up this mess. Can we keep it clean for ten minutes?'"

19. I owe this insight to Dan Conway, who generously suggested the line of analysis offered in this paragraph. Evidence of this decline is Mr. Incredible's admission, after his complaint about humanity's penchant for getting itself into trouble: "Sometimes I think I'd just like the simple life, you know? Relax a little and raise a family."

# 9

# MUGGLES, MAGIC, AND MISFITS

## Michel Foucault at Harry Potter's Hogwarts

*Jamie Warner*

Welcome to Hogwarts! At this school of witchcraft and wizardry, magical boys and girls will learn to hone their potential in spell-casting, potion-making, divination, and the mystical arts. They will learn how to fly on brooms, play Quidditch, and duel with wands, and they will be taught the proper way to greet a Hippogriff. Students will also be monitored day and night, their actions under constant surveillance. Anyone caught breaking the rules will be disciplined. Punishments can range from a loss of "house points," needed for receipt of the coveted House Cup, to detention, suspension, a revocation of privileges, or even expulsion. Students will also be monitored at all times by the Ministry of Magic, who, through the Improper Use of Magic Office (a division of the Department of Magical Law Enforcement), will make sure that no underage witch or wizard performs magic and that no magic is performed in the presence of Muggles (nonmagical persons). Surveillance, discipline, and conformity: Never forget your place, young witches and wizards!

J. K. Rowling's *Harry Potter* series—the story about eleven-year-old Harry, who, out of the blue, gets a letter informing him of his acceptance to Hogwarts School of Witchcraft and Wizardry—has captivated literally hundreds of millions of people. As a franchise, *Harry Potter* is among the most successful in history. It is widely reported that by 2008 the number of books sold had surpassed the 400 million mark and the books had been translated into sixty-seven languages. The last movie, *Harry Potter and the Deathly Hallows: Part 2,* broke opening weekend box-office records around the world with a total of $476 million in ticket sales.[1] Harry's adventures, leading up to the final battle with the dark wizard, Lord Voldemort, have caught the imagination of people across the globe. It is a phenomenon of epic proportions.

Potter is popular, but where are the politics? At the most explicit of levels, Harry Potter's author, J. K. Rowling, provides her readers with the outlines of a political system. Not surprisingly, it looks much like her home, Great Britain, and thus there is both a "Minister" and a "Ministry of Magic," both very important to the story through the seven books. In the world of Harry Potter, this somewhat parallel political system is completely hidden to nonmagical people ("Muggles").[2] In fact, according to Rowling, wizards and witches have lived as a community within a community, with only occasional contact with Muggles, since 1689, when the International Statute of Secrecy was signed.[3]

There are also plenty of less overtly and explicitly structural but still very "political" themes in the books, and many scholars have written about themes such as sexuality, gender, race, and more.[4] However, one of the most critical and underappreciated aspects of the *Potter* series, as a broader work of political theory, is its presentation of different manifestations of power. Most obviously, there are the Nietzschean themes of power and ethics that are present in the struggles between Voldemort's Death Eaters and the rest of the wizarding community (for example, Professor Quirrell's claim at the end of *The Sorcerer's Stone* that "there is no good and evil, there is only power, and those too weak to seek it").[5] Less obvious are the forms of power that are present in all aspects of the magic-using world, from the Ministry of Magic to Hogwarts itself. Such power structures directly reflect Michel Foucault's concept of "disciplinary power" as put forward in his book *Discipline and Punish: The Birth of the Prison* and allow us to hone in and analyze how power works on a deeper level.[6] Specifically, using Foucault's description of the disciplinary tactic of hierarchical observation not only leads us to see more depth and nuance in the texts but also gives us insight into Foucault's ideas and our own "Muggle" politics.

## The Panopticon: I Always Feel Like Somebody's Watching Me

In *Harry Potter and the Half Blood Prince*, Professor Dumbledore argues that "Voldemort himself created his worst enemy, just as tyrants everywhere do! Have you any idea how much tyrants fear the people they oppress? All of them realize that, one day, amongst their many victims, there is sure to be one who rises against them and strikes back!"[7] Dumbledore continues his warning to Harry that Voldemort remains "always on the lookout for the one who would challenge him" and that therefore, through his magic and his minions, he maintains perpetual surveillance over the wizarding world. Voldemort's goal is to identify those who might oppose him and punish or remove them, so as to create and consolidate his own position of power. Interestingly, although the Dark Lord Voldemort is the antagonistic villain who threatens Potter and his friends (not to mention the entire magical and nonmagical worlds), his attempts to monitor the world and conform it to his designs are not at all unlike the rigid structure and enforcement of rules at Hogwarts, where free will and genuine action on the part of students are actively suppressed and discouraged through the establishment of collective norms and values that are administratively enforced. In both cases power seeks to control toward conformity.

Before attempting to see how disciplinary power allows us a more detailed and subtle discussion of power at Hogwarts, however, we first need to look more closely at Foucault's argument. In his book *Discipline and Punish*, Foucault claims that a new kind of power has evolved, beginning around the eighteenth century, a kind of power that is excluded from traditional conceptions of power. This power is "mild, subtle, insidious and disciplinary."[8] The liberalizing tendencies of democratic institutions in that period limited the overt and obviously repressive power of the king, the church, and the aristocracy (this time period, the late 1700s to the mid-1800s, for example, gave rise to both the American and the French revolutions) but masked the institutionalization of a more insidious type of power. We are implicated in it whether we realize it or not, in the sense that it defines what is "normal." While this might not seem nearly as problematic as the potentially limitless power of a king, it is even more dangerous, more powerful, if you will, because we internalize these definitions of normality and then police ourselves.

In *Discipline and Punish: The Birth of the Prison*, Foucault lists a series of disciplinary tactics, techniques, and procedures that were and are variously employed by various institutions since the eighteenth and nineteenth centuries. This is not at all what we are used to when we discuss "power." He does not mean an overwhelming show of military force or variations of agenda-setting by politicians but instead assorted methods of the spatialization of bodies and the timing, duration, and repetition of their activities, the hierarchical observation of which has allowed us to both reward good behavior and punish the smallest of infractions (Sit up straight. Be on time. Work hard. Pay attention). These tactics are not necessarily original to these two centuries, but they became widespread as the growing institutions of that time period (factories, prisons, schools, asylums, hospitals, and government institutions) and the newly instituted social sciences combined to form a matrix of power-knowledge relations that climaxed in theory, according to Foucault, in the figure of the Panopticon.

The Panopticon was the architectural wonder of English philosopher Jeremy Bentham; it was designed to be a place where "morals [are] re-formed—health preserved—industry invigorated—instruction diffused—public health burdens lightened." Such benefits, according to Bentham, could be derived "all by a simple idea of architecture."[9] This "simple idea of architecture" consisted of a central tower in which a prison guard or schoolmaster or psychiatrist or foreman could stand and watch each and every inmate or student or patient or worker. The cells would be arranged in a circle around the tower with only the side of the cell facing the tower visible from the outside. Each cell would also be backlighted so the body inside would be in plain sight of the watchman in the tower at all times. While the inmate or student or patient or worker could be plainly seen, those watching inside the tower would not be visible to those being watched. It would be impossible to know whether anyone was inside the tower watching at any given time. Bentham thought this to be the ultimate instrument of correction. Since those confined had no idea when or whether anyone was watching, they would eventually learn to internalize this external authoritative gaze and police themselves: "So it is not necessary to use force to constrain the convict to good behavior, the madman to calm, the worker to work, the schoolboy to application, the patient to the observation of the regulations. . . . He who is subjected to a field of visibility, and who knows it, assumes responsibility for the constraints of power; he makes them play spontaneously upon himself; he inscribes in himself the power relations in which he simultaneously plays both roles; he becomes the principle of his own subjection" (203).

Foucault uses the Panopticon to illustrate the effectiveness of this new type of power at its logical extreme. The Panopticon is also a metaphor for modern life. We have become, according to Foucault, a panoptic society. While the law has progressively limited the overt power of traditional institutions and recognized more and more people as equal subjects with rights, this internalized panoptic policing of ourselves according to such disciplinary norms has worked to homogenize and then individualize us only according to the appropriate norms. From the moment we are born, we are constantly watched and measured against norms. We know what is "normal" for just about every behavior in society. We know the "normal" range for IQs, for hair color, for the height of five-year-olds, for classroom behavior, for sexual conduct, for responses to lie detector tests. There is intense social pressure to conform to the normal or risk exclusion as a case to be treated or a problem to be solved. On the whole, he argues, most of us submit to this social pressure to be normal and become our own jailers—modern, disciplined subjects. What, Foucault implies, is lost as we strive for normality? Persons who fail to measure up to these somewhat arbitrary, historically situated norms, purposefully or not, become the Other, the "abnormal," and are excluded from society in prisons, asylums, and hospitals. There they are carefully watched, documented, and put through an even more strenuous regimen of correction and rehabilitation.

## Hierarchical Observation, Real and Imagined

While Foucault argues that a myriad of small tactics and techniques, a "micro-physics of power," are used in disciplinary power,[10] one of the most important of these many and overlapping techniques is what he calls "hierarchical observation." I would argue that this is the lynchpin that holds the others together. It is done with the help of seemingly banal things, such as the placement of beds in a hospital or encouraging comments from a supervisor. According to Foucault, the very position of buildings, walls or half walls, doors, windows, and furniture can affect how people behave, because people act differently if they think they might be watched. As institutions began to be very aware of this principle in the late eighteenth and early nineteenth centuries,

> [a] whole problematic then develop[ed]: that of an architecture that is no longer built simply to be seen (as with the ostentation of palaces), or to observe the external space (cf. the geometry of fortresses), but to permit an internal, articulated and detailed control—to render visible those who are inside it; in more general terms, an architecture that would open to transform individuals: to act on those it shelters, to provide a hold on their conduct, to carry

the effects of power right to them, to make it possible to know them, to alter them. Stones can make people docile and knowable. (172)

The institution of supervisory positions at institutions as diverse as factories and elementary schools (individuals who watch those below them and then are, in turn, watched by their supervisors) works the same way as the decisions about architecture that Foucault discusses. Many small, seemingly unrelated decisions, he argues, become geared toward establishing permanent inspection: "Hierarchized, continuous, and functional surveillance may not be one of the great technical inventions of the eighteenth century, but its insidious extension owed its importance to the mechanisms of power that it brought with it. . . . It functions like a piece of machinery" (176–77). People are constantly watching and being watched.

We must not forget, however, that these techniques are not necessarily designed with the explicit goal of domination. Foucault argues that they do make people "docile," especially if the power is successful and they internalize the possibility of external gazes and then police themselves, but he also insists that these techniques make us "useful." Foucault says: "Discipline increases the forces of the body (in economic terms of utility) and diminishes these same forces (in political terms of obedience)."[11] This is not all bad. My classroom is a much more useful place for learning when students have internalized being watched in an educational institution—and thus aren't texting and messing around on Facebook during class, for example.

Magic, however, has the power to create the ultimate Panopticon, surveillance beyond Jeremy Bentham's wildest dreams (or Foucault's worst nightmare). Foucault points out, "The perfect disciplinary apparatus would make it possible for a single gaze to see everything constantly," and magic certainly has that potential.[12] If we look at the Harry Potter series through this lens, we see many different methods of surveillance beyond that which is available in the Muggle world, starting right away in the first book of the series when the almost-eleven-year-old Harry gets a letter inviting him to attend Hogwarts. The letter is addressed not just to the house where he lives with his aunt and uncle, but specifically to "Mr. H. Potter, The Cupboard under the Stairs, 4 Privet Drive, Little Whinging, Surrey."[13] How would anyone from Hogwarts know that Harry's relatives make him sleep in a small broom cupboard under the stairs? When Harry's Uncle Vernon refuses to let Harry have that first letter, more letters begin arriving, so many that Uncle Vernon nails the mail slot shut.[14] Letters then begin arriving through any available cracks in the house and the chimney; they follow the family to a hotel and finally to a shack on a rock out at sea, where Harry is at last given his letter in person. Someone must be watching.

Once Harry gets to Hogwarts, he finds a combination of both nonmagical and magical methods of surveillance. One of the most effective is quite nonmagical: the caretaker Filch and his cat, Mrs. Norris. They patrol the dark stone halls of the school to make sure that no students are making mischief or are out of their beds at night, and Harry and his friends spend quite a lot of time avoiding them. In fact, students at Hogwarts are watched in many of the ways Foucault describes in *Discipline and Punish*. In addition to being watched by Filch, they are also watched by other students, who hold supervisory positions such as "prefect" and "head boy" and "head girl" and who run constant surveillance. And then they are watched and evaluated by their professors academically in ways that all of us would recognize: lots of constant homework and tests culminating in standardized exams (O.W.L.s [Ordinary Wizarding Levels] and N.E.W.T.s [Nastily Exhausting Wizarding Tests]), the scores from which allow or refuse them entrance into certain professions upon graduation.[15] In many ways, Hogwarts is a normal school with a mission like any other educational institution: to mold its charges into reputable and skilled individuals. Foucauldian discipline is working quite nicely.

But there are other ways students are watched at Hogwarts that are quite different from that which Foucault describes. For example, the halls are watched not only by Filch and Mrs. Norris, but also by the portraits that line the walls and the ghosts that inhabit the school.[16] Once followers of Voldemort take over the Ministry of Magic, magical means of communication, such as the owl post and the floo network, are monitored.[17] Students are watched outside of school, too. For example, the Ministry of Magic is notified as soon as a student performs underage magic, and in the final book of the series, a jinx is put on the evil Lord Voldemort's name, so the location of anyone who uses it can be instantaneously traced.[18] Aside from physically watching to ensure proper behavior, however defined, there are also magical ways to do more serious surveillance, not just surveillance of bodies and actions but direct observation of what is going on inside a person's head. For example, the Sorting Hat, a hat that first-year students put on as soon as they enter Hogwarts for the first time, can see your most important qualities as a person, and it sorts you into one of the four "houses" at Hogwarts accordingly: Griffindors (brave and daring), Hufflepuffs (hardworking and loyal),

Ravensclaws (witty and smart), and Slytherins (cunning and ambitious).[19] The Mirror of Erised will show you your heart's desire when you look into it.[20] More ominously, there is a magical truth-serum potion, called "veritaserum" that is used on one of Lord Voldemort's servants by the Headmaster, Albus Dumbledore, and also on students by Dolores Umbridge, who replaces Dumbledore for a short but memorable time in the fifth book, even though the Ministry of Magic supposedly has very strict guidelines about the use of the potion.[21] Perhaps the most interesting and important, not to mention creepiest, magical inner surveillance in the series is "Legilimency," or "the ability to extract feelings and memories from another person's mind."[22] It's not as blunt as what we might call mind reading, as explained to Harry by his least favorite professor, the potions teacher, Severus Snape, but is still very effective:

> Only Muggles talk of "mind reading." The mind is not a book to be opened at will and examined at leisure. Thoughts are not etched on the inside of skulls, to be perused by any invader. The mind is a complex and many-layered thing, Potter. . . . It is true, however, that those who have mastered Legilimency are able, under certain conditions, to delve into the minds of their victims and to interpret their findings correctly. The Dark Lord, for instance, almost always knows when someone is lying to him. Only those skilled at Occlumency are able to shut down those feelings and memories that contradict the lie, and so utter falsehoods in his presence without detection.[23]

This is very advanced magic, but because Harry is mentally and emotionally connected to Lord Voldemort through the scar Voldemort left on Harry's forehead when he tried to kill him as a one-year-old child, Voldemort might also be able to use Legilimency on Harry from afar, even unknowingly.

## Zones of Shade

Even with the increased number of ways to watch and thus influence and normalize behavior, the magical world of Harry Potter also provides an extraordinary number of what Foucault calls "zones of shade," or places where the machinery of hierarchical observation fails, where one cannot be watched.[24] These secret or hidden places work against the power of the Panopticon, allowing Harry and his friends ways to disrupt the power structure, to plot and plan and rebel against the rules. Indeed, the entire plot through all seven books hinges on the fact that Harry is not "docile" and "useful" at all, but, because of his celebrity status as the "Boy who Lived," the only person ever to survive the killing curse, he instead operates somewhat outside the parameters of "normality," as storybook heroes often do. To do this, however, requires thoughts and actions that are shielded from the gaze of others, including both villains and well-meaning adults.

There are many, many magical ways to hide.[25] Occlumency, mentioned in the quotation above, is a very important one. While Legilimency is the art of looking into someone else's mind for hints of that person's emotional state, Occlumency is the opposite: closing one's mind down, shielding it from the gaze of others. The "great Snape debate" that occurs between the publishing of the sixth and seventh books—Is Severus Snape good (as Dumbledore insists) or bad (as Harry feels)?—hinges on Snape's amazing talent for Occlumency, shutting out perhaps the greatest Legilimens of all time, Lord Voldemort, so he can operate as a double agent. In fact, Snape operates almost completely shaded from practically every gaze, including both Voldemort and the reader, for that matter, and not until the end of the last book do we find out his true leanings.

Although Snape's Occlumency is crucial to Harry's final defeat of Lord Voldemort, it is certainly not the only magical zone of shade. Two interesting and indispensable ways to avoid being watched come to Harry as Christmas gifts: the Marauder's Map and an Invisibility Cloak. A gift from the resident mischief-makers and class clowns, Fred and George Weasley, the Marauder's Map is a piece of parchment that shows all of Hogwarts, including secret passages leading into and out of the school. More importantly, it also shows, with tiny, labeled dots, the location of every person in the school. With the map, Harry is able to avoid those whose job is to watch. While the Weasley twins embody the spirit of the map, which is activated only when it is touched by a wand while saying "I solemnly swear that I am up to no good," and use the map for silly pranks, Harry uses it for much more serious sneaking around.[26]

The Invisibility Cloak is given to Harry as an anonymous Christmas present his first year at Hogwarts (the unsigned note says only that it was originally his father's and that Harry should "Use it well," although we find out later that it was actually a present from Dumbledore).[27] This zone of shade opens up an entire new world to Harry: "Suddenly, Harry felt wide-awake. The whole of Hogwarts was open to him in this Cloak. Excitement flooded through him as he stood there in the dark and silence. He could go anywhere in this, anywhere, and Filch would never know" (205). This was a zone of shade like no other in that it was mobile, not only allowing hidden thought and activity, but allowing the wearer (or wearers) of the Cloak the freedom to move around undetected by the authorities. We find out in the final book of the series that it is actually one of the three Deathly Hallows, objects that, when united under one master, allow that person to master death.[28] Although an advanced wizard like Dumbledore may be able to make himself invisible with a spell,[29] young Harry and his friends use the Cloak on almost every adventure they have, from helping Hagrid, the groundskeeper, sneak his pet dragon Norbert out of Hogwarts in the first book (240), to allowing Harry to reenter Hogwarts during the final battle to fight Voldemort.[30]

In addition to spells and magical objects that allow one to operate unseen, the very architecture of Hogwarts works against the idea of the Panopticon, since it was built more than a thousand years ago, well before the time when Foucault argues that disciplinary power evolved.[31] Even with all the magical ways to watch, normal day-to-day student life at Hogwarts seems to be more shaded than that of students in secondary schools in the United States. The hallways of Hogwarts, for example, are dark and mysterious, lit only by sunlight during the day or torches and the occasional wand at night. It is even a challenge for new students to find their classrooms in the daylight. There are 142 staircases at Hogwarts, "some that led somewhere different on a Friday. . . . Then there were the doors that wouldn't open unless you asked them politely, or tickled them in exactly the right place, and doors that weren't really doors at all, but walls just pretending."[32] While the outside of Hogwarts is hidden to Muggles by a spell that makes the castle look like a "moldering old ruin," the inside also houses many unwatched places and thus, many secrets.[33] There are many places to get lost—and to hide away from prying eyes. There are even places that Dumbledore himself admits to not knowing:[34]

> Only this morning, for instance, I took a wrong turning on the way to the bathroom and found myself in a beautifully proportioned room I have never seen before, containing a really rather magnificent collection of chamber pots. When I went back to investigate more closely, I discovered that the room had vanished. But I must keep my eye out for it. Possibly it is only accessible at five-thirty in the morning. Or it may only appear at the quarter moon—or when the seeker has an exceptionally full bladder.

Harry snorted into his plate of goulash. Percy frowned, but Harry could have sworn that Dumbledore had given him a very small wink.[35]

Dumbledore was talking about one of the most interesting hiding places at Hogwarts: the Room of Requirement. The Room of Requirement first appears in the fifth book of the series, after the arrival of another powerful gaze, Ministry bureaucrat Dolores Umbridge. Ostensibly, she is sent to become the new Defense against the Dark Arts professor, who will teach students the theory, but not allow them to practice, how to defend themselves against dark wizards. Soon, however, Umbridge is appointed by the Ministry to the post of "Hogwarts High Inquisitor." According to the wizarding newspaper, *The Daily Prophet,* "This is an exciting new phase in the Minister's plan to get to grips with what some are calling 'falling standards' at Hogwarts. . . . The Inquisitor will have powers to inspect her fellow teachers and make sure that they are coming up to scratch."[36] In addition to observing all the Hogwarts teachers and forcing them to stop teaching most practical applications of magic, one of her first big moves, a classic by dictators of every stripe to prevent dissent, is to disband, on threat of expulsion, any groups, teams, societies, clubs, and organizations that she has not explicitly approved (351–52). Harry and his friends want to avoid her panoptic gaze and practice magical defense. But where?

Dobby the House Elf provides Harry with the answer: the Room of Requirement. According to Dobby, "it is a room that a person can only enter . . . when they have a real need of it. Sometimes it is there, and sometimes it is not, but when it appears, it is always equipped for the seeker's needs."[37] We find that Dobby has used it himself to allow fellow house elf Winky to sleep off hangovers, Filch has found extra cleaning materials there, and tricksters Fred and George Weasley have used it to hide from Filch (387, 391). When Harry and his friends Ron and Hermione stand outside its supposed location and wish for a secret room where twenty-eight students can practice Defense against the Dark Arts, the Room of Requirement appears, complete with bookcases full of books, dark magic detectors like Sneakoscopes, Secrecy Sensors, and silk cushions on the floor to protect them when they practice stunning spells (390). Dumbledore's Army (D.A.) is thus born, allowing Harry and the rest of the students a safe place to challenge the increasingly hostile scrutiny of Umbridge and the Ministry: "He and the D.A. were resisting under her very nose, doing the very thing that she and the Ministry most feared" (392, quotation on 397). While the D.A. is eventually caught by Umbridge, it is only because one of the students in the group reveals the secret. Unless you know exactly what the room is used for, no gaze can penetrate. In the final book, after the Death Eaters take over Hogwarts, Dumbledore's Army regroups and uses the Room of Requirement as a hideout and staging area for raids.[38]

As befits a story as complicated as the Harry Potter series, the Room of Requirement is not only used by the "good guys" to pull pranks or hide from menacing authorities like Dolores Umbridge; it is also used by Harry's arch-enemy, Draco Malfoy, a fellow student who hides out in the Room of Requirement plotting the murder of Dumbledore for much of the sixth book. Harry knows that Draco is using the Room of Requirement, but Draco is protected from Harry's gaze because Harry doesn't know why Draco is using the room and thus can't ask for the room to open for him.[39] In the final book, we learn that the room was used long ago for its most sinister purpose: to house one of Lord Voldemort's Horcruxes, an object magically transfigured to hold part of one's soul. While that portion of soul exists, the maker of the Horcrux cannot die. This is dark magic indeed, as a Horcrux can be created only by committing the ultimate act of evil: murder. Voldemort made not one but seven Horcruxes and hid them in various places protected by complicated and dangerous enchantments. The Horcrux he hides in the Room of Requirement, however, has no magic protecting it. Voldemort thought, mistakenly, that he had been the only one to find the Room of Requirement and relied completely on its ability to provide "shade" to this most important of objects. Unfortunately for Voldemort, the protection from Harry's prying eyes was only temporary.[40]

## Harry Potter and Political Theory

If Harry Potter had been a nicely disciplined subject, he would have been killed, Voldemort would be running the Ministry of Magic, and the Muggles would be enslaved. But like most heroes, Harry was neither docile nor useful, in Foucauldian terms. More specifically, if Hogwarts had been a "normal" educational institution, where the ability to watch—and thus control—students was at a premium, Harry would have had neither the knowledge nor the skills to vanquish the Dark Lord. However, both the architecture of Hogwarts and the magical objects that were given to Harry (one by Dumbledore himself) provided zones of shade that allowed Harry the freedom he needed to develop along a different path, to become supremely "useful" (you can't get any more useful than defeating the arch-enemy), but in a very different way than the Panopticon normally allows.

Focusing Foucault's theoretical lens on a make-believe world might seem like a waste of time, or perhaps just a disciplinary exercise designed to help us practice our craft. After all, Foucault was talking about our world, the "real" world, and there are plenty of things to argue about right here without talking about invisibility cloaks and rooms that can morph to fit your unspoken needs. I would claim, however, that not only does thinking about hierarchical observation, for example, within the context of Harry Potter allow us to see new themes in the books themselves; it also forces a fresh perspective when we look back at the world Foucault wanted us to analyze. I argue that finding magical examples of both surveillance and zones of shade shows both the applicability and the limits of Foucault's analysis. By examining how well Foucault's concepts and ideas match up in the world J. K. Rowling created, we can turn a more critical eye to the world we create every day.

It was remarkable to me to see just how many zones of shade exist in the world of Harry Potter, which begs the question about our own world. We don't have the magical zones of shade that are available with magic, but the Panopticon has yet to be implemented in the seamless way that Jeremy Bentham hoped. There are still zones of shade where we can gather to think our own thoughts and learn new skills away from prying eyes. But are they disappearing? Think of the ways we can be watched today, with our consent: social media, No Child Left Behind, assessment reports, cell phones, video cameras at red lights, supervised or organized play. What does it mean that so much of our life is continually assessed by others, others who dole out rewards and punishments for those who docilely follow the rules? The combination of Michel Foucault and Harry Potter gives us much to ponder.[41]

## Notes

1. See Guy Dammann, "Harry Potter Breaks 400m in Sales," *Guardian,* June 18, 2008, www.guardian.co.uk/books/2008/jun/18/harrypotter.news (accessed November 21, 2011); and Brooke Barnes, "Millions of Muggles Propel Potter Film at Box Office," *New York Times,* July 17, 2011, www.nytimes.com/2011/07/18/movies/harry-potters-opening-weekend-breaks-box-office-records.html (accessed November 21, 2011).

2. J. K. Rowling, *Harry Potter and the Sorcerer's Stone* (New York: Scholastic, 1997), 53, hereafter referred to as *Sorcerer's Stone.*

3. J. K. Rowling, *Harry Potter and the Deathly Hallows* (New York: Scholastic, 2007), 318, hereafter referred to as *Deathly Hallows*. For a detailed description of the explicitly political world that Rowling creates, see Benjamin H. Barton, "Harry Potter and the Half-Crazed Bureaucracy," *Michigan Law Review* 104 (May 2006): 1523–38.

4. See, for example, Tamar Szabó Gendler, "Is Dumbledore Gay? Who's to Say?" in *The Ultimate Harry Potter and Philosophy: Hogwarts for Muggles*, ed. Gregory Bassham (Hoboken, NJ: Wiley, 2010), 143–56; Elizabeth E. Heilman and Trevor Donaldson, "From Sexist to (Sort-of) Feminist: Representations of Gender in the Harry Potter Series," in *Critical Perspective on Harry Potter*, ed. Elizabeth H. Heilman, 2nd ed. (New York: Routledge, 2009), 139–61; and Jackie Horn, "Harry Potter and the Other: Answering the Race Question in J. K. Rowling's *Harry Potter*," *Lion and the Unicorn* 34, no. 1 (2010): 76–104.

5. *Sorcerer's Stone*, 291.

6. Michel Foucault, *Discipline and Punish: The Birth of the Prison* (New York: Vintage Books, 1979).

7. J. K. Rowling, *Harry Potter and the Half-Blood Prince* (New York: Scholastic, 2005), 510, hereafter referred to as *Half-Blood Prince*.

8. Peter Digeser, "The Fourth Face of Power," *Journal of Politics* 54, no. 4 (November 1992): 993.

9. Foucault, *Discipline and Punish*, 207.

10. Ibid., 203.

11. Ibid., 138.

12. Ibid., 173.

13. *Sorcerer's Stone*, 34.

14. For those who are not familiar with the storyline: Harry lives with his aunt and uncle, the Dursleys, because his parents were killed by Lord Voldemort when he was one year old. Voldemort also tried to kill Harry, but his killing curse rebounded, giving Harry a very distinctive lightning-bolt-shaped scar and turning Voldemort into a shadow of his former self. Although Harry's parents had magical abilities that they passed on to Harry, the Dursleys are Muggles, with a very negative view toward magic, which Rowling uses to start the series: "Mr. and Mrs. Dursley, of number four, Privet Drive, were proud to say that they were perfectly normal, thank you very much. They were the last people you'd expect to be involved with anything strange or mysterious, because they just didn't hold with such nonsense." Ibid., 1.

15. For more information on the standardized exams, see J. K. Rowling, *Harry Potter and the Order of the Phoenix* (New York: Scholastic, 2003), chap. 31, "O.W.L.S.," 703–28, hereafter referred to as *Order of the Phoenix*.

16. *Sorcerer's Stone*, 132.

17. *Order of the Phoenix*, 612.

18. *Deathly Hallows*, 389, 445. Harry thrice gets in trouble with the Ministry for using underage magic: once that is actually Dobby the House Elf's doing (*Sorcerer's Stone*, 20–21), once when he purposely inflates Uncle Vernon's sister, Aunt Marge (J. K.

Rowling, *Harry Potter and the Prisoner of Azkaban* [New York, Scholastic, 1999], 29, hereafter referred to as *Prisoner of Azkaban*), and once when Harry does a patronus charm to save his cousin, Dudley, from a Dementor, for which he is tried and acquitted by the Wizengamot (*Order of the Phoenix*, 32–33).

19. *Sorcerer's Stone*, 117–22.

20. Ibid., 207–9. Harry's greatest desire was to be with his parents and have a family.

21. J. K. Rowling, *Harry Potter and the Goblet of Fire* (New York: Scholastic, 2000), 683, 517, hereafter referred to as *Goblet of Fire*. Also see *Order of the Phoenix*, 744.

22. *Order of the Phoenix*, 530.

23. Ibid., 530–31.

24. Foucault, *Discipline and Punish*, 177.

25. To list just a few: Polyjuice potion can temporarily transform you into someone else. J. K. Rowling, *Harry Potter and the Chamber of Secrets* (New York: Scholastic, 1998), 205–26, hereafter referred to as *Chamber of Secrets*. You can also magically turn yourself into an animal (*Prisoner of Azkaban*, 349–57) or do the complicated Fidelius Charm, in which a secret is magically hidden inside someone's soul until the "secret keeper" divulges it (205). Harry's parents were betrayed by their secret keeper, which led to their deaths at the hand of Lord Voldemort. The headquarters of the Order of the Phoenix, 12 Grimmauld Place, was also under the Fidelius Charm (*Order of the Phoenix*, 59–78). In the final book, Harry could not have done his tasks without the books, pictures, clothing, tent, and equipment that Hermione had fitted in her little beaded bag with an Undetectable Extension Charm (*Deathly Hallows*, 162).

26. *Prisoner of Azkaban*, 192.

27. *Sorcerer's Stone*, 202.

28. *Deathly Hallows*, 714–15.

29. *Sorcerer's Stone*, 213.

30. *Deathly Hallows*, 733.

31. *Chamber of Secrets*, 150.

32. *Sorcerer's Stone*, 131–32.

33. *Goblet of Fire*, 166.

34. What exactly Dumbledore knows is quite interesting in the series. There are certainly times when he appears to know everything that goes on in the castle, which brings up an intriguing point: If he does know what is happening at Hogwarts, why does he allow dangerous things to happen to children?

35. *Goblet of Fire*, 417–18.

36. *Order of the Phoenix*, 307.

37. Ibid., 386–87.

38. *Deathly Hallows*, 577–78.

39. *Half Blood Prince*, 458–59.

40. *Deathly Hallows*, 620, 626–37. For a discussion of the Room of Requirement using another Foucauldian concept, heterotopia, see Sarah K. Cantrell, "I Solemnly Swear

I Am Up to No Good: Foucault's Heterotopias and Deleuze's Any-Spaces-Whatever in J.K. Rowling's Harry Potter Series," *Children's Literature* 39 (2011): 195–212.

41. I would like to thank my "Harry Potter and Political Theory" class in the summer of 2011 for fantastic discussions and thought-provoking papers, some of which inspired my thinking here.

# 10

# FEMINISM, SEXISM, AND THE SMALL SCREEN

## Television's Complicated Relationship with Women

*Denise Du Vernay*

> This is so weird. It's like something out of Dickens. Or Melrose Place.
> —Lisa Simpson

Culture critics have argued about the stupidity and dangers of television almost since the advent of the medium. We've been warned against spending too much time in front of the "boob tube" or the "idiot box" so many times that we don't even register the warnings anymore. Some of us read Neil Postman's seminal *Amusing Ourselves to Death* in media studies courses in college. While his arguments were certainly persuasive, I distinctly recall being happy when I finished it so I could watch *The Simpsons*. We know the evils of TV: it makes us want to buy things we don't need. The beautiful stars and advertisements for beauty products make us feel ugly and fat (and, of course, watching TV makes us fat because it is a passive activity that frequently involves snacking, drinking soda or beer, and not much moving). It "rots your brain" in some other vague ways that my parents were never quite able to articulate. But the truth is that television has changed in the past two decades, making consumers susceptible to new attacks that even Neil Postman didn't warn us about. The popularity of reality TV and the advent of the TiVo and DVR have made product placement the rule, whereas it was previously the exception in both reality and scripted shows. Clever editing, alcohol, bribery, and sleep deprivation are used to create drama on reality shows,[1] frequently to the detriment of female contestants and the image of women in general.

Reality TV is one reason why many feminists are compelled to focus on culture critique. Certainly, many feminists continue to strive for equality in the workplace, rally against funding cuts for women's health services, voice anger and frustration against legislation designed to nick away at hard-fought reproductive freedom, and argue in favor of comprehensive sex education and many other issues. So, with all of these issues still nagging at the conscience of the feminist activist or scholar, why would one choose to study and discuss pop culture? Why waste one's time analyzing television? The reason is simple: while television shows generally do not depict accurate representations of human beings and the way society functions, they do affect culture. Even with video games and the Internet, American children are watching more television now than ever before, approximately four and a half hours per day.[2] From television children learn about society, plus gender relations, power structures, sexuality, and even how to perform their gender. And what they're learning consists of heteronormativity, sexism, and even misogyny. Girls come in two categories: good girls and sluts. Women are gold diggers and not to be trusted. And they're certainly "not here to make friends."[3]

While reality TV is reinforcing negative stereotypes, creating gender wars and intra-gender wars, and persuading millions of Americans to buy products that share parent companies with the broadcasters, scripted television, especially dramas, are telling a different story. In fact, past decades have seen two simultaneous, but very different, changes in television. Although the major networks offer too much in the way of cheap (and I mean that in all connotations) reality shows, scripted television has gotten smarter. Sometimes, these smart scripted shows even offer feminist messages and positive images of women. There are countless means an individual might employ to determine whether a show is feminist (how many female characters there are, what positions they hold, etc.), but for the sake of simplicity, a materialist feminist criterion is that if a show seeks to keep women "in their place," it is an antifeminist show. Various tactics are used by television and other media to stifle women: using sexist language that reinforces to boys and girls the notion that being a boy is better, manufacturing a feeling of mistrust among women, and not allowing women to be sexual and condemning them if they are (often referred to as slut-shaming), while simultaneously showing women and girls that their value relies on their appearance and whether or not men find them sexy.

Judged on the use of these tactics, most reality shows are antifeminist; fortunately, some scripted shows depict women as complicated, interesting, and not bound by traditional gender roles and rules of sexuality.

## Feminism 101

The types of feminism seen and discussed (and often misunderstood) most often in contemporary American culture are radical feminism and materialist feminism.[4] The variety of feminism that gives feminists an overall unsavory reputation is radical feminism, which arose in the 1970s and is generally considered antimale. An argument can be made that radical feminists are cultural feminists and that their analysis comes from "a reification of sexual difference based on absolute gender categories." In other words, radical (cultural) feminists believe there are inborn qualities in being female or male and that this system "gives rise to a formulation of femininity as innate and inherently superior to masculinity."[5] This type of feminism relies on a specious belief in intrinsically feminine characteristics and also presupposes a sisterhood—a unification of women and girls based solely on their sex. This is a dangerous, essentialist view that also leads to exclusion of the male sex. Also, in light of contemporary neuroscience research that proves no measurable differences in brain function between the sexes, thus suggesting that most or all sexual difference is learned, there is no basis for believing in "femininity," let alone the superiority of femininity over masculinity.

Most feminists are not this militant or negative, but radical feminists are the most vocal, especially on the blogosphere.[6] In fact, the blogosphere has created derogatory words, such as *dood* and *mansplain,*[7] which are used to attack men, often when they dare to chime in on feminist blogs. Name-calling seems counterintuitive and hypocritical to some global goals of feminism (haven't women fought for years against being called "bitch" or being accused of having PMS every time they have a bad day?), but such attacks seem to occur more and more often on feminist blogs. Sadly, many people, especially misinformed men and young people,[8] envision man-haters when they hear the word *feminist* in large part because of this vocal minority.[9] The negative connotation prevents them from identifying as feminists, even if they believe in basic tenets of feminism (equal pay for the same work, family leave for both parents, inviting more women to golf at Augusta, etc.).

Negative connotations of feminism also prevent people from speaking out against inequalities large and small, including antifeminist television shows, for fear of being labeled a "humorless shrill."

On the other end of the spectrum is materialist feminism,[10] which "deconstructs the mythic subject Woman to look at women as a class oppressed by material conditions and social relations,"[11] removing notions of feminine superiority. Materialist feminism takes its cues from Marxist theory and views feminism as political, begun in movements built upon changing the power relations between men, women, society, and the status quo. The goals of materialist feminism do not arise from a desire for women to take jobs traditionally held by men (that ideology is closer to what is frequently called liberal feminism), but rather for women not to have their sexuality, femininity, and fecundity decided for them.[12] Materialist feminism is also good for men in that it strives to remove gender stereotypes regarding parenthood and jobs, for example (gone would be the expression "male nurse").

Looking at women as a social class is inclusive and, in my view, productive: A materialist feminist isn't looking for improvements only for women and girls, but for any group (or class) that has been held back. A materialist feminist strives for a lovely ideal, a society that assesses a person based solely on his or her character, education, experience, and other qualities, and not on skin color, attractiveness, biology, sexual orientation, or religion. A materialist feminist is not upset if a white man gets a job instead of, say, a woman of color, if the white man is truly more qualified. (However, the materialist feminist may question the system that afforded that particular man more educational and professional opportunities than his competitors. She or he would rather work to combat social and educational injustices than blame the individual who benefits from the situation. This is why people of all backgrounds, including white males, can be, and often are, materialist feminists).

## Feminism and Popular Culture

Although the focus of this chapter is mainly television, pop culture is not limited to television, of course. There is no shortage of sneers among readers and moviegoers surrounding the popularity of so-called chick lit and chick flicks. Building on Susan Faludi's seminal 1991 text *Backlash: The Undeclared War against American Women,* many feminist critics report that the pop culture of the 1990s and early 2000s is bad for feminism and is damaging the progress that feminism made in the preceding decades, in that pop culture has expanded on the lie perpetuated by the media, especially news and business magazines such as *Newsweek* and *Forbes,* that women were rejecting feminism. The media actually invented a neotraditionalist "movement."[13] Culture critic Susan Douglas points the finger at *Beverly Hills, 90210* (which began in 1990, followed two years later by its spin-off *Melrose Place*) as the program that started the new trend: when television stopped moving in the right direction. Previously, shows like *Roseanne, Murphy Brown,* and *L.A. Law* were challenging stereotypical notions of family, women, and femininity, and then along came some very superficial, rich teenagers, gluing teens to the TV and derailing progress. As British culture theorist Angela McRobbie states, "elements of contemporary popular culture are perniciously effective in regard to this undoing of feminism."[14] The perceived undoing, along with other examples of backlashes to feminism, is often referred to as postfeminism, although Douglas refers to postfeminism, perhaps more aptly, as "enlightened sexism." Postfeminism deals with the pervasive idea that feminism has happened, that it has come of age,[15] and that its work here is done. Douglas has renamed postfeminism through her discovery that this mistaken notion of feminism being over has opened the door for greater sexism in television: "Under the guise of escapism and pleasure, we are getting images of imagined power that mask, and even erase, how much still remains to be done for girls and women, images that make sexism seem fine, even, and insist that feminism is now utterly pointless—even bad for you."[16] As I will discuss below, enlightened sexism has opened the door not just for girl-on-girl hate but also for advertisers and countless television shows to use damaging sexist language without controversy or public outcry.

Of course, in reality the work of feminism is far from over;[17] there is no strong, feminist society in danger of being toppled over by pop culture, and those who tend to announce that feminism has achieved its goals most likely do so out of a genuine concern that their power position is under fire or that equality might actually be accomplished. There is fear in their words.[18] Many men's rights activists and conservatives who argue against feminism point to laws that make sexual discrimination illegal as evidence that there is no such thing as sexism and thus no longer a need for feminism. While feminists acknowledge and welcome such protections, one only needs to look at the relatively small number of women who hold powerful positions in government and business to realize that equality hasn't been achieved. Specifically in filmmaking, the numbers are dismal. According to the Center for the Study of Women in Television & Film at San Diego State University, in 2010, of the 250 top-grossing films, women wrote 10%, directed 7%, and made up only 15% of executive producers. In television, the numbers are perhaps better but still not equitable. In the 2010–2011 television season, 22% of executive producers were women, 15% of writers were women, and 11% of directors were women. Reality programs employ the greatest number of women in behind-the-scenes roles at 28%, with dramas at 25% and comedies at only 22%. Interestingly, of all television characters in that same programming season, only 41% were female. Perhaps if more women had creative and executive positions in television, there would be more female characters (and female characters of higher quality); we do know that shows with at least one female writer or creator feature more female characters than shows without female creators and writers.[19]

While these numbers are telling, the concerns shared by feminists regarding pop culture are not limited to the statistics. Previously, if feminists were looking at pop culture, they may have been concerned with how many female leads there were in prime time, or which shows (if any) were LGBT-friendly; or they may have been conducting content analyses such as the Bechdel Test.[20] Currently, feminist media scholars (such as McRobbie, Douglas, and Jennifer Pozner) have more subtle, nuanced criteria for determining the values and dangers in popular culture.[21] As a materialist feminist, my concern is with how much of the popular culture, namely television, affects girls and boys in positive or negative ways and what the takeaway message and attitudes are. For example, how often do shows that are deemed appropriate for all ages have instances of slut-shaming or sexist language? Many shows (plus the ads that pepper the commercial breaks) perpetuate sexual double standards and use sexist language. These practices are so ubiquitous that much of the time we don't even notice. At the time of this writing, a commercial appears frequently during prime time in Chicagoland for a chain of convenience stores called AM PM. In one version, a dorky man is so proud of the burger he has made that he says, "Thanks for playing, ladies" to the two jockish men in the store with him. In the same vein, the "man up" series of Miller Lite commercials is even more offensive: they frequently feature babes in the roles of bartenders who disparage male "customers" for being too girly to deserve a Miller Lite. If a bartender in a commercial refused to give a Miller Lite to a man she deemed too black or too Jewish (or fill in any other characteristic here) to deserve the beer instead of too girly, an outcry would cause the ad to be pulled and an apology provided (and rightly so). Various comedians have taught us the rules of comedy: although the dominant group is fair game, you can only make fun of a group *not* in power *if* you are a member of that group. For some reason, however, women (and so-considered girly men) are not afforded the same courtesy. Most kids realize that it is not okay to call someone's shoes or a math test "gay" or "retarded," but girlish insults persist.

ABC's sitcom *Modern Family* has it both ways in an episode entitled "The Musical Man." The show makes a sexist-language joke and immediately points out that the joke is not fair. Upon hearing one male character bash another male character by implying his shirt came from a women's clothing store, Gloria (Sofia Vergara) deadpans, "It's funny because women are so inferior." The viewer notices, of course, that she is not laughing. With her ample cleavage and oozing sex appeal, Gloria is not the obvious choice as the feminist voice of reason on the show, which might actually make her the best pick to deliver such a line.

## So-Called Reality Television

The depiction of women and girls in reality television shows such as *My Super Sweet Sixteen* and *The Real Housewives* franchise gives children and teens the wrong idea—that women are not doing phenomenal things every day (or worse, that they don't have the desire to).[22] Reality shows tend to show women and girls that their value is in their looks (*Toddlers & Tiaras* and *America's Next Top Model*), that women are catty backstabbers who are not to be trusted (the *Real Housewives* and *Real World* franchises, and most elimination reality shows, including even my personal favorite, *Top Chef*), that women who own their sexuality or who behave sexually for any reason other than to please or keep a man are sluts (*The Bachelor* and basically any show with a hot tub), and that women are gold diggers (*The Bachelor*, *Joe Millionaire*, and basically any show with a hot tub). Reality shows also perpetuate the belief that only heterosexual relationships are appropriate, including even MTV's lower-class version of *The Bachelor, A Shot at Love with Tila Tequila*, whose entire premise was the star's bisexuality. The competition began with an equal number of straight men and lesbian women vying for Tequila's "love." In the end, Tequila has stated, the producers would not allow her to select the female contestant she wanted as the winner but instead coerced her to choose a man.[23]

Popular culture has a huge role in shaping the gender and personal identification of children, which is just one of the reasons why popular culture's offerings deserve scrutiny and analysis.[24] Numerous studies have proved that people's opinions about themselves and others are influenced by stereotypes and gender priming. Behaviors and performance of gender are not "hardwired," as many pop psychology books would have us believe; rather, social identities are flexible depending on context and expectations.[25] Girls and women are encouraged to be sexy but given the clear message that it's not okay to want sex or sexual satisfaction. If that doesn't confuse a kid, I don't know what would. In addition, studies have shown that adolescents, especially LGBT kids, turn to television and film for information about sex rather than to the adults in their lives.[26] With many states offering no sex education (or worse, abstinence-only sex education), it is indeed disturbing to consider the messages children and adolescents are receiving regarding sexual behavior and romance.

If pop culture is discussed rather than just passively consumed, even media that do not offer feminist messages or characters can become teachable moments in feminism. As Andi Zeisler reminds us, pop culture is a "key route to making the concept of feminism—which still manages to send many women and men into a kind of nervous tizzy—both resonate and relatable." Therefore, parents and teachers have unlimited opportunities and material to teach children and students about feminism on a daily, low-impact basis: no heavy lectures are necessary. Discussing with young viewers the attitudes depicted on a television show, for example, creates critical thinking skills and better consumers of pop culture; this is a much more practical and useful task than attempting to ban television and other media. Gender studies scholar Merri Lisa Johnson explains, "Pop culture is a ubiquitous part of our lives. It is therefore necessary to address it, to develop a reading practice that attends to its contradictions in content, its role in our lives, and in its attitudes towards feminism."[27] I would take the sentiment further and suggest that a study of the effects of pop culture is imperative.

## Scripted Television

It takes some searching to find them, but many scripted dramas in recent years have demonstrated prowoman, feminist depictions. To be prowoman, the characterizations of female characters needn't be without flaws; a realistic depiction of women as complex and interesting, flaws and all, is more desirable than characters who are too good to be true. Take Buffy (from

Joss Whedon's *Buffy the Vampire Slayer* series): she is strong but sometimes vulnerable, intelligent but also occasionally guilty of hubris. She falls in love, struggles with authority, and has great clothes and hair. None of these things weakens her character or her role-model status because she is realistic (as realistic as the chosen slayer can be, in any case). *Buffy* had a good run, but it ended in 2003 and there hasn't been anything like it since.[28] Quality shows like *Freaks and Geeks* and *My So-Called Life* had short lives, but because of their honesty and realistic characters, they have enjoyed cult success on DVD and cable.

Today, there are scripted shows that do feminism and entertainment a service. Shows like *Justified, Mad Men, Breaking Bad,* and *The Good Wife* feature female characters who are complex with story lines that don't revolve solely around relationships, motherhood, and other such acceptable female concerns.

In *Justified,* Margo Martindale plays Mags Bennet, the head of a crime family. She doles out the punishments and completes business transactions as swiftly as any man. By and large, her sex is not made an issue on the show.

*Mad Men,* a show almost as consumed by Don Draper as Don Draper himself, has an unmistakable feminist subtext, perhaps because the show has many regular female writers. The female characters (with the exception of Betty) are as interesting and complex as their male counterparts in regard to their concerns, talents, personal lives, and opinions. Pregnancy out of wedlock is depicted accurately as the woman's problem; Peggy does not tell her baby's father about the pregnancy until long after she has placed the child for adoption. Another character, Joan, also faced an unplanned pregnancy and has opted to be a single mother while keeping her corporate job. Issues of early-1960s sexism in the workplace are treated matter-of-factly, with no overt commentary about how it was wrong and backward; the viewer picks it up on his or her own.

*Breaking Bad* features two strong female roles, sisters Skyler White and Marie Schrader. Although much of the drama unfolds around their husbands (in the first two seasons, their roles are mainly "wife" parts), the character-izations of Skyler and Marie are realistic, yet positive. Both are flawed, but both become heads of their respective households. In the case of Marie, it is out of necessity (her husband, Hank, is injured on the job and becomes despondent and childlike). Skyler analyzes the dangerous and complicated situation (that most sane people would run from, never looking back), puts her accounting and negotiating skills to work, and takes over: season 4 finds

Skyler in charge of a money-laundering business and giving direction to her husband on how best to handle their financial situation.

*The Good Wife* has a clever, ironic title that is, unfortunately, misleading: the show is not about a "wife," and it is certainly not a "chick show." The show's main character is a woman, Alicia Florrick (played by Julianna Margulies), whose husband, Peter, a former Cook County State's Attorney, is incarcerated for a corruption and prostitution scandal. Alicia, also an attorney, has been out of the workforce for many years to raise her two children, now teenagers, and finds herself a junior at a downtown Chicago law firm. That is where Peter's importance starts and ends; his existence, problems, and return to politics are mostly an irritation in her life as lawyer and mother. The show is a courtroom drama in the spirit of *L.A. Law*, with its ripped-from-the-headlines cases and humor thrown into the mix, plus just a dash of *Ally McBeal*-style quirk and romantic intrigue (but, thankfully, without the whining, painfully short skirts, and unisex bathrooms). Alicia is similar to Skyler White in that she finds herself making tough decisions regarding her career, her marriage, and how to best run her household and similarly does not avoid issues that are ugly or hard to deal with. She also finds, like Skyler, that she had the vigor to do all of these things the whole time. Both characters have emotion along with strength; they are complex and interesting people. These roles make both shows a pleasure to watch.

Alicia is not the only interesting female on *The Good Wife*; Christine Baranksi plays Diane Lockhart, a senior partner in the firm. While her screen time is considerably less than some of the other players', Diane is a striking character. On the surface, she embodies liberal feminism: she is a woman who plays in the old-boys club as well as any man. She is smart and ethical but sneaky when the situation requires it. Diane is very liberal, but not doctrinaire—if she were, she most certainly would not allow herself to fall for a conservative ballistic expert and shoot guns with him. Kalinda Sharma (played by Emmy winner Archie Panjabi), the firm's investigator, is also written with due consideration of the complexity of the human female. In dark clothes and with her hair up, she wears what Panjabi jokingly refers to as Kalinda's "boots of justice."[29] Yes, she is sexy, but it's Kalinda's mysterious personal life, backstory, surprising wit, and intimidating strength that make her the viewers' favorite. Her character is bisexual, and, refreshingly, her sexual orientation is not sensationalized by the show. With the channels saturated by reality shows bent on slut-shaming, it is a rare delight to see a show that allows a female character to own her sexuality.

## Sneaky Sexism

Instead of diminishing over time, the phenomenon of slut-shaming seems to be growing in intensity. And certain television shows only serve to exacerbate the problem. As if the orchestrated fights and girl-on-girl make-out sessions on reality shows aren't enough, shows on ABC Family (which, one would think, would be family-friendly) also serve to perpetuate sexual double standards.

On the surface, ABC Family's *Make It or Break It* appears to break out of the mold we're so used to regarding depictions of teenage girls as vapid, as serving as the butt of jokes, or as simply an important character's girlfriend. In most sports-oriented shows, boys and men are the athletes and women and girls are the supporting mothers, wives, girlfriends, sisters, and teachers. Not so on *Make It or Break It;* the girls are the athletes, and they take it seriously. Yes, as gymnasts they spend a fair amount of screen time in leotards (but at least leotards are realistic and functional, not merely ornamental—awfully convenient, I know), but the fact that the show focuses on female athletes with boys in supporting, onlooker roles is refreshing. This is a show about the sport; the romances and family dramas are secondary.

What is troubling about *Make It or Break It* is the reliance on stereotypes, rich white privilege, and religious overtones. The first two seasons focused on four top gymnasts, all with Olympic aspirations, training together at a gym in Boulder called "The Rock": Payson Keeler, Kaylie Cruz, Lauren Tanner, and Emily Kmetko. Payson is the sweetest and most innocent and, not coincidentally, the most likable of the group. She's a fan favorite because she overcomes a back injury through hard work and perseverance. Unfortunately, she's also the one with the requisite crush on her coach (one of them had to have it). Kaylie (a Latina and the only minority lead character) is the former champion who battles an eating disorder (again, one of them had to). Lauren is blond, sexy, dangerous, and heartless; and Emily comes from trailer stock and is the only one of the four on a scholarship, so her actions are even more carefully monitored than the others (she is, after all, getting free money).

Their coach enforces a rigid "no dating" rule, which on the surface seems to be in the girls' best interests; the goal is to keep their minds on training and the prize. Instead, however, the idea that the girls' coach has ownership over their sexuality is disturbing and follows the same trend so commonly seen on reality shows: a woman's sexuality is for everyone but herself. Lauren, whose father is wealthy and is in charge of The Rock, frequently breaks the rules and is sexually active, but she manages to manipulate the situation and not get into any serious trouble, not unlike a certain former reality star and future heir of the Hilton fortune. When a new coach takes over, the dating restrictions are lifted, although they remain in place for Emily because she is not allowed to date under the terms of her scholarship contract. To honor the contract, she ends her relationship with her boyfriend indefinitely and has goodbye sex with him (her first time). Disturbingly, Emily refers to the act as something that she "can give him." She doesn't think to use protection because she doesn't menstruate, but, of course, she becomes pregnant anyway. She is literally sent away to her godmother's home, where she will have the baby. The message is that unless you're rich, if you break the rules and/or "give sex" to someone not your husband, expect to be punished and maybe even banished.

Emily's single mother, Chloe, has had her sexuality used against her as well. Because of her lack of education, she works as a cocktail waitress in a strip club. She attempts to keep it a secret for fear of embarrassing Emily, who eventually finds out. Chloe has previously been involved with Lauren's father, Steve, but at the end of season 2, Steve is engaged to Summer, a religious woman who works for him at The Rock. Summer's "values" (which seem to consist of maintaining her virginity and not much else) are a big issue on the show. Obviously, the woman with "values" deserves to land the rich husband much more than the single mother willing to take a job that requires her to get tarted up on a nightly basis in order to feed her family.

## Getting beyond Female Competition and Slut-Shaming

Twenty years after Susan Faludi first outlined the tactics in the war against American women, many of our television shows continue to perpetuate negative stereotypes of women, advocate sexual double standards and slut-shaming, and discourage women and girls from trusting each other. These are the reasons why feminists and culture scholars are (and should be) examining American television. The general pop culture consumer is best served by taking a materialist feminist approach when choosing which shows to watch and how to frame conversations with others (especially children) regarding these shows. We should ask ourselves and others questions as we watch: How are power relations between men and women depicted? Does the subtext or the narrative strive to protect the status quo?

Are female characters punished for acting out against expectations placed on them (be they sexual, academic, economic, or related to appearance)? Are women shown to be backstabbing and untrustworthy? Does the show have a heteronormative agenda? How realistically are the characters drawn?

When asking these questions, we may find many of the answers to be disheartening. For example, the narrative of *Make It or Break It*, a show aimed at teenage girls, appears concerned with the Olympic aspirations of several hardworking gymnasts, but the subtext projects a heteronormative standard and a society that punishes women for their sexuality and rewards women who suppress it. This message coincides with the dominant messages offered by reality TV shows in which women's sexual attractiveness is currency and female sexuality exists solely for the enjoyment of men.

Furthering the media-driven sexism, television dialogue and advertisements achieve cheap laughs at the expense of women and girls with derogatory language deemed acceptable to the general public because of enlightened sexism. Each time a father tells his son that he throws like a girl or that boys don't cry, and each time a man teases a friend about being girly or a coach calls his male athletes "girls," a message is sent to anyone listening that being female is inferior.

Not all humor is made at someone else's expense, but for a society that generally approves such humor if the butt is the dominant group, sexist humor is confusing and inappropriate. Although women and girls do not hold the majority of the power in any element of contemporary culture, from political office to film editing, antifemale jokes abound. Referring to this "enlightened sexism," Douglas explains that the reason for the paradox lies in the media-created myth that feminism has accomplished equality for women, and then some, supposedly causing many women to be unhappy and unfulfilled with their liberation. The myths of gender equality and fairness have opened the doors for mockery and wisecracks on television and film, which leach into everyday conversation to the detriment of women and girls. Such language affects girls' self-image and even achievement while perpetuating ideas of male superiority to boys and men. Since boys understand that the worst insults they can dish out or receive are ones that compare them to girls, imagine how bad it must be to actually be a girl!

I wish there were a forecast in sight for the elimination (or at least a dip in popularity) of reality TV, but unfortunately, reality TV does not seem to be a passing fad. Aside from the obvious financial incentives networks have in producing reality shows, the public has shown itself willing to be a consistent audience. The Academy of Television Arts & Sciences has also given validity to the genre; reality shows enjoy many of their own Emmy categories, divided into two separate categories for competition reality shows and noncompetition shows,[30] just as scripted shows are divided into drama and comedy categories. James Poniewozik, television critic for *Time Magazine,* stated in early 2011 that reality TV "is simply now another genre of TV, like sitcoms or dramas."[31]

While all reality shows employ many of the same disturbing tactics to varying degrees, some are fairer in their characterization of women than others. In general, the talent-based competition shows where men and women compete more or less as equals are markedly less sexist and heteronormative than shows such as *The Bachelor* that pit women against women to win marriage or a man as the prize (although all competition reality shows manufacture tension and the "I'm not here to make friends" mentality between female opponents especially, often through clever editing and sleep deprivation). Also, there are bright spots in scripted television such as in *The Good Wife* and *Mad Men,* shows with complex female characters who are permitted to own their sexuality and have personal and professional aspirations separate from marriage or motherhood. The popularity of the film *Bridesmaids,* which showed that a female ensemble cast can bring the funny (and the money), might also be a positive sign that more female-created and female-produced scripted shows will hit our DVRs in coming years.

And if those examples aren't comforting enough, we can take solace in knowing that television indefinitely has Lisa Simpson to speak up on the side of reason, fairness, and tolerance.

## Notes

1. Jennifer Pozner discusses these tactics in her book *Reality Bites Back: The Troubling Truth about Guilty Pleasure TV* (Berkeley, CA: Seal Press, 2010). National Public Radio has also discussed the issue of sleep deprivation's use to heighten drama; an example can be found here: www.npr.org/templates/story/story.php?storyId=90406338. And in 2004, a reality show called *Shattered,* which was based solely on recording sleep-deprived contestants' strange behavior, was produced in the United Kingdom.

2. V. J. Rideout, U. G. Foehr, and D. F. Roberts, "Generation M2: Media in the Lives of 8- to 18-Year Olds," Kaiser Family Foundation, (2010) (accessed August 30, 2011), www.kff.org/entmedia/mh012010pkg.cfm.

3. The mantra "I'm not here to make friends" has become a running joke among

viewers of reality shows, as shown by the many YouTube videos made of clips of contestants using the line, such as this one: www.youtube.com/watch?v=b0bOw11qxBc.

4. While the descriptions of various schools of feminist thought are found in many sources, my main resource is Jill Dolan's *The Feminist Spectator as Critic* (1988; Ann Arbor: University of Michigan Press, 1991).

5. Ibid., 5, 6.

6. When a man contributes to the comments sections of certain feminist blogs, unless he is simply agreeing with someone, he can expect to be attacked. I personally have been scolded and told "Be careful what you say on here" for defending the opinion of a man who commented on a blog. The man was defending the idea of "Boobquake."

7. *Dood* is an alternate spelling of *dude*, and *mansplain* is a blend of *man* and *explain*, which is used when a radical feminist either feels that a man is explaining something to her in a condescending manner or perceives that a man is talking about a topic that he isn't authorized to talk about, such as feminism or oppression.

8. Online forums such as the "Men's Rights" Reddit abound with conversations by those who reject radical feminism. Sadly, through their misunderstanding of the term, there is an assumption that all feminist thinkers or those who identify as feminist subscribe to radical, antimale views. Within many of the discussions found, there are straw-man logical fallacies: all feminists are attacked for the words and actions of the most fringe speakers.

9. When I begin a theory lecture in sophomore-level college courses, I put the word *feminist* on the board and ask students to shout out the first things that come to mind. "Manhater" and "dyke" are among the tamest responses.

10. Not all feminists can be classified as "radical" or "materialist" feminists; as with most political identifications, individuals hold nuanced views and philosophies.

11. Dolan, *Feminist Spectator as Critic*, 10.

12. Chris Weedon, *Feminist Practice and Poststructuralist Theory*, 2nd ed. (Oxford: Blackwell, 1997), 1.

13. Chapter 4 of Susan Faludi's *Backlash: The Undeclared War against American Women* (New York: Crown, 1991) outlines in great detail how antifeminism was invented by the media with trend stories based on anecdotal (or no) evidence that working women weren't happy and would prefer to stay at home. These articles appeared in such publications as *Newsweek, Fortune, Forbes, Atlantic, U.S. News & World Report*, and the *Wall Street Journal*. A *New York Times* article from 1980 entitled "Many Young Women Now Say They'd Pick Family over Career" was proved completely false by Faludi. The media also popularized the invented concept of "cocooning." The so-called opt out revolution myth continues to be perpetuated in the media but has been debunked by numerous fact checkers, including E. J. Graff in the article "The Opt-Out Myth," *Columbia Journalism Review*, March–April 2007, www.cjr.org/essay/the_optout_myth.php.

14. Susan Douglas, *The Rise of Enlightened Sexism: How Pop Culture Took Us from*

*Girl Power to Girls Gone Wild* (New York: St. Martin's Griffin, 2010), 23; Angela McRobbie, "Post-Feminism and Popular Culture," *Feminist Media Studies* 4, no. 3 (2004): 255.

15. Ann Brooks, *Postfeminisms: Feminism, Cultural Theory, and Cultural Forms* (London: Routledge, 1997).

16. Douglas, *Rise of Enlightened Sexism*, 6.

17. According to research by Kristin Rowe-Finkbeiner, in 1975, 18% of all American women of ages twenty-five to twenty-nine had completed at least four years of college. While that percentage increased to 32% in 2002, the increase was seen most with white women, with a jump of 20% (from 19% to 39%). African American women experienced an 8% increase (from 10% to 18%) while Latinas saw only a 3% increase (from 7% to 10%). These numbers are not acceptable to materialist feminists and certainly did not usher in a time of postfeminism. Source: Kristin Rowe-Finkbeiner, *The F Word: Feminism in Jeopardy—Women, Politics, and the Future* (Berkeley, CA: Seal Press, 2004).

18. An extreme  example is Rush Limbaugh's frequent use of the word *feminazi*.

19. Martha Lauzen, "Boxed In: Employment of Behind-the-Scenes and On-Screen Women in the 2010–11 Prime-Time Television Season," Center for the Study of Women in Television & Film, 2011, http://womenintvfilm.sdsu.edu/files/2010–2011_Boxed_In_Exec_Summ.pdf.

20. The Bechdel Test (or Rule) originated in a 1985 comic strip called *Dykes to Watch Out For,* by Alison Bechdel, in which a character states she will watch a movie only if it meets certain criteria: "1. It has at least two women in it, 2. Who talk to each other 3. About something other than a man."

21. See Pozner's *Reality Bites Back.*

22. I could go on here; there is no shortage of shows that depict women and girls as vapid, materialistic, trashy, or just plain stupid. And I'm not just talking about MTV shows like *The Hills* or VH1's *You're Cut Off.* Negative stereotypes of women lurk where you'd least expect them. Consider Discovery Health, which is guilty of depicting women as clueless with its dramatic reenactments on *I Didn't Know I Was Pregnant.* In addition, *Wife Swap* chooses the most radical of women, often cultlike in their adherence to a particular lifestyle, in the hopes of creating high drama.

23. Pozner, *Reality Bites Back,* 262.

24. For an extensive discussion of how culture shapes expectations and even ability, see Cordelia Fine, *Delusions of Gender: How Our Minds, Society, and Neuroscience Create Difference* (New York: Norton, 2010).

25. Ibid., 12–13.

26. Victor Strasburger, "Adolescents, Sex, and the Media: Oooo, Baby, Baby—a Q & A." *Adolescent Medicine Clinics* 16 (2005): 272.

27. For an example of a feminist discussion of a show that does not seem to easily lend itself to a feminist analysis, see my chapter "I'm Just a Squirrel," in *SpongeBob SquarePants and Philosophy: Soaking up Knowledge under the Sea,* ed. Joseph J. Foy (Chicago: Open Court, 2011); Andi Zeisler, *Feminism and Pop Culture* (Berkeley, CA:

Seal Press, 2008), ix; Merri Lisa Johnson, *Third Wave Feminism and Television: Jane Puts It in a Box* (New York: IB Tauris, 2007), 20.

28. At the time of this writing, it is early in the first season of Sarah Michelle Gellar's show, the CW's *Ringer*. So far, unfortunately, it seems to rely on gender stereotypes, although the show's main character, Bridget, is complex enough to make the show worth a watch.

29. Panjabi made this statement in an article on The Daily Beast: www.thedailybeast .com/articles/2011/02/14/the-good-wife-archie-panjabi-on-playing-the-mysterious-kalinda.html.

30. In 2001, the first Prime Time Emmy for Outstanding Reality Program was awarded. Two years later, the Academy of Television Arts & Sciences added a separate Prime Time Emmy for the Outstanding Reality–Competition Program category. There are additional Emmys specific to reality shows, such as for outstanding host and many technical aspects. In addition, reality shows are frequently nominated for Emmys in various variety, nonfiction, and music categories.

31. Michael Ventre, "Will 2011 Be the Year Reality TV Dies?" *Today Online* (MSNBC.com), January 3, 2011, http://today.msnbc.msn.com/id/40753472/ns/today-entertainment/t/will-be-year-reality-tv-dies/.

**Part 4**

# THE PROMISES AND PROBLEMS OF LIBERAL DEMOCRACY

# 11

# FROM JOHN WAYNE TO JOHN McCLANE

The Hollywood Action Hero and the Critique of
the Liberal State

*Carl Bergetz*

America is in constant conflict. On one side of the divide rests America's
political foundation—the philosophy of liberalism and the companion
governing system of liberal democracy. Liberal democracy cherishes the
Enlightenment values of reason, discourse, and compromise and ensures
due process, checks and balances, and tolerance for a plurality of viewpoints
and identities.[1]

On the other side paces the most successful, accessible, and identifiable
product of American culture—the Hollywood action-hero movie. It likes
to blow things up.[2]

Both are major national exports. Both are quintessentially American.
And both . . . well . . . this country just may not be big enough for both of
them.[3]

The action-hero movie values emotion over reason, intuition over
empiricism, order over rights, uncompromising action over debate and
due process, suspicion over tolerance, and the need for the violent oblitera-
tion of problems. The action hero does not redeem or validate anything
fundamental about American juridical or political ideals or Enlightenment
values. Rather, the action-hero genre repudiates foundations of American
liberal political theory, reminds us of its inefficacies, and evokes a need for
something different. But the action-hero movie is not simply or broadly

"illiberal" or right-wing.[4] On closer analysis, the metagenre reflects a criticism and prescription that is very specific, quite foreign, and fundamentally un-American: the legal and political theory of a German jurist—and former Nazi—Carl Schmitt.[5]

As explained below, the action-hero film reflects key elements of Schmitt's critique of liberalism and prescriptions for sovereignty, and these reflections suggest a connection between Schmitt's theories and the American psyche.[6] Thus, an analysis of these films can provide a means to understand not only Schmitt's positive and normative theories, but Americans' view of their own political and legal ideals as well. Significantly, the intersection between these films and Schmitt's theories shows the complexity and fragility of a country where political and cultural ideals are in conflict.[7]

## About Schmitt

Schmitt's critique of liberalism and his positive and normative theories on sovereignty and democracy have always been a source of controversy in political theory, but his work has received increased attention in recent years.[8] In the wake of 9/11, some have argued that neoconservatives and others on the American Right have evinced a distinctly Schmittian influence, specifically in the justifications for enhanced interrogation techniques, the noncombatant status of terrorist suspects, and the right to take preemptive strikes against sovereign nations.[9] Theorists on the Left have increasingly referenced and examined Schmitt's views to show whether and how liberalism and constitutionalism can withstand his unavoidable critique.[10]

But Schmitt is perhaps most entertainingly seen and examined in Hollywood action-hero movies, from the Western of yesteryear to the superhero movies of today. To detect the reflections of Schmitt—whether in a political speech, a policy paper, or a movie theater—we will need a brief overview of his core concepts.

First, Schmitt's works critique liberal constitutional democracy as a political framework that cannot resolve the problems of pluralism, preserve order, address existential threats, or prevent collapse from internal or external enemies. Schmitt argues that liberal institutions, with their faith in rationality, openness, and compromise, are at odds with the reality of politics and the human condition and thus are ineffectual.[11]

Second, in *The Concept of the Political* (1932), Schmitt draws the "friend-enemy" distinction as a basis for sovereign autonomy. The enemy is, "in a specially intense way, existentially something different and alien, so that in the extreme case conflicts with him are possible" and intense enough to become violent.[12]

Third, in *Political Theology* (1922), Schmitt sets out his famous principle, "The sovereign is he who decides on the exception." At the core, Schmitt is stating that only the sovereign can declare the moment at which he is entitled to exempt himself from the law in order to address the existential threats to the state. The sovereign is free from the strictures that normally apply to anyone else's legal power. He "stands outside of the normally valid juridical order and yet belongs to it."[13]

Schmitt's "sovereign dictator" stands in contrast to the "commissarial dictator" of Roman law. Rome's deliberative body would appoint a temporary dictator to address a specific problem, and that person was legally commissioned to operate outside of the bounds of law to address the problem within set bounds of time and duty. Once the task was accomplished, the "commissarial dictator" would relinquish his power, and the normal conditions of law and politics would return.[14]

Schmitt contends that crisis is the norm, not a temporary situation. Therefore, the sovereign cannot be constrained by law, because all political problems present the possibility of existential conflict. The sovereign must be free to determine when it is necessary to stand outside the law in order to preserve order or create a wholly new order. Liberal constitutional constraints like checks and balances are fictions glossing over this sobering reality.[15]

## Mr. Schmitt Goes to Hollywood

A word about fictions: Schmitt's concepts are clearly about the sovereign; however, the action-hero genre rarely deals with an actual sovereign (notable exceptions are *Independence Day* and *Air Force One*).[16] The action hero is rather an agent of the sovereign or a metaphor for him—usually a sheriff, a policeman, a soldier, or a special agent—who possesses abilities and a status that place him in position to declare the state of exception and step outside the rule of law to eliminate threats.

In many comic book hero films of relatively recent vintage, the hero is not a state official. This "private action hero" is, like the main character of *The Dark Knight* or *Iron Man*, a superequipped (and superrich) vigilante. This plot could be interpreted as an allegory for antistate conservative theory, from libertarianism to anarcho-capitalism. However, careful review of such films reveals a closer connection between the private action hero and the state. The private action hero typically acts at the behest of the state, in uneasy alliance with the state, or with the state's reluctant permission.

Whether the protagonist is an actual sovereign, an official state agent, or a partner of the sovereign, the action-hero film can be broken down into key elements that evoke and illustrate the conservative political theory of Schmitt described above:

1. A hero who literally or metaphorically is representative of the sovereign;
2. a villain who poses an existential threat to a community, can be deemed alien to that community, and can be eliminated only through violence;
3. ineffective liberal democratic institutions and actors who serve only to enable the enemy and are unable to resolve the problem;
4. a hero who is of the community yet outside of it and thus is able to understand the enemy and how to destroy him;
5. an escalating narrative conflict and climax in which the hero effectively and essentially declares a state of exception in acting outside the bounds of the law to preserve order;
6. the intimation that continual threats are the norm; and
7. in the denouement, the conveyance of the hero's distrust or contempt for liberal democratic principles and the suggestion of the need for a new order.

An examination of iconic and trendsetting action-hero movies, from Westerns to superhero movies, can help explain Schmitt's theories, provide a different insight into this genre, and aid in understanding the conflict between our popular culture and our political ideals.

## The Western at *High Noon*

While the action-hero film evolved from other well-established genres, including war films, police procedurals, and comics, the dominant parent of the metagenre was the Western. The Western setting presents a backdrop ripe for the action hero: a fledgling, frail civilization on the fringes of savage land constantly besieged by external existential threats from American Indians and internal threats of lawlessness.[17]

Such threats were omnipresent throughout hallmark Westerns, such as *Stagecoach* (1939), *The Searchers* (1956), *Rio Bravo* (1959), and *True Grit* (1969). Not coincidentally, these films all featured the man who created the modern action hero: John Wayne. Wayne (with major assists from John Ford and Howard Hawks) transformed the action hero from a "perfect" and "pure" lawman into a "dirty fighter," beginning the evocation of Schmittian ideas.[18] But while an understanding of Wayne and his films is important, a non-Wayne Western—one that Wayne loathed and against which he waged a personal war—more fully reflects the elements of Schmitt's criticisms and prescriptions.

In 1952, during the Korean War and America's Second Red Scare, *High Noon* was released. The most-viewed movie in the history of the White House screening room and a favorite film of presidents from Eisenhower to Clinton, *High Noon* displays specific Schmittian elements that became touchstones for all action-hero movies.[19] The hero, Marshal Will Kane (Gary Cooper), is a state official—an agent of the sovereign. The enemy, Frank Miller (along with his gang), is an existential threat to both Kane and the law and order within the town. Kane once sent Miller to jail, ending an apparent reign of terror.[20] But civilization's processes and procedures have enabled the enemy. The fecklessness of liberal democracy is more overt than in previous genre films and lies at the root of the film's conflict.

> WILL KANE. I sent a man up five years ago for murder. He was supposed to hang. But up North, they commuted it to life and now he's free. I don't know how. Anyway, it looks like he's coming back.[21]

Later in the film it is noted that "politicians up North" saved Miller "from hanging." The more general failings of the legal process are noted when ex-marshal Martin Howe gives the following reasoning for his refusal to fight the villains:

> MARTIN HOWE. You risk your skin catching killers and the juries turn them loose so they can come back and shoot at you again. If you're honest, you're poor your whole life and in the end you wind up dying all alone on some dirty street. For what? For nothing. For a tin star.

No one is willing to help Kane. Not even, it appears, Kane's new bride, Amy Fowler (Grace Kelly), who reasons that she became a Quaker due to her opposition to guns and violence, regardless as to who is right or wrong. She prays, "There's got to be some better way for people to live."

But there is not any better way in *High Noon*. The tactics Kane must use to dispense justice are those of base, lethal force that stand in opposition to reason, civility, and compromise. In fact, these latter ideals provide some with a convenient rationale for avoiding any action. When Kane comes to the church to look for deputies, the religious service turns into a democratic town-hall meeting (once the children are dismissed so as not to hear the "difference[s] of opinion"). Some people lobby for Kane to take action, others recommend that Kane leave and let the new marshal take over the next day to handle the situation, and others suggest that the "politicians up North" who caused the problem should save them. Accommodation of Miller and his gang is even advocated to avoid violent conflict and appease investor interests of the "North."

But Kane knows violence is the only solution. While of the community, Kane is simultaneously not of the community and understands how the enemy operates. The town's debate resolves nothing, and Kane must take exception. Kane does reject earlier advice to arrest part of the gang so that he'll only have to deal with Frank Miller, rationalizing tersely that no laws have yet been broken. However, that reasoning rings hollow, as Kane instead waits for the entire gang to arrive at noon so he can kill them all. And despite the clichés about the genre, none of them are killed in a face-to-face showdown. Kane kills the first villain with a bit of misdirection and the second from a hayloft's hidden higher ground. Kane's avowed pacifistic fiancée shoots the third villain in the back. After she is taken hostage by gang leader Frank Miller, she claws at his face, providing a moment of separation to give Kane a clear shot at eradicating the final enemy.

At the end, there is no sunshine in *High Noon*. Clearly, the "dirty little village" of Hadleyville will be besieged by conflict again, without an official like Kane. Yet Kane rejects his office and symbol of sovereign status, tossing his badge into the dirt. He shows contempt for his community—an outpost of liberal democratic civilization that dithered, debated, and rationalized its way out of action and into a paralysis of fear.

Like all great art, *High Noon* is something of a Rorschach test. The movie is generally considered to be liberal, even subversive, and for good reason. The screenwriter, Carl Foreman, was a former Communist and a critic of the House Un-American Activities Committee (HUAC), for which he refused to "name names." He readily admitted that *High Noon* was an allegory for the events surrounding that episode of American history. However, viewed outside the context of the HUAC controversy, *High Noon* can be seen as a marked movement toward the Hollywood action-hero story that evokes key Schmittian illiberal concepts. But at the time, the movie didn't sit well with conservatives, particularly John Wayne.

After *High Noon* was released to critical and commercial acclaim, Wayne took both political and cinematic action against the film. First, he publicly decried the movie as un-American, partly because Wayne had misunderstood the final scene, in which Wayne incorrectly believed Cooper crushed his badge beneath his boot. Wayne prompted HUAC to act against the screenwriter, and Foreman ended up blacklisted and in self-imposed exile from the United States. Even as late as 1972, Wayne was still priding himself for driving Foreman out of the country.[22]

Wayne and filmmaker Howard Hawks produced *Rio Bravo* (1959) as a purported cinematic response to Foreman's film. While Wayne does get help from a ragtag bunch of townies and retains his badge at the end, *Rio Bravo* as well as Wayne's other action-hero films are not exactly reaffirmations of America's founding ideal of liberal democracy. Instead, Wayne's films, from the ridiculous to the sublime, recall elements of Schmitt's criticisms of liberalism and prescriptions for sovereignty. On the ridiculous end, in an express attack on HUAC targets like Foreman, Wayne starred as a HUAC investigator who breaks up a Communist terror plot in *Big Jim McLain* (1952). The film overtly wrapped itself in the flag yet simultaneously disparaged America's liberal constitutionalism, specifically Fifth Amendment protections that inhibited HUAC's efforts to destroy the enemy.[23]

On the sublime side was John Ford's *The Man Who Shot Liberty Valance*, which pitted the conservative man-of-action (Wayne's Tom Doniphon) against the liberal man-of-thought-and-words (Jimmy Stewart's Ransom Stoddard). The liberal tenderfoot Stoddard believed that justice under laws—not men—could tame the uncivilized. Like Schmitt, Wayne understood that the one who protects the law cannot be constrained by it. And between them was the town thug Liberty Valance (Lee Marvin). As Schmitt would predict, the enemy was the "other" who necessitated violent conflict and the state of exception. In the end, Stoddard gets credit for shooting Valance in a fair and justified showdown and setting the town on a course to civilization. But in actuality, Doniphon was the dirty fighter who truly killed Valance, committing "murder" by shooting Valance in the back.

Upon hearing the real story years later, a reporter utters the famous line

"When the facts become legend, print the legend." A myth was necessary to justify the frontier town's transformation into a liberal democratic outpost. But as Schmitt would argue, the various institutions of liberal democracy were ineffectual in the final conflict—whether the press (newspaper offices are destroyed by Valance), the political process (which Valance disrupts), or the feckless marshal (at whom Valance scoffs). All the talking, deliberation, due process, and democracy in the world wouldn't have saved the town. But murder did. And the idea that liberal democratic civilization, represented by Stoddard, can provide peace and contentment is dubious—since in the ending we understand that the liberal institutions have been built on a fiction, we feel Stoddard's wife's longing for the true hero and "murderer," and we witness a funereal image of a "tamed" West.[24]

## Good Cop, Dirty Cop

In 1971, amid political and cultural tumult, Wayne's heir apparent Clint Eastwood came out blasting with *Dirty Harry,* and the modern action movie was truly born, combining character, structural, and thematic elements of the Western but leaving behind the time, setting, and trappings of the frontier and the cowboy.[25]

As Schmitt would critique, liberal democratic institutions (represented by the Mayor, the D.A., the Judge, Dirty Harry's police superiors, and other bureaucrats) are unable to deal with the threat of an inexplicably evil enemy (the "Killer"). Only the brutal, uncivilized tactics of the hero, Dirty Harry Callahan, operating in the state of exception, can preserve that civilization and obliterate the countercultural enemy. As in *High Noon* and Wayne's movies, deliberation and due process are ineffectual:

> MAYOR. I don't want any more trouble like you had last year in the Fillmore District. Understand? That's my policy.
> CALLAHAN. Yeah, well, when an adult male is chasing a female with intent to commit rape, I shoot the bastard, that's my policy.
> MAYOR. Intent? How did you establish that?
> CALLAHAN. When a naked man is chasing a woman through an alley with a butcher knife and a hard-on, I figure he isn't out collecting for the Red Cross.[26]

Torture and brutality are necessary tactics, and rights assist the enemy:

KILLER. (begging Callahan for mercy) No, no, no, no. Don't do anything more. You tried to kill me . . . Please no more, I'm hurt, can't you see I'm hurt? . . . Let me have a doctor . . . Please give me the doctor, don't kill me.

. . .

I have the right for a lawyer, don't shoot me, I have rights, I want a lawyer.

After Callahan's torture and illegal search of the Killer, liberal democratic rules and institutions release him:

DISTRICT ATTORNEY. You're lucky I'm not indicting you for assault with intent to commit murder.

. . .

Where the hell does it say you've got a right to kick down doors, torture suspects, deny medical attention and legal counsel. Where have you been? Does *Escobedo* ring a bell? *Miranda?* I mean, you must have heard of the Fourth Amendment. What I'm saying is, that man had rights.

The Judge agrees:

JUDGE. Now, the suspect's rights were violated, under the Fourth and Fifth and probably the Sixth and Fourteenth Amendments.

Liberal constitutional principles and high court interpretations serve to protect the Killer and enable him to kill again. As Schmitt might note, liberal civilization helps the uncivilized destroy civilization itself. But Callahan, the agent of the sovereign who is both of the community and also not of the community, understands how to handle the problem.

Dirty Harry goes on to shoot the Killer dead—in defiance of his superiors' orders—by declaring a state of exception. To effectuate his role and duty, he cannot be constrained by the law. Callahan then tosses his badge away (like Kane's final act of contempt for the dilatory liberal community in *High Noon*).[27] The conclusion is that liberal constitutionalism, quite literally, must change. As Schmitt would suggest, the system is simply incapable of dealing with real-world conflicts, rationalizing them as containable through process. But Dirty Harry will need to return, because the Killer is a nameless horde, a constant existential threat to a new Wild West of urban America.

## Die Harder with a President

Of course, Dirty Harry did return, in many sequels and imitations, for the next two decades. By the 1980s, the cops and soldiers became increasingly specialized and supersized. But in 1988, the action-hero genre was rejuvenated.[28]

John McTiernan's *Die Hard* took the *Dirty Harry* framework and ingeniously tweaked the characters and settings by presenting a more humorous and human hero in an unfamiliar, confined location pitted against highly skilled enemies. But *Die Hard* and its derivations still display Schmittian elements. These heroes of these films, by dint of their official status and training, have an ability to take on the fight that few others would. Further, as in *Dirty Harry*, the hero of *Die Hard*, Bruce Willis's John McClane, decides on the exception and refuses to be constrained by the law in his efforts to preserve order and destroy the enemy.

> McCLANE (trying to arrest a terrorist). Drop it, dickhead. It's the
>     police.
> VILLAIN. You won't hurt me.
> McCLANE. Oh yeah? Why not?
> VILLAIN. Because you're a policeman. There are rules for policemen.
> McCLANE. Yeah. That's what my captain keeps telling me.[29]

McClane proceeds to kill him and use his corpse to terrorize the team of primarily foreign terrorists led by Hans Gruber (Alan Rickman). Like most film terrorists, the villains of *Die Hard* pose a constant, asymmetrical, and somewhat inscrutable threat. And finally, like *Dirty Harry*, *Die Hard* recalled the Western thematically, textually, and symbolically—specifically *High Noon*. Exchanges such as the following between Hans and McClane expressly make such references—and show the Schmittian "other" quality of the enemy.

> HANS. You know my name, but who are you? Just another American
>     who saw too many movies as a child. Another orphan of a
>     bankrupt culture who thinks he's John Wayne . . . Rambo . . .
>     Marshal Dillon.
> McCLANE. Actually, I was always partial to Roy Rogers actually. I
>     really liked those sequined shirts.

HANS. Do you really think you have a chance against us, Mr.
  Cowboy?
MCCLANE. Yipee-ki-yea . . . mother fucker.

Holding McClane's wife Holly hostage, Hans takes aim at the modern-day
cowboy, and the final scene from the 1952 classic is reenacted.

HANS. Put down the gun . . . Well, this time John Wayne does not
  walk off into the sunset with Grace Kelly.
MCCLANE. That was Gary Cooper, asshole . . .
HANS. No more jokes, drop it or she gets it between the eyes!
MCCLANE (slowly puts down his gun). Whoa, Hans, now you're the
  cowboy?
HANS. "Yippe-ki-yea, mother fucker"? Now you are fucked.
MCCLANE. Holly, now . . . !

Taking McClane's cue, Holly drives Hans away with an elbow. McClane pulls
out a hidden gun, shoots Hans, and agrees with Hans's opinion that indeed
Americans "are cowboys."[30]

Other parallels to *High Noon* and reflections of Schmitt abound in *Die
Hard*. Like Kane, McClane seeks help early on, but the Los Angeles Police
Department is slow and cynical in its response and tries to rationalize and
negotiate around the situation, just as the townsfolk of Hadleyville did. The
press and the FBI, unlike McClane, misunderstand the enemy and provide
more harm than help. Key narrative differences separate *Die Hard* from
*High Noon* (and *Dirty Harry*), since McClane doesn't reject his office at the
end of the film. Rather, McClane seems truly duty-bound, wherever he is. In
fact, the President may want to get McClane's appointment book and crank
up the threat level wherever he is, because enemies are inevitably nearby.

Of course, if the President took a cue from Wolfgang Peterson's *Air Force
One* (1997), he wouldn't need McClane's help. In this *Die Hard* derivation, the
sovereign himself plays the hero. The film truly begins in a state of exception,
with President James Marshall (Harrison Ford) delivering a speech in Russia
about the violent overthrow of an apparent terrorist regime in Kazakhstan in
which Americans and Russians got their "heads out of the sand" and "stood
up to brutality." No longer would there be negotiating with such terrorists or
brutal regimes. President Marshall threatens: "It's your turn to be afraid."[31]

After the terrorists overtake the eponymous aircraft and hold the President, his family, and his aides captive, the Leader of the Free World remains true to his "Be Afraid" speech, telling his Vice President at the White House via satellite phone "We can't give in to their demands; it won't end there." Of course, the enemies, á la *Die Hard,* underestimate the President and utilize tactics that might persuade a more reasonable, compromising person to accede to demands. Back in Washington, the very reasonable, process-obsessed Vice President and Secretary of Defense, pondering how to proceed, seek answers in the text of the U.S. Constitution. Relying on the Twenty-Fifth Amendment, the Attorney General opines that because the President is essentially a hostage under duress, he may be declared incapacitated and no longer Commander-in-Chief.[32]

However, the sovereign is oblivious to these constitutionalist inquiries as he takes action in the state of exception. Unlike the compromisers and legal positivists, the President knows the enemy can only be dealt with violently, and the sovereign himself does the honors. In the end, the President annihilates the enemy without act of legislature, without regard to possible constitutional limitations, and despite objections and calls for compromise (but with a little help from the First Lady, recalling *Die Hard* and *High Noon*).

For some obvious reasons, *Air Force One* may be the most Schmittian feature in a metagenre filled with Schmittian elements. Significantly, it presaged the Bush Doctrine, neoconservative policies, and unitary executive theory memoranda of post-9/11 America. Perhaps, once the Schmittian action hero had moved from agent of the sovereign to the sovereign himself, the genre needed to rise to the fantastical heights of the superhero. And the next decade gave us more iterations of that species of hero than the previous one gave us Bruce Willis clones. However, the most successful of these films stood out with the most profound reflections of Schmittian themes.

## From *High Noon* to *Dark Knight*

In Christopher Nolan's *The Dark Knight,* the constant threat of the criminality and corruption of Gotham is augmented by a sociopathic terrorist, Heath Ledger's Joker, whose crimes are inscrutable in motive. This enemy is truly a Schmittian "other"—the Joker has no physical, mental, or cultural connection to the community of Gotham—not even to the existing criminal element.

Police Commissioner Gordon, District Attorney Harvey Dent, and Batman coordinate to combat the "normalcy" of rampant criminality and terror through employment of various extralegal measures. The sovereign agents of Gotham—even the judge, who orders a highly unorthodox mass imprisonment of thugs—effectuate a state of exception. But Batman is their public contractor in the area of law enforcement. He tortures, maims, and terrorizes in ways perhaps officials cannot but are willing to permit. Even the prosecutor, Dent, knows that the state of exception must always be declarable and that only overwhelming force can eliminate the criminal element.

Nearly all aspects of Schmitt's theories are present in *The Dark Knight*. But perhaps most interesting, *The Dark Knight* questions, as Schmitt does, whether liberal constitutionalism can truly make sense in a real world full of senseless threats. As in *Liberty Valance,* the projection of undeserved heroism onto the respectable, civilized official betrays the fundamental problem of liberal jurisprudence in handling the crises and chaos of real society. At the end, in an exchange between Gordon and Batman, the Dark Knight has his own take on the "print the legend" concept:

> BATMAN. You either die a hero or live long enough to see yourself become the villain. I can do those things because I'm not a hero, not like Dent. I killed those people. That's what I can be.
>
> . . .
>
> You'll hunt me. You'll condemn me. Set the dogs on me. Because that's what needs to happen. Because sometimes the truth isn't good enough. Sometimes people deserve to have their faith rewarded.[33]

## Life Imitating Art Reflecting Political Theory

The Hollywood action-hero movie is remarkable escapism—escape to a place very different from our own lives and reality, a place where the frustrations regarding inaction in our political and judicial systems can be alleviated. Still, Americans might be concerned that this product of popular culture—so exportable and identifiable around the globe—reflects criticisms and prescriptions that are so illiberal. The action-hero movie suggests in some measure that liberal democratic ideals are a dangerous fictional overlay—an attempt to govern in a way that is at odds with the true normal state of affairs—and that Schmitt's state of exception must lie at the core of our political and juridical reality.

Over the past forty years, presidential politics and policies have never been too far removed from both Schmitt's influences and action-hero references.[34] Recall Nixon's admiration for Wayne, his repeated viewings of *Patton* before the bombing of Cambodia, and his declaration that "when the President does it, that means it is not illegal."[35] Both Reagan and Bush I had a penchant for referencing *Dirty Harry* when discussing economic policy. During partisan showdowns and the 1995–1996 government shutdowns, Clinton found strength in his viewings of *High Noon*.

Before his inauguration, George W. Bush half-joked, "If this were a dictatorship, it'd be a heck of a lot easier, just so long as I'm the dictator."[36] Then came 9/11, and his administration provided legal and political cover for preemptive strikes and enhanced interrogation techniques and proclaimed the noncitizen yet noncombatant status of terror suspects, while Bush made "Wanted: Dead or Alive" quips lifted from the Western genre and a fighter jet carrier landing evocative of *Independence Day* and *Air Force One*. Perhaps these are unconnected clips. But these incidents and intonations over the past four decades can be spliced to show that not only our popular culture but also our politics and policies at some level repudiate our founding ideals and have more in common with an illiberal German jurist than we may want to admit.

## Notes

1. "Liberal democracy" or "constitutional democracy" (the terms are used interchangeably here) has had different meanings to different peoples and has taken many forms, from republics to constitutional monarchies. All liberal constitutional democracies were the targets of Schmitt's criticisms, but the constitutional republic of the United States is the point of reference here. See generally John Dunn, *Democracy: A History* (New York: Atlantic Monthly Press, 2005); Roland N. Stromberg, *Democracy: A Short, Analytical History* (Armonk, NY: M.E. Sharpe, 1996).

2. The Hollywood action-hero genre, as explained throughout, refers to an evolving agglomeration of genres in which representative films share certain thematic, visual, and narrative qualities. For an excellent and thorough history and analysis of the genre or metagenre, see Eric Lichtenfeld, *Action Speaks Louder: Violence, Spectacle, and the American Action Movie* (Middletown, CT: Wesleyan University Press, 2007).

3. American popular culture is a major economic export, and Hollywood films are significant revenue generators. Furthermore, since the 1980s, the top-grossing movie lists each year have been replete with action-hero movies, and such films have become proxies for American life and identity to much of the world. See Allen J. Scott, "Hollywood in the Era of Globalization," *YaleGlobal*, November 29, 2002, http://yaleglobal.yale.edu/content/hollywood-era-globalization (accessed September 5, 2011); Paul Fahri and

Megan Rosenfeld, "American Pop Penetrates Worldwide," *Washington Post,* October 25, 1998, A1, www.washingtonpost.com/wp-srv/inatl/longterm/mia/part1.htm (accessed September 5, 2011); "The Return of Cultural Diplomacy," *Newsweek,* December 30, 2008, www.thedailybeast.com/newsweek/2008/12/31/the-return-of-cultural-diplomacy.html (accessed September 5, 2011).

4. Interpreting the Hollywood action-hero movie as illiberal or even fascist is certainly not novel. See, e.g., Pauline Kael's infamous review of *Dirty Harry* as a "right-wing fantasy" and an "attack on liberal values." Pauline Kael, *5001 Nights at the Movies* (New York: Henry Holt, 1991). Joseph Campbell's "monomyth"—which underlies the narrative themes and basic plotlines of most action-hero films—has origins in ancient and primitive cultures that were organized far more hierarchically than democratically. In Campbell's description of the monomyth, the hero leaves his community both as a rite of passage and with a charge of protection and salvation, always returning with a boon for his community, to rejuvenate and redeem it, even to validate and reaffirm traditional values of that community—which are often patriarchal, dominance hierarchies. See generally Joseph Campbell, *The Hero with a Thousand Faces* (Princeton, NJ: Princeton University Press, 1968). In *The Myth of the American Superhero,* John Shelton Lawrence and Robert Jewett provide an overview of popular culture in various media and find a fascist undercurrent in which heroes must use extralegal means to save feckless democracies. John Shelton Lawrence and Robert Jewett, *The Myth of the American Superhero* (Grand Rapids, MI: Eerdmans, 2002), 6–8. In contrast to Joseph Campbell's classical monomyth, which is built around adventures outside the community as a rite of initiation back into the community, Lawrence and Jewett's "American monomyth" defines the hero as a Christ-like redeemer who gives his life for others to destroy an evil threat, returns a community to its idyllic conditions, and "recede[s] into obscurity." However, as explained in this chapter, viewing many iconic action-hero movies through the lens of Carl Schmitt's theories reveals that the action hero is not redemptive of much that could be considered American or Christian. Rather, the action-hero movie reflects specific criticisms of liberalism, and even Judeo-Christian traditions, and suggests a need for something new in a political and juridical sense, as Schmitt would prescribe.

5. See Jan-Werner Mueller, *A Dangerous Mind: Carl Schmitt in Post-War European Thought* (New Haven, CT: Yale University Press, 2003); Peter M. R. Stirk, *Carl Schmitt, Crown Jurist of the Third Reich: One Preemptive War, Military Occupation, and World Empire* (Lewiston, NY: Edwin Mellen Press, 2005).

6. Schmitt wrote his theories well before the action-hero movies discussed were made, and, as shown in this chapter, the genre evokes very specific aspects of his work. However, no contention is made that his theories directly or indirectly influenced Hollywood filmmaking. Schmitt's three cornerstone works, the ideas of which are analyzed in this chapter, all were originally written between 1921 and 1932: *On Dictatorship* in 1921, *Political Theology* in 1926, and *The Concept of the Political* in 1932. The editions cited here are the following: Carl Schmitt, *Political Theology* (Chicago: University of

Chicago Press, 2005); Carl Schmitt, *The Concept of the Political* (Chicago: University of Chicago Press, 2007); Carl Schmitt, *Dictatorship* (Cambridge: Polity Press, 2011). The earliest film discussed herein is *Stagecoach,* which was released in 1939.

7. A substantial body of fairly recent scholarship has examined films for their political themes and messages as well as their portrayal of politicians. See, e.g., Jonathan Rosenbaum, *Movies as Politics* (Berkeley: University of California Press, 1997); Terry Christensen and Peter J. Haas, *Projecting Politics: Political Messages in American Films* (Armonk, NY: M.E. Sharpe, 2005); Ernest Giglio, *Here's Looking at You: Hollywood, Film, and Politics* (New York: Peter Lang, 2005); Philip John Davies and Paul Wells, *American Film and Politics from Reagan to Bush Jr.* (Manchester, UK: Manchester University Press, 2002).

8. See David Luban, "Carl Schmitt and the Critique of Lawfare," *Case Western Reserve Journal of International Law* 44, nos. 1–2 (March 28, 2011): 457; *Georgetown Public Law and Legal Theory,* Research Paper No. 11-33, p. 10, http://scholarship.law.georgetown.edu/facpub/621 (accessed August 28, 2011).

9. See, e.g., Sandy Levinson, "Thinking Out Loud about John Yoo (and about Carl Schmitt)," *Balkinization,* April 12, 2008, http://balkin.blogspot.com/2008/04/thinking-out-loud-about-john-yoo.html (accessed August 28, 2011); David Abraham, "The Bush Regime from Elections to Detentions: A Moral Economy of Carl Schmitt and Human Rights," University of Miami School of Law Legal Studies Research Paper No. 2007-20, May 2007, http://ssrn.com/abstract=942865 (accessed August 28, 2011); Scott Horton, "The Return of Carl Schmitt," *Balkinization,* November 7, 2005, http://balkin.blogspot.com/2005/11/return-of-carl-schmitt.html (accessed August 28, 2011); Damon Linker, "Carl Schmitt and the American Right," *New Republic,* March 3, 2009, www.tnr.com/blog/damon-linker/carl-schmitt-and-the-american-right (accessed August 28, 2011); Christopher Kutz, "Torture, Necessity, and Existential Politics," Stanford Public Law Working Paper No. 121, December 2005, http://ssrn.com/abstract=870602 (accessed August 28, 2011).

10. See, e.g., Giorgio Agamben, *State of Exception* (Chicago: University of Chicago Press, 2005); Chantal Mouffe, "Carl Schmitt and the Paradox of Liberal Democracy," in *Law as Politics: Carl Schmitt's Critique of Liberalism,* ed. David Dyzenhaus (Durham, NC: Duke University Press, 1998).

11. See Schmitt, *Political Theology;* Heiner Bielefeldt, "Carl Schmitt's Critique of Liberalism: Systematic Reconstruction and Countercriticism"; and Ernst-Wolfgang Boeckenfoerde, "The Concept of the Political: A Key to Understanding Carl Schmitt's Constitutional Theory," both in Dyzenhaus, *Law as Politics.*

12. See Schmitt, *Concept of the Political,* 27; Robert Howse, "From Legitimacy to Dictatorship—and Back Again: Leo Strauss's Critique of the Anti-Liberalism of Carl Schmitt," in Dyzenhaus, *Law as Politics,* 65; Mouffe, "Schmitt and Liberal Democracy," 165–71.

13. See Schmitt, *Political Theology,* 5; Agamben, *State of Exception,* 35.

14. John P. McCormick, "The Dilemmas of Dictatorship: Carl Schmitt and Constitutional Emergency Powers," in Dyzenhaus, *Law as Politics*, 222–26.

15. See Bielefeldt, "Schmitt's Critique of Liberalism"; David Dyzenhaus, "Why Carl Schmitt?" in Dyzenhaus, *Law as Politics*.

16. See generally McCormick, "Dilemmas of Dictatorship."

17. See Will Wright, *Six Guns and Society: A Structural Study of the Western* (Berkeley: University of California Press, 1977); Robert B. Pippen, *Hollywood Westerns and American Myth: The Importance of Howard Hawks and John Ford for Political Philosophy* (New Haven, CT: Yale University Press, 2010).

18. Wayne once explained his creation: "I made up my mind that I was going to play a real man to the best of my ability. I felt many of the Western stars of the Twenties and Thirties were too goddamn perfect. . . . They were too goddamn sweet and pure to be dirty fighters. Well, I wanted to be a dirty fighter if that was the only way to fight back . . . who gets angry, who fights clean whenever possible but will fight dirty if he has to. You could say I made the Western hero a roughneck." Randy Roberts and James Stuart Olson, *John Wayne: American* (New York: Simon & Schuster, 1995), 131.

19. Bill Clinton estimates that he saw *High Noon* "half a dozen times during its run in Hope" when he was growing up and "more than a dozen times since." Reports of White House screenings indicate that he watched it around twenty times during his two terms as president. No other president had such an admitted connection with a movie—not Nixon, who obsessed jingoistically over *Patton* during the Vietnam War, and not Reagan, who starred in so many of his own films and sometimes conflated movies with reality. Clinton expressly admitted that he drew inspiration from the movie and Cooper's seminal action hero: "Over the long years since I first saw *High Noon*, when I faced my own showdowns, I often thought of the look in Gary Cooper's eyes as he stares into the face of almost certain defeat, and how he keeps walking through his fears toward his duty. It works pretty well in real life too." Bill Clinton, *A Life* (New York: Knopf, 2004), 20–21.

20. Dialogue in the film notes that before Kane arrested Miller, "a decent woman couldn't walk down the street in broad daylight" and the town "wasn't a fit place to bring up a child."

21. *High Noon*, directed by Fred Zinnemann, written by Carl Foreman, from John W. Cunningham's story "The Tin Star," produced by Stanley Kramer Productions and released by United Artists in 1952.

22. Garry Wills, *John Wayne's America* (New York: Touchstone / Simon & Schuster, 1997), 273.

23. The year before *High Noon*, Wayne's *Flying Leathernecks* (1951) was released, in which he played World War II Marine Air Corps pilot Major Daniel Kirby. That same year, a young congressman and member of the House Un-American Activities Committee, Richard M. Nixon, went to the Senate to commend the film as "an original story portraying the immortal achievements of our Marine Corps air arm." This may

have been a bit of payback, as Wayne had supported Nixon in his earliest congressional bid. Mark Feeney, *Nixon at the Movies* (Chicago: University of Chicago Press, 2004), 86.

24. Pippen, *Hollywood Westerns and American Myth*, 80–82.

25. *Dirty Harry* was originally titled *Dead Right*. *Dirty Harry* was the movie that gave rise to so many films that have filled our theaters, as well as so many studio executives' pockets, during the past four decades. Those films included the myriad rough-and-tumble urban cop, private detective, and vigilante films and television shows of the 1970s, the *Dirty Harry* sequels, the *Death Wish* films, the *Walking Tall* films, *Taxi Driver, McCloud, The Streets of San Francisco,* and *Starsky & Hutch.* It also inspired the "super-cop" and "super-soldier" action movies of Arnold Schwarzenegger, Sylvester Stallone, Steven Seagal, Jean-Claude Van Damme, and Chuck Norris during the 1980s and 1990s. In this vein, there are the "genre-mashing" productions (combination fantasy-comedy-superhero action movies and television series) from the past two decades: *The Matrix Trilogy,* the *Mission Impossible* films, the *Bad Boys* movies, *Batman Begins, Spider-Man 1–3,* the *Bourne* trilogy, the *Transporter* films, the *Rush Hour* films, and television's *24.*

26. *Dirty Harry,* directed by Don Siegal, written by Harry Julian Fink, Rita M. Fink, and Dean Riesner, with John Milius and Jo Heims, and produced and distributed by Warner Bros. Pictures in 1971.

27. The myriad sequels establish that Callahan wanted the badge and his official status back—and that the streets of San Francisco needed him.

28. *Die Hard* was the first book in an action-hero genealogy of biblical proportions: *Die Hard,* the original, well-executed concept begat a solid sequel (*Die Hard 2*); which begat immediate imitators, both middling (*Toy Soldiers, Passenger 57, Cliffhanger*) and entertaining (*Under Siege, Speed*); which begat another, not-as-solid sequel (*Die Hard with a Vengeance*); which in turn begat another round of middling (*Executive Decision, Daylight*) and entertaining (*The Rock, Con Air*) imitators, which begat unintentional jokes (*Speed 2, Under Siege 2, Sudden Death*), which begat an intentional joke (*Snakes on a Plane*), which begat a resurrection (*Live Free or Die Hard*). Hallelujah.

29. *Die Hard,* directed by John McTiernan, written by Jeb Stuart and Steven E. de Souza, from Roderick Thorp's novel *Nothing Lasts Forever,* produced and released by Twentieth Century Fox Film Corporation in 1988.

30. The connections between *Die Hard* and the Western—and *High Noon* in particular—are explored, along with an analysis of *Die Hard*'s religious and spiritual references and significance, in John C. Lyden, *Film as Religion: Myths, Morals, and Rituals* (New York: New York University Press, 2003), 146–51.

31. *Air Force One,* directed by Wolfgang Peterson, written by Andrew W. Marlowe, produced by Columbia Pictures Corp., and distributed by Sony Pictures Entertainment in 1997.

32. See U.S. Const. amend. XXV, §4.

33. *The Dark Knight,* directed by Christopher Nolan, written by Jonathan Nolan,

Christopher Nolan, and David S. Goyer, based on Bob Kane's characters, and produced and distributed by Warner Bros. Pictures in 2008.

34. For an analysis of the impact of popular movies—including action-hero films—on presidential politics, rhetoric, and symbolism, see Neal Gabler, *Life: The Movie* (New York: Vintage Books, 1998), 108–16.

35. "'I Have Impeached Myself'—Edited Transcript of David Frost's Interview with Richard Nixon Broadcast in May 1977," *Guardian,* September 7, 2007, www.guardian .co.uk/theguardian/2007/sep/07/greatinterviews1 (accessed August 28, 2011).

36. "Transition of Power: President-Elect Bush Meets with Congressional Leaders on Capitol Hill," *CNN.com Transcripts,* December 18, 2000, http://transcripts.cnn.com/ TRANSCRIPTS/0012/18/nd.01.html (accessed August 28, 2011).

# 12

# J. R. R. TOLKIEN'S *THE HOBBIT,* OR, *THERE AND BACK AGAIN*

## Recovering a Platonic-Aristotelian Politics of Friendship in Liberal Democracy

*Mary M. Keys*

It is well known that J. R. R. Tolkien's tales *The Hobbit* and *The Lord of the Rings* have been immensely popular with democratic audiences, from their publication in the mid-twentieth century to their ongoing adaptation for the big screen. Perhaps not well known, however, is the surprising extent to which these same stories draw from and indeed embody central insights in political theory, especially from the Platonic and Aristotelian traditions. The narrative of *The Hobbit* presents contemporary readers with a literary view, fresh and wonderful, of property, justice, and friendship. One could even consider the story as offering readers a dialogue about justice and friendship. Made more delightful by the presence of protagonists who are hobbits, wizards, dwarves, and elves, *The Hobbit* "holds up the mirror to the only nature we know, our own," as W. H. Auden wrote of *The Fellowship of the Ring.*[1] In its subcreation of "imagined wonder," the narrative sets in vibrant (and pathetic) relief the core human aspirations of justice and friendship. In so doing, it can open our eyes to some possibilities and problems of justice and friendship in this world; to the interconnectedness of the two; and to the arguably greater value of the latter for persons and polities.[2] I will emphasize these aspects in sketching the tale of *The Hobbit,* bearing in mind Tolkien's caution to persons engaged in this sort of "scientific" enterprise against "ignorance or forgetfulness of the nature of a story (as a thing told in its entirety), [which] has often led such enquirers into strange judgments."[3]

We can only understand the extent to which these stories apply to our politics, however, if we appreciate the intellectual relevance of Tolkien's stories, admitted by their author to belong to the genre of *fairy tales* or *fairy stories*.[4] This chapter addresses the significance of Tolkien's stories through a three-part exploration. The first part makes a theoretical case for the relevance of fairy story to political science and philosophy based especially on Tolkien's essay "On Fairy-Stories." In this text, the master craftsman explains how he understands his literary art; its relation to reason, nature, and truth; and its value for human life. Among the functions Tolkien considers fairy story's fantasy apt to fulfill, the one he terms "recovery" is of special importance for our topic here. The second part of the chapter reflects on Tolkien's portrayal of property, justice, and friendship in *The Hobbit,* as an excellent example of this "recovery." The final section considers what relevance this sort of recovery, facilitated by Tolkien's fantasy, might have for citizens of liberal democracies today.

## Fairy Stories, Truth, and Literary "Recovery"

If we ask what relation Tolkien's fairy stories properly have to the study of political science and philosophy, the answer would seem at first sight to be "none," for at least four reasons.

First, according to both common opinion and scholarly classification, fairy stories are considered by definition *children's* literature.[5] They are written for, appreciated by, and perhaps at times useful to precisely that "class" of human beings who are immature, little educated, and too inexperienced in social and political affairs to be appropriate students of political science and philosophy. If Aristotle doubts the preparedness for political studies of most young people and perhaps even of most adults,[6] he never even contemplates the possibility of teaching political science to children. From Plato's and Xenophon's works we likewise gather that, while older teenagers and young adults grouped around Socrates to engage his moral and civic dialectic, the first thinker "to bring philosophy down from the heavens and into cities" was not a pied piper for youngsters aged twelve and under. And this concurs with contemporary common sense.

A second and related reason why Tolkien's tales and political philosophy seem poles apart has to do with *fairies* and the realm of faerie they are said to inhabit. Fairy stories are mainly about these *imaginary* beings and their imaginary principalities, and even about imaginary worlds. By comparison, the much-maligned city founded in speech in Plato's *Republic* appears a model of social-scientific realism.[7] Of all types of narratives, fairy tales most require of their readers a robust "suspension of disbelief," or, put more positively in Tolkien's own terms, a generous grant of "literary belief."[8] Both in the telling and in the hearing, fairy stories thus appear at polar opposites from scientific or philosophic inquiry and education and from the real-world polities studied by political science.

Third, one can easily conclude from what has been said that the sole benefit fairy stories offer to adult humans is mental and emotional relaxation, a temporary *escape* from the here and now, from the weight of grown-up responsibilities and concerns. The causes of fear and unease that we may put out of mind through indulging in fairy stories include social and political problems and possibilities, the stuff of citizenship and statesmanship as well as the matter for social science and theory. Tolkien's tales may thus benefit some students of political science and practitioners of the political art, but only instrumentally and indirectly, affording them a mental getaway now so that they may study and work more energetically later. Fairy stories still seem to have no intrinsic value for more ennobling forms of leisure; they appear unhelpful for genuine learning about matters of serious human concern, including the social and political.

A fourth and very concrete reason to doubt that Tolkien's tales could assist students of political philosophy is that Tolkien himself often appears little interested in politics, and even to think very little of politics, at least as we commonly use the word. This impression is conveyed most strongly in some of his published letters: "world policies and events" typically tend to "trample" rather than support ordinary human life and relationships; Tolkien's own "political opinions" incline increasingly toward "Anarchy" or "'unconstitutional' Monarchy," that is, to either the absence of formal government or the least *political* of Aristotelian regime types; a character named Denethor in *The Lord of the Rings* evinces the tragic flaw of having "become a 'political' leader," "tainted with mere politics"; and Tolkien and his friends secretly undertake to "wean" a colleague from involvement in "politics (academic)."[9]

To appreciate Tolkien's contribution to political philosophy, we need to find a response to these objections.[10]

## CHILDREN, GROWN-UPS, AND FAIRY STORIES

In a 1967 interview with the *Sunday Times,* Tolkien playfully reveals that his decision decades earlier to write and market *The Hobbit* as a children's book was something of a front. Tolkien had observed that the critics, not to mention the children, tend to go much easier on children's tales than on fiction written for adults ("OFS," 37–38). Tolkien indeed wrote for children, including his own children, but not exclusively or even primarily: "That's all sob stuff [about his intent to write exclusively for children or even for the private enjoyment of his own children]. *No, of course I didn't. If you're a youngish man and you don't want to be made fun of, you say you're writing for children.* At any rate, children are your immediate audience and you write or tell them stories, for which they are mildly grateful: long rambling stories at bedtime."[11] Tolkien's is a more age-inclusive approach to the fairy-story craft.

Why should this be so? In "On Fairy-Stories," Tolkien reasons that in the first place, children do not constitute a strictly separate class of readers, much less a "special kind of creature"; they are simply "normal, if immature, members of a particular family, and of the human family at large" ("OFS," 34). He reiterates this basic view some three decades later, in his 1967 interview with the *Sunday Times:* "Children aren't a class. They are merely human beings at different stages of maturity. All of them have a human intelligence which even at its lowest is a pretty wonderful thing, and the entire world in front of them. It remains to be seen if they rise above that."[12] What normally differentiates children from adults is, on the one hand, the longer experience and the broader and more advanced understanding generally possessed by adults and, on the other hand, the greater humility, innocence, and capacity for wonder possessed by most children ("OFS," 37–38, 42–43). Yet children and adult human beings do not have radically diverse tastes and desires.

As a matter of historical record, Tolkien notes that the most revered fairy tales, collected and revised by Andrew Lang and others as especially appropriate for children, were not originally children's stories but were myths, epics, and tales told by adults for adults, or for an entire, age-inclusive community. More essentially, Tolkien maintains that fairy stories are one full-fledged branch of the literary art. Like other forms of art, fairy story flows from and reflects certain natural *human* desires, not merely children's desires. If fairy tales as a literary type are pitched exclusively to young readers, then the art form as a whole cannot flourish or reflect its essential humanity, and children and adults will share in the loss. "Fairy-stories . . . cut off from a full adult art, would in the end be ruined; indeed insofar as they have been [so cut off], they have been ruined." Conversely, just as the art of painting can be adapted for children and taught in simple terms to children but is *perfected* in forms best appreciated by adults who are possessed of wider experience and are more sensitive to depth and refinement, so too with the telling and hearing of tales:

> *If fairy-story as a kind is worth reading at all it is worthy to be written for and read by adults. They will, of course, put more in and get more out than children can.* Then, as a branch of a genuine art, children may hope to get fairy-stories fit for them to read and yet within their measure; as they may hope to get suitable introductions to poetry, history, and the sciences. Though it may be better for them to read some things, especially fairy-stories, that are beyond their measure rather than short of it. Their books like their clothes should allow for growth, and their books at any rate should encourage it. ("OFS," 43, emphasis added)

One important way at least some adult readers can "put more in," or bring more to the reading of myth or fairy tale, is precisely through their greater experience with and interest in social and political matters. They may well find that the reading of Tolkien's tales revives their awareness of some puzzles of social and political life and theory, especially in the ethical dimensions of those puzzles.

### REASON, FANTASY, AND "SUB-CREATIVE" ART

For Tolkien, identifying the proper readership of his literary genre opens the way to appreciating its "values and functions" for human life. Tolkien proposes that fairy tales offer "in a peculiar degree or mode" these four contributions: "Fantasy, Recovery, Escape, Consolation, all things of which children have, as a rule, less need than older people" ("OFS," 43–44). It would seem that "fantasy" at least must be in contradistinction or even opposition to the *rational* activities of science and philosophy. Yet Tolkien places fantasy among the "rational not . . . irrational activit[ies]" of human beings ("OFS," 45n2). Precisely insofar as human beings are rational animals (as Aristotle famously argued), "fantasy is a natural human activity." To flourish, fairy stories and their fantasy require sharpness and clarity of reason on the part of their authors and readers alike ("OFS," 51).

Tolkien's use of the word *fantasy* is closely linked with his theory of art as "sub-creation." Both flow from and give expression to our nature as human beings, as rational animals. Reason is contemplative and practical, directed toward both understanding and acting in accord with the truth of things. Practical reason's scope in turn encompasses both doing and making; it is perfected by prudence and by art. In the latter capacity, we act upon and express our being "made in the image and likeness of a Maker" ("OFS," 52), a God who freely and not of any necessity chooses to create as a manifestation of and for the sharing of love. The nature of created reason thus appears such that at least some human beings will want to employ it to direct their potent faculty of *imagination* in "combin[ing] nouns and redistribut[ing] adjectives" drawn from their perception of and speech about the real or "primary" world. In this way they can create, in a derivative, limited, yet meaningful sense, new beings and fresh or "secondary" worlds in speech. We know "green" and we know "the sun" as separate from one another in the natural or primary world. Through our imagination we can combine them to "create" in a literary sense, to imagine and *to say* and communicate "a green sun" ("OFS," 46). We recognize "trees" and "humans"; a literary artist working with images and words joins their attributes to produce a wondrous world with "ents" or "tree-herds," rational animals with many treelike features, evincing an unusual understanding of and concern for trees.

On Tolkien's own account, it is important to grasp that this entish literary fantasy, to give just one example from the "secondary world" of *The Lord of the Rings,* requires the prior perception of and distinction between trees and humans in the *primary* world. The deeper the author's understanding of real humans and real trees, the more "real" or "true," consistent or compelling will be his portrayal of his novel literary creation. Tolkien thus insists that "Fantasy . . . does not destroy or even insult Reason; and it does not either blunt the appetite for, nor obscure the perception of, scientific verity. On the contrary" ("OFS," 51). Fantasy's excellence appears actually to *depend* upon this rational appetite and sharp sense perception. Faerie and political science are not natural enemies or absolute strangers; they share some common roots and ought at the very least to coexist in peaceful, respectful diversity.

According to Tolkien, the genuine goals of literary subcreation and fantasy do not involve delusion or manipulation.[13] Instead, subcreative art should aim to craft a wonderful, desirable world in speech, intended and experienced as a genuine *common good.* Fantasy "uncorrupted . . . seeks shared enrichment, partners in making and delight, not slaves." Freedom is doubly of the essence of Tolkien's fairy stories, for fantasy is founded on the "recognition" of real-world "fact, but not a slavery to it" ("OFS," 50–51). And this once again applies to both writers and readers who seek citizenship (or at least asylum and safe conduct) in faerie. If the author of a tale is a master of the fairy-story craft, according to Tolkien an exceedingly difficult one, fraught with pitfalls and perhaps least likely of success among literary arts, the "secondary world" he or she fashions will possess an "inner consistency" that elicits many readers' *freely,* even spontaneously given literary assent to the tale as "true" to that subcreated world and its laws.

Here some significant parallels emerge between Tolkien's theory of fantasy and elements of especially Aristotelian, Augustinian, and Thomistic political thought. Fairy stories, like social and political relations, are by nature intended to strive for common or shared goods, facilitating friendships as well as just ordering and participation. They are to express and somehow protect the freedom that all humans by nature (according to Augustine and Aquinas, at least) ought properly to possess. In reading Tolkien's theoretical account of his literary art, the student of political theory is thus invited to reflect on some influential accounts of the political science and art, as a spur to formulate or refine her or his own views. The roads of faerie and political science share common sources in human rationality, sociability, and speech.[14] Their respective aspirations and agents bear close resemblances: both fairy stories and politics are profoundly "social or human" activities, arts dealing with the sharing of common goods and the prospects of happiness.[15]

In Tolkien's literary theory, there is another interesting, precise point where the paths of faerie and of political philosophy intersect, namely where fantasy (or fairy story or myth) is said to constitute "a human right" ("OFS," 52). It is a human right as an activity of human reason, a form of art or making with its irreplaceable (and unpredictable) contribution of shapes and colors to weave into the grand tapestry of human existence. Some people will naturally find themselves inclined to desire, and hence to create and to enjoy such literature; and it is by nature right that they be permitted to do so, for their personal welfare and for the common good. This right is one part or expression, one aim, as Tolkien would have it, of the law instilled in the minds and hearts of humans, the primordial or natural law whereby we understand that "good is to be done and pursued, and evil avoided."[16] The law and the right once again bear witness to our being "made" and "measured" by a "Maker," the archetypal artist who is also the most provident of legislators and a lover of freedom.[17]

## FAMILIARITY, "ARRESTING STRANGENESS," AND "RECOVERY"

Tolkien's definition of *fairy* story is bound up with "the nature of Faërie: the Perilous Realm itself," home to elves or fairies and to many magical creatures—to wondrous "things not found within recorded time," as he puts it in his poem "Mythopoeia."[18] Faerie appears to be for Tolkien either a synonym for or a species of the "secondary world" fashioned by subcreative art, an "indescribable, though not imperceptible," and inescapably strange land containing some strange inhabitants ("OFS," 13–15). If a story does not "use" or at least in some way "touch upon" faerie, if it fails to convey a feel for "the air that blows in that country," then it cannot appropriately be called a fairy tale. Even if fairy story is considered to constitute or reflect a human right, there is still much about it that is foreign to our human experience, much that is for us "other." I will argue later that even this "arresting strangeness" and the otherness of fairy story can contribute to our pursuit of political-philosophical wisdom.

Not all in faerie is foreign to us, however, as Tolkien is eager to emphasize. In terms of the content of the tale, he suggests that if it is well conceived and well told, we should find in its secondary world much that is familiar from our own human and natural world. Tolkien's vision of fairy story depends upon faerie, but not on the inclusion of *fairies* [or elves] as characters, and certainly not as protagonists. In some significant passages, Tolkien underscores the *humanity* of fairy tales precisely as tales told by human beings to and for human beings. It is therefore generally appropriate that the protagonists of these narratives should themselves be human: "Most good 'fairy-stories' are about the *adventures* of men in the Perilous Realm or upon its shadowy marches. Naturally so" ("OFS," 14, emphasis in original). "In stories in which no human being is concerned; or in which the animals are the heroes and heroines, and the men and women, if they appear, are mere adjuncts; and above all those in which the animal form is only a mask upon a human face, a device of the satirist or the preacher, in these we have beast-fable and not fairy-story" ("OFS," 19).

Tolkien underscores one "realist" cause for the humanity of well-crafted fairy story and its protagonists: we human beings, as both readers and writers, generally find our exploits and ourselves especially interesting. By contrast, stories actually *about* "fairies" or "elves" are "in modern English ... relatively rare, and as a rule not very interesting" ("OFS," 14). Affection is strongest when its object is both good and one's own.[19] One could also note that it is proper to *human* beings to experience and to communicate their lives and those of others, factual or fictitious, in the form of narrative. The human being is by nature "the story-teller," and our very mortality sharpens and adds urgency to our tales.[20] Humans are not tied to the purely historical; we yearn for an eternal and transcendent good. Yet our condition as material and spiritual creatures imparts to our existence an inherently historical dimension, which in turn makes us tend to craft and to tell stories in myriad forms.

In this aspect of his vision of the fairy-story art's foundation, Tolkien stresses again and anew its fundamental *humanity.* Tolkien likewise underscores the humanity of genuine politics and hence the necessary subordination of the narrowly political to the broadly human if politics itself is to achieve its *telos.* Tolkien locates the origins of the humanity of fairy stories in their arising from "certain primordial human desires" ("OFS," 17) and for the satisfaction and further "whetting" or "enkindling" of these desires.[21] He mentions explicitly the "primal desire at the heart of Faërie: the realization, independent of the conceiving mind, of imagined wonder," "the desire to survey the depths of space and time," and "[the desire] to hold communion with other living things" ("OFS," 17, 19). In these desires human beings again appear as rational, desiring by nature to know universal truth; as social, desiring broader and deeper communication and conversation with others; and as artistic or creative, wanting to make beautiful and useful things—all within the proper yet ample scope of the finite mind's "measured measure."[22]

Considering the human desire "to survey," to see and to comprehend, in its relevance to his literary art, Tolkien takes issue with Andrew Lang's contention that children evince a special "wish to believe." In his own experience, Tolkien has observed them rather as wanting *to know.*[23] Tolkien further observes that they are especially desirous to know the truth about good and evil, right and wrong. Children are typically far more interested in this aspect of *the truth* of a story, at least in broad strokes ("Was he good? Was he wicked?"), than in knowing whether or not it actually happened ("OFS," 38–39 and notes). As human agents are the chief characters in fairy stories and also in politics, so too in reading the one and studying the other the central questions we wonder about will commonly concern good and evil, justice and injustice, benefit and harm, happiness and misery, right and wrong.[24]

Besides the familiarity of these human dimensions, the fairy tale's "secondary world" necessarily contains many natural things and artifacts recognizable from our real-world experience. Bread and water, earth and sky, fire and ice, stone and sun, field and hoe, and a host of other familiars will normally be found in faerie ("OFS," 14). The human artist cannot create ex nihilo, out of nothing, but rather must borrow generously from what is *given* him or her to perceive and to say. The literary master may then imagine, refashion freely, and recombine properties, nouns, and modifiers, thus conceiving and crafting in speech new forms, new kinds, and new individuals. At the peak of the art of fairy story, the master craftsman can aspire to reveal the nature of the "old" or the given more perfectly through the new and imagined ("OFS," 54–55). Even behind or within the novelty of fantasy and subcreation, if Tolkien is right, we can expect to reexperience familiar realities that we have already actually seen, heard, touched—and perhaps forgotten, or never really *contemplated*.

At this juncture, where fantasy's "arresting strangeness" ("OFS," 45) meets primary-world familiarity, we encounter another of the chief functions Tolkien considers fairy tale to fulfill in human life. This task he calls "recovery,"[25] and with its consideration we round out our inquiry into fairy story's relationship with political philosophy. Long experience with world and art, with literature and nature, as well as perhaps with society and politics, brings with it "a danger of boredom or anxiety to be original," to take for granted what has become *too* familiar, or to seek violently to refashion it, or even, one trembles to think after the tragic social experiments of fascism and communism in the twentieth century, to "liquidate" it in order to attempt to make ex nihilo ("OFS," 52–53). Tolkien affirms:

> Before we reach such states we need recovery. We should look at green again, and be startled anew (but not blinded) by blue and yellow and red. We should meet the centaur and the dragon, and then perhaps suddenly behold, like the ancient shepherds, sheep, and dogs, and horses—and wolves. This recovery fairy-stories help us to make. In that sense only a taste for them may make us, or keep us, childish. Recovery (which includes return and renewal of health) is a re-gaining—regaining of a clear view. I do not say "seeing things as they are" and involve myself with the philosophers, though I might venture to say "seeing things as we are (or were) meant to see them"—as things apart from ourselves. We need, in any case, to clean our windows; so that the things seen clearly may be freed from the drab blur of triteness or familiarity—from possessiveness. ("OFS," 53)

If Tolkien is correct in his appraisal of fairy tale's ability to assist in such "recovery," then this literary genre ought to offer at least three forms of aid to students and the study of political philosophy. First and foremost, fantasy's "arresting strangeness" may reawaken us to *wonder* at foundations and aspirations of society and politics that have long been buried under the accumulation of intellectual and political history, under elaborate institutional structures and forms, or hidden behind our daily business and boredom. In confronting these *familiar* realities in the *foreign* realm of faerie, we may experience them in all their pathos and beauty, their oddness, fearsomeness, and awesomeness. The human being, human faces and voices, rulers, citizens, and subjects, law, judgment, poverty, pity, counsel, exhortation, courage and cowardice, war and peace . . . these can be restored to our minds' contemplation by being more vividly and poignantly experienced through our senses, pricked by faerie. As the old adage goes, *nihil in intellectus quod nisi prius in sensu* (there is nothing in intellect that is not first in sense). The artist's appreciative presentation of the *particular* and its uniqueness and value is a powerful prelude to theorizing about general kinds and abstract wholes. We cannot know *fraternity* unless we have experienced brothers or sisters, and the subcreative artist can *re-present* them to us if we have become somehow estranged. As Tolkien notes, "fairy-stories deal largely, (or the better ones) mainly, with simple or fundamental things, untouched by Fantasy, but these simplicities are made all the more luminous by their setting" ("OFS," 55).

Second, even those readers indisposed to recognize in the fairy-story setting the mystery of the familiar may find their wonder aroused precisely by those strange, unfamiliar creations of the author's imagination and speech, the "things *not* found in recorded time" or within the primary world as we know it. Over time, or even in an instant, this amazement may spill over or branch out to include the familiar. Persons may develop (or receive) a deeper and perhaps even habitual capacity for awe at the strange, largely unknown denizens of the world around them and thus come to perceive even very ordinary things in the primary world with extraordinary freshness and clarity (cf. "OFS," 52–53). This is what Tolkien seems to suggest when he writes, "[In fairy-story, we] should meet the centaur and the dragon, *and then perhaps* suddenly behold, like the ancient shepherds, sheep, and dogs, and horses—and wolves" ("OFS," 53, emphasis added). Likewise, through even a "taste" for fairy tales, we may find ourselves confronting human beings and citizens, friends and enemies, wrongdoers and those wronged, the letter of the law and its spirit, as if for the first time, with a deeper sense of all that we do not know about them and an intimation of why we should care about them. Thus the author's fantastic fairy stories may, even precisely *as fantastic,* assist us in recovering some preconditions for serious social science.

Finally and significantly, Tolkien stresses that recovery entails a renewed appreciation for the *otherness* of persons, beings, and practices. The wonder evoked by fairy tale can effect in us a sort of spring cleaning of the senses and the mind, helping

> to clean our windows; so that the things seen clearly may be freed from the drab blur of triteness or familiarity—from possessiveness. . . . This triteness is really the penalty of "appropriation": the things [and persons] that are trite, or (in a bad sense) familiar, are the things we have appropriated, legally or mentally. We say we know them. They have become like things which once attracted us by their glitter, or their colour, or their shape, and we laid hands on them, and then locked them in our hoard, acquired them, and acquiring ceased to look at them. ("OFS," 53–54)

It would seem that recovering our capacity to perceive *others* as such can help reawaken our sense of justice, as the virtue and the rule of actions that properly regard the otherness of persons and the things that are their due. If our gaze is fixed on the things and persons around us only insofar as they relate to ourselves, insofar as they are (or could be) *ours,* then we put ourselves at risk of glossing over justice or misinterpreting its requirements. Moreover, an awareness of "otherness" also properly undergirds our friendships: at the very least, it assists us in respecting the freedom of the friend, in fending off the excessive possessiveness that stifles relationships of justice and friendship alike. Even "another self" is not rightly reducible to myself, is not strictly speaking "mine" or "me."

The value for social and civic life and thought of this other-regarding dimension of literary recovery seems undeniable. Whether "the political good is justice" or whether the good of friendship is found to constitute an even higher "social and civic" aim,[26] the fantasy of faerie and the wonder at *otherness* it evokes can assist us in appreciating and investigating anew a key aim of politics. As Wilson Carey McWilliams has written of *The Lord of the Rings,* Tolkien's tales can assist "those citizens who would *recover* the habit of imagination, of moral clarity, and of political vision."[27] Fairy story likewise can help free us from an excessive (if natural) desire to acquire, to appropriate others "legally or mentally" to ourselves and our self-regarding passions and ambitions. In this way too Tolkien's fantasy can aid "humility" in representing to us the humanity proper to politics and political science (cf. "OFS," 53–54).

## Tolkien's *Hobbit* and a Fresh Perception of Justice and Friendship

Such are the aspects of Tolkien's theory of fairy story that seem most apropos of the study of politics. Yet one may well wonder whether Tolkien's account of the "recovery" that fairy story can bring about is not exaggerated. This section considers one literary test case for Tolkien's thesis: the fairy story that first put our author on the literary map, *The Hobbit, or, There and Back Again.*[28]

Tolkien indicates that *The Hobbit* presents to its readers an especially *human* and therefore for us a natural vision of the world and of persons, relationships, and events; in this it differs from *The Silmarillion*, where as it were divine, angelic, and especially "elvish" perspectives predominate, as well as from *The Lord of the Rings*, where the vantage point is midway between the elvish and the human, or rather a "blend[ing]" of the two.[29] Tolkien also stresses that his hobbits "are . . . really meant to be a branch of the specifically *human* race."[30] Since politics likewise comprises a fundamentally *human* art and science, reflecting and elucidating the ways we humans understand, evaluate, and craft our common lives together both in and among our polities, *The Hobbit* is especially apropos.

The adventure of that most respectable hobbit, Bilbo Baggins, began with "an unexpected party" in his most respectable hobbit-hole. Bilbo was an experienced, grown-up hobbit, about fifty years old but with a youthful attitude. He was fond of parties and guests, for he was comfortably well off and took pleasure in sharing his leisure and his goods with others. In this case, however, his hospitality and his provisions seemed unusually, and uncomfortably, out of his rightful control. Bilbo did not even know the thirteen dwarves who invaded his abode one afternoon, and their manners clearly did not measure up to Shire standards.[31] He did know Gandalf, the wizard who, unbeknownst to Bilbo, had invited the dwarves, and who moreover had recommended the hobbit to them as their companion on the long and dangerous journey they were about to undertake.

The purpose of the expedition was the recovery of stolen treasure and the exaction of vengeance on the robber, one Smaug the dragon, who had cruelly murdered many among their family and friends or (for the younger among the dwarves) their forebears and kinsmen and who had destroyed the dwarves' great polity, the Kingdom under the Mountain. In the same assault, Smaug had devastated the neighboring town of Dale, once a prosperous place inhabited by human beings. In short, the quest was about exacting and restoring justice, chiefly through the recovery of property.

Yet from the beginning, Tolkien tells this tale with an ironic and playful twist. Through the words and actions of various characters, the meaning and value of property, of the concept *one's own* and hence also of justice strictly speaking, are repeatedly called into question.[32] In recruiting Bilbo to help regain the dwarves' lost goods, for instance, Gandalf is rather free with Bilbo's own goods: not only with the hobbit's food and drink, but also with his home. To tip the dwarves off to the location of the correct hobbit-hole and to jolt the unwilling Baggins into opening it, the wizard first scratches and later dents "Bilbo's beautiful green front door" (30, 23). Gandalf thus seems curiously unconcerned about property, at least about what is due to Bilbo as proprietor. The wizard does express an interest in *profiting* the hobbit (19), although strangely enough in a conversation that repeatedly underscores the uncomfortably high chances of fatality entailed by the quest. Even the dwarves, desirous as they are of their lost treasure, tease Bilbo about his solicitousness for his household goods, composing this little ditty in his honor:

Clip the glasses and crack the plates!
Blunt the knives and bend the forks!
That's what Bilbo Baggins hates—
Smash the bottles and burn the corks! (25)

Whereas Bilbo's heart is especially in his household management, evincing perhaps the greater naturalness of his way of life, the dwarves' thoughts are focused on the beautiful artifacts their people had made and on the once magnificent halls of their former dwelling under the Mountain. Their affection is given to "the beautiful things made by [mainly their own] hands and by cunning and by magic . . . a fierce and jealous love, the desire of the hearts of dwarves." Their chief aim on this "errand" is "to claim our long forgotten gold" (27–28), even before, it seems, avenging their dead—whence the double irony that, at Gandalf's prodding, they employ the most respectable hobbit available on account of his excellent credentials at "*burglary*": why, when their "errand" is not theft but rather the *reclaiming* of stolen goods, and when the hobbit they hire has an impeccably clean record? To Bilbo's consternation at his new professional title, one of the dwarves replies: "You can say *Expert Treasure-hunter* instead of *Burglar* if you like. Some of them do. It's all the same to us. Gandalf told us that there was a man of the sort in these parts looking for a Job at once, and he had arranged for a meeting here this Wednesday tea-time" (31).

Against both his better judgment and his self-preservation instinct, Bilbo meets the dwarves the next morning as they set off, and in so doing he seals the contractual agreement whereby "Burglar Bilbo" promises to assist "Thorin and Company" (named for the leader of the expedition and heir to the former Kingdom under the Mountain) in their peculiar, risky, and apparently shifty business venture. If they succeed, one-fourteenth of all profits (however defined) will be his; if they fail, all his travel and/or funeral expenses will still be covered by the "Company." As they set off in search of the Lonely Mountain where Smaug now reigns from a heap of treasure, Bilbo leaves behind the goods and properties to which he is most attached, those material comforts his heart most desires and that land most possessed of his affections. He hopes of course to return to them, but for now he freely detaches himself from their secure enjoyment, albeit painfully and with difficulty, for the sake of an intangible adventure that he also, deep down, desires. The dwarves, by contrast, are moving ever closer to the properties they most wish to (re-)acquire, toward highly valued goods that are by right their own but not yet theirs to enjoy. This opposite interior movement along one and the same road may help explain the sharp disagreement concerning the right and the good that erupts between Bilbo and Thorin at their journey's end.

In principle at least, a friendship Aristotle would term "useful" has been formed between hobbit and dwarves.[33] Their common business venture involves goods that they desire but could not attain unaided. The Company burglar is first called into action as such early on, when the Company is cold and famished in a forest and three trolls are found enjoying their stolen fare around a fire. Bilbo's words and deeds in this affair raise further questions about what is *owed,* about justice in speech and in deed (45–53). Is Bilbo right to attempt burglary of trolls' (stolen) gold and provisions, and if so on what grounds? Ought he to tell them the truth or (as he later opts) to mislead them regarding his companions or purported lack thereof? It seems possible at any rate that extraordinary circumstances can sometimes alter what one would generally judge to be another's due, in speech as well as in deed, and that one owes it to one's friends not to compromise their safety unnecessarily. The fledgling friendship between hobbit and dwarves is on this occasion (and on many others that follow) tested and forged beyond the bounds of contract when, to succor his companions' needs, Bilbo risks his safety to burgle other than the specified stolen dragon-treasure, and again when the dwarves on their part nearly perish in an attempt to save the captured burglar from the trolls' cooking pot. Only with their mutual friend Gandalf's aid do they all (except the trolls) escape alive in the end.

As the "Company" continues its march and advances through dangers, the tale of their adventures and perils shows up more difficulties in ascertaining and achieving what is just. Some of these challenges again stem from the unusual circumstances surrounding the group's quest and its setting in faerie. In one key moment, for instance, Bilbo finds a ring deep beneath a mountain, where a gang of goblins has carried him and his companions. (This is in fact "the One Ring," as readers of *The Lord of the Rings* later come to know it.) Bilbo later learns that this ring "belongs" to a small slimy creature named Gollum, but since the latter evidently wishes to eat him and the ring proves magical and Bilbo's only hope of escape, he judges it necessary to keep it (but, significantly, *not* to use it to kill his unarmed would-be killer). In the course of their negotiations, the two engage in a high-stakes duel of riddles: if Bilbo wins, Gollum will escort him out of the mountain to light and safety; if Gollum wins, Bilbo becomes Gollum's next meal. At one point in the game, Bilbo, flustered and afraid, accidentally asks a question that is not properly a riddle. Gollum fails to answer it, and Bilbo holds the game won; but has he really won, on fair or just terms? Bilbo's benign intent compared with Gollum's murderous designs does seem to justify altering the venerable rules of engagement, especially so since Bilbo did not intend to cheat; yet one still senses that Bilbo is not entirely happy with his conduct on this occasion. He would much prefer that things be done by the book, or rather in accord with the revered rationality embedded in an ancient custom; but necessity compels him to accept a less respectable result—and to take advantage of it to flee for his life.

Out of the mountain at last, Bilbo is reunited with his friends, who once again have escaped with Gandalf's help. To attend to other "business" of his own, the wizard soon leaves them, on the edge of the dark and perilous forest called Mirkwood, which they must cross to reach the Lonely Mountain. While they are lost in the forest, the group's provisions fail. On the brink of starvation, they are captured by Wood-elves, all, that is, except Bilbo,

whose ring renders him invisible. Bilbo follows them to the elf-king's forti-
fied palace. Here the dwarves are treated decently by the elves, yet they are
imprisoned on account of the long mistrust between the two peoples. This
mistrust, we learn, had its roots in an ancient dispute about property and
about what was on one occasion due to whom. Elves interpret this event and
its causes in one way, while the dwarves have an alternative memory and
account. Neither view is verified in the story, but it seems likely that there is
something (if not an equal portion) of the truth about right, but not justice
entire, on each side.[34] The narrator does imply that in this instance the elves
may have been more at fault, because of their king's somewhat excessive
desire for gems and precious metal and for the honor a rich treasury would
bring him, a desire more difficult to fulfill given that the Wood-elves do not
mine or work metal and show no interest to learn. Moreover, the author
writes that the Wood-elves tended to suspect or mistrust *strangers.* As a result
of this unfriendly stance, the elves now misinterpret the starving "Thorin and
Company's" begging for harassment and even "crime" or assault. Knowing
the elf-king's liking for beautiful treasure (but not for doing the mining or
*working* with metals and gems to make it), Thorin judges it unwise to tell him
the whole truth about the quest that brought his Company to the forest. The
dwarves land in prison, where they are at least well fed, while the invisible
Bilbo is thrust back on a wearisome life of *burglaring* in the palace to keep
body and soul together and to prepare to rescue his friends (which in the
end of course he does). Differing and perhaps necessarily partial perceptions,
excessive desires to acquire, and long-standing unfriendly mistrust hinder
what is *due* from being ascertained and achieved throughout this episode.

The problematizing of property and, with it, of justice reaches its high
point at the story's climax. Thorin and Company reach the Lonely Mountain with the aid of Burglar Bilbo. They steal into a secret entrance in the
mountainside. Bilbo performs his famous function ably, managing first to
lift a golden cup from under the dragon's nose and later to engage Smaug in
clever conversation with the aim of discovering a weak spot in the dragon's
armor, which he in fact does. But the immensity of the treasure hoard and
Smaug's keen sense of smell quash any hopes of even an invisible hobbit's
burglaring back the whole. Their Company does not appear to include any
"warriors or heroes" capable of dragon-slaying, and Gandalf has not rejoined
them. Worst of all, during Bilbo's dialogue with the dragon, he momentarily
lets his wit and daring go to his head, naming himself (among other more
heroic epithets) "Barrel-rider" and thus revealing his recent association

with Lake-town, a settlement of human beings dwelling near the Lonely Mountain. Bilbo soon realizes his blunder and is humble enough to admit it to the dwarves. A friendly bird flies off to warn the town's inhabitants of their impending peril and to tell them of the unprotected spot in Smaug's jewel-crusted belly. At Lake-town Smaug meets his match in a warrior named Bard, but despite the dragon's demise, the town is destroyed and one-third of its people perish. The rest are left in cold, hunger, and sorrow. The Wood-elves come to the relief of Lake-town; and together men and elves in arms march to the Lonely Mountain, where the dwarves are presumed dead and the treasure available to compensate for so much unmerited harm. But instead they find Thorin and Company alive and well and reveling in *their own* recovered treasure.

Even before the arrival of Lake-men and Wood-elves announcing the dragon's death, Bilbo was concerned about the dwarves' covetousness and its likely consequences. A first foray into the treasure chamber had mesmerized his companions. They "cried out to one another, as they lifted old treasures from the mound or from the wall and held them in the light, caressing and fingering them. . . . They gathered gems and stuffed their pockets, and let what they could not carry fall back through their fingers with a sigh" (228). Bilbo also felt moved by the magnificence of it all and had in fact quietly pocketed the most precious gem of all, the Arkenstone. Yet the hobbit managed to gather his wits and in the end to escape the treasure's maddening spell. "Long before the dwarves were tired of examining the treasures, he became wary of it and sat down on the floor; and he began to wonder nervously what the end of it all would be." Bilbo reflected then that a warm and cheerful draught from a friend's wooden bowl would really be preferable to a whole pile of the hoard's jeweled goblets (228–29).

Maddened by the Lake-men's claims on his wealth and infuriated by the mere presence of his former jailers, Thorin sticks to his (far-outnumbered) guns and especially to his narrow vision of the right. As heir to the Kingdom under the Mountain, he still assumes that the treasure comprises only *his* just and rightful inheritance. Never mind that the very hospitality of the Lake-men to the dwarves in their need, coupled with the carelessness of the dwarves' contracted burglar, has led to a grievous injustice committed against the townspeople. Never mind that the Lake-man Bard has slain the dragon and so made the actual repossession of the dwarves' property possible. Never mind that the dragon's plunder under the mountain included goods stolen from the former men of Dale, from whose chieftain Bard had descended. Thorin might eventually come to honor the last claim, and he would certainly pay his Company's bills for their food and lodging in Lake-town, once the elves and armed men had gone away. Yet he remains unmoved even by pity at such great human suffering, caused (albeit unintentionally) to *others* by his *own* quest. His passionate yearning for his own is too exclusive and too powerful to allow him to open his eyes, freshly to perceive and so more broadly to understand just what under the circumstances is truly due to whom. "[The] lust of [gold] was heavy on him," and the desire for properties "about which were wound old memories of the labours and the sorrows of his own race" (250).

So Thorin remains stubborn and a bloody conflict threatens to break out. Some of the younger dwarves are grieved, wishing they could "welcome" the elves and men "as friends" (248); yet they do not presume to contradict Thorin. Only Bilbo is confident that Thorin's conduct is fundamentally unjust and unwise, likely to harm also the dwarves themselves in the end; he is miserable, yet finally he hatches a plot designed to prevent such unnecessary strife and bloodshed. His leverage comes once again from his burglary, specifically of the Arkenstone, which belonged to Thorin's grandfather and which the dwarf-king desires above all else. Bilbo initially reasoned, or rather *rationalized,* that his pocketing the gem was justified by Thorin's promise to let him choose his own fourteenth-share of the treasure; but Bilbo's conscience still bothered him. He might well have returned it earlier but for fear of Thorin's rage. Now, however, the situation has become so extreme that Bilbo's courage is roused, and he decides to deliver the Arkenstone over to the other side for them to barter with. He does this not to betray his friends but to save them, King Thorin included, from Midas's curse and from committing injustice against others. The exact attribution of property in the Arkenstone is no longer of prime importance; at this moment, moreover, it is difficult even to determine to whom it really belongs.

> Bilbo, not without a shudder, not without a glance of longing, handed the marvelous stone to Bard, and he held it in his hand, as though dazed.
>
> "But how is it yours to give?" he asked at last with an effort.
>
> "O well!" said the hobbit uncomfortably. "It isn't exactly; but, well, I am willing to let it stand against my claim, don't you know. I may be a burglar—or so they say; personally I never really felt like one—but I am an honest one, I hope, more or less. Anyway I

am going back now, and the dwarves can do what they like to me. I hope you will find it useful. . . . I don't think I ought to leave my friends like this [by remaining safely with the elves and men], after all we have gone through together." (257–58)

Gandalf is in the camp disguised as an old man and overhears all this; he warmly approves of Bilbo's deed. Thorin, however, is enraged and rejects Bilbo utterly as a traitor: "Take him, if you wish him to live; and no friendship of mine goes with him" (262). Yet after a surprise assault by a powerful common enemy at last unites dwarves, elves, and humans in a common cause, Thorin and Bilbo finally do part in friendship and a more just, indeed generous distribution of goods is achieved at Thorin's own behest. Thorin has fought bravely in the common defense and been grievously wounded. He lies dying under the Lonely Mountain and takes his leave of the rehabilitated Company Burglar:

"Farewell, good thief," [Thorin] said [to Burglar Bilbo]. . . . "I go now to the halls of waiting to sit beside my fathers, until the world is renewed. Since I leave now all gold and silver, and go to where it is of little worth, I wish to part in friendship from you, and I would take back my words and deeds at the Gate. . . . There is more in you of good than you know. . . . Some courage and some wisdom, blended in measure. If more of us valued food and cheer and song above hoarded gold, it would be a merrier world. But sad or merry, I must leave it now. Farewell!" (272–73)

Bilbo in turn takes his leave of Thorin, thanking him for the undeserved privilege of sharing in his perils, for which the hobbit is grateful. Then Bilbo weeps long and bitterly for Thorin's death, confirming what the reader has increasingly noticed as the story has progressed: that the hobbit rather easily has come to care more for his companions for their own sakes than for the adventure they shared with him and that facilitated their friendship, and much more than for the reward they had contracted to pay him. Bilbo's ability at the story's outset to distance himself from his property and to share his possessions through hospitality, even with uninvited guests at "an unexpected party," foreshadows both his openness to new insights concerning justice and, especially, his affinity to form fuller friendships. Bilbo easily transcends the useful, chiefly instrumental friendship their business contract began, and the attitude of deeper *friendliness* that he cultivates opens for him a fuller perspective on justice than mere compact or strict legal due could afford.

Throughout the journey Bilbo has likewise come to realize more and more his dependence for a meaningful life on society with particularly close friends, even as he matures and becomes more confident of his own abilities. Midway through the quest, Bilbo finds himself for the first time lost and alone in the forest. He kills an attacking giant spider with his small sword and feels "much fiercer and bolder" than ever before. Yet his first thought after the victory is for his missing friends and how to find them. He muses, "What a mess we are in now! We! I only wish it was *we:* it is horrible being all alone" (154, emphasis in original). Later on, while the dwarves are locked in the Wood-elves' jail cells, Bilbo sometimes uses his invisible ring to slip out of the palace gates and explore the forest. But this is risky business, wandering alone in the woods, incapable of hunting and uncertain of finding and reentering the hidden palace. So "when [Bilbo] did go out, which was not very often, he did no good. He did not wish to desert the dwarves, and indeed he did not know where in the world to go without them" (169). And when he organizes their escape with the help of his new ring, it is a fully common venture: "We must all keep together and not risk getting separated. All of us must escape or none" (174).

Gollum, by contrast, the previous owner of the ring as we encounter him in *The Hobbit,* has chosen or at least resigned himself to a solitary life. There has long been for him no meaningful "other," neither a friend with whom to converse or share things that are good, nor even simply an individual apart from himself to whom to render what is her or his due. Even Gollum cannot live completely without conversation, so he objectifies himself and converses with that imaginary or pseudo-other, his pseudo-friend, "my precious." Genuine others like Bilbo are reduced to mere curiosities or even to foodstuffs. Outside of himself, only a useful, inanimate object has value for Gollum: the ring, perceived and desired as a purely private good, also personified and referred to as "my precious [present]."[35] He is anxious to *appear* friendly to Bilbo for a time, but not to make a friend nor even to persevere in external affability longer than suits him.[36] Thorin, in an analogous though much less extreme manner, has only a reduced group of friends, or kinsmen, with whom he is willing to share *his* treasure; and he is for a while so focused on that external good that he cannot properly perceive even those select friends as *others,* as persons existing apart from himself and his desire. He thus cannot clearly conceive *their* good nor determine what is really *their* due. The pathos comes full circle in that as a consequence Thorin cannot judge rightly what is *his own,* until misfortune strikes hard and he at last lets his eyes be opened. Whether the wretched and now ringless Gollum can experience a similar conversion facilitated by or leading to a fresh vision of persons and things, of friendship and justice, remains at *The Hobbit*'s end an unanswered riddle. It seems highly unlikely, but perhaps it is not yet impossible.

The story of *The Hobbit* ends where it began, in Bilbo's beloved home in the Shire and with Bilbo's property in jeopardy. After only a year away, Bilbo returns to find that he is presumed dead. His house is again full of uninvited guests, and this time his belongings are being auctioned off. Many people actually seem disappointed to find him alive, reluctant as they are to return their fine new acquisitions. Bilbo finally has to buy back some of his own furniture. In the end his household goods are mostly recovered, but not his formerly good name: his reputation for respectability has gone the way of most burglars'. He is held in high esteem among his *young* nieces and nephews on the (also somewhat suspect) Took side of his family, "but even they were not encouraged in their friendship by their elders" (285). Bilbo seems untroubled by this unjust loss of repute; he takes up poetry writing and often returns to visit the elves.

Years later his old friends Gandalf and Balin[37] come to visit Bilbo, bringing him encouraging news of peace and prosperity in the lands around the Lonely Mountain. Wealth abounds, the land is again green and fertile, government among humans is improved with Bard at its helm, and commerce bustles up and down the Running River. Significantly, the narrator stresses not that justice entire finally reigns in those lands, but rather that friendly relations have been restored and strengthened among their peoples. Such is *The Hobbit*'s formula for a social and civic "happily ever after" (qualified by an appropriately realistic disclaimer that "it *seemed* [things] were going very well" there): "and *there was friendship in those parts* between elves and dwarves and men."[38]

## Tolkienian Recovery in Modern Liberal Democracy

The "imagined wonder" of Tolkien's *Hobbit* thus can aid us in recovering a fresh awareness of the strangeness of ownership; of the difficulty of discerning what is strictly right or just, and the need for both knowledge and, perhaps especially, friendliness or benevolence if we are even to approximate what is due in more complex situations;[39] and of the importance as well as the fragility and limitations of friendship in social and civic relationships. In these regards, the recovery of a clearer (and, paradoxically, *more problematic*) perception prompted by Tolkien's tale seems especially apropos for us denizens of modern liberal democracy. We can tend to view our world through a predictable prism of privacy and rights-claims and individualistic outlooks, that is, through a glass clouded by anxious desires to acquire and to succeed. If we allow this fairy story to open our eyes to a broader view of our own humanity and its neediness, foibles, and aspirations, it can, as Alexis de Tocqueville wrote of classical Greek and Latin literature in the modern democratic era, help "prop us up on the side where we lean."[40] And by shaking some of our "settled convictions" about the just and the beneficial, this "child's tale" can help clear the way for adults to engage afresh in philosophical and social-scientific inquiry.

Tocqueville considers classical Greek and Latin literature to be essentially aristocratic in spirit and thus an excellent counterweight to democratic tendencies in the arts. The former is all attention to detail, beauty, refinement, and idealism; the latter seeks ease, excitement, novelty, and naturalism. There are virtues in each approach, but if isolated and allowed to follow its natural bents, each "literary spirit" has its peculiar pitfalls. The aristocratic ethos can end in an esoteric incommunicability of artificial, even petty and sterile formalism; the democratic spirit can swing toward the hastily written, the reductive, and the bizarre.[41] Tocqueville likewise contrasts the tendency of aristocratic historians to focus on the roles of individual persons in shaping the course of events, on the one hand, with the common bent of democratic history to gloss over human agency and responsibility and identify the causes of particular events in mass movements, material processes, and sweeping social currents, on the other hand. Once again, either of these approaches in isolation is likely to obscure the full truth of things.[42] In literature at least (and one can extend the analogy to history), Tocqueville indicates the possibility of periods governed by a sort of mixed regime, contested, perhaps short-lived, yet flourishing, when "as the literary genus of democratic nations meets that of aristocracies, both seem to want to reign in accord over the human mind. Those are passing, but very brilliant periods."[43]

Tolkien's tales seem to reflect just such a meeting of aristocratic and democratic spirits, as works by a poet and storyteller with a love for the particular and a keen sense of history (he at least once described his "subcreation" as more properly of an imaginary historical period than of an imaginary world). Tolkien's stories are painstakingly crafted by a lover of language who has read widely in ancient and medieval texts, including Norse, Latin, and Greek, and who has an appreciation for tradition, custom, and literary form. Yet at the same time, Tolkien's theory of art as subcreation leads him to provide the novelty and unpredictability, the freedom from established forms, that democratic cultures often crave. Tolkien's view of the quest genre as an excellent vehicle for subcreation through story lends itself to adventurous tales full of variety and action, both favorites of democratic audiences.

With regard to the historical dimension, Tolkien's quests are set in specific (if imaginary) periods—in the case of *The Hobbit* and especially *The Lord of the Rings*, at the close of one era and the birth of another. As Tocqueville maintains of the transition from aristocratic to democratic era in the primary world, so too in Tolkien's imaginary epic there are forces at work that individual agents cannot control and which they would try to master or reverse at their own peril. There is a keen and even sorrowful sense in Tolkien's tales of all that is slipping away in the sands of time, together with a moderate hopefulness toward the future and what might yet be achieved. And, perhaps most importantly, there is in "middle-earth" a sphere of causality that is properly each character's own, comprising personal tasks, decisions, and responsibilities, upon which (under and aided by Providence)[44] the fate of others also depends. In their subcreated wonder, Tolkien's tales re-present to modern readers the rightful priority of humanity over the narrower needs of a particular polity and likewise the priority of the personal over the artificial and mechanical. Indeed, his disdain for the chauvinism that often underlies moments of purportedly universalist expansion, as well as his deep concern for the tendency of mass society and technological rationalism to obfuscate the primordial dimension of the personal, free, and responsible, underlies Tolkien's sometimes deprecatory comments about "modern" politics, or "mere" politics.[45] "If we could get back to personal names [in speaking about politics]," writes Tolkien to his son Christopher, "it would do a lot of good."[46]

Both Tolkien and Tocqueville perceive humanity in terms of its potencies for greatness and for misery; moreover, both share in a fiery passion for human greatness.[47] What most distinguishes their visions is perhaps this: while the social scientist Tocqueville is more level-headedly amenable to democratic social states and institutions, the poet Tolkien can love, delight in, and marvel at the concrete, ordinary, provincial, and even petty human *person* in a way that Tocqueville apparently cannot. Tolkien's "hero is a hobbit,"[48] which is to say, one of us: small, "unimaginative," and comfort-loving, yet possessed of a "pretty wonderful" intellect (even the dullest of us), and capable of surprising courage and heroism in a pinch. "This last great Tale [comprising both *The Hobbit* and *The Lord of the Rings*] is seen mainly through the eyes of Hobbits: it thus becomes anthropocentric. But through Hobbits, not Men so-called . . . to exemplify a recurring theme: the place in 'world-politics' of the unforeseen and unforeseeable acts of will, and deeds of virtue of the apparently small, ungreat, forgotten in the places of the Wise and Great (good as well as evil)."[49]

## Notes

1. W. H. Auden, "The Hero Is a Hobbit," *New York Times Review of Books*, October 31, 1954.

2. Cf. Aristotle, *Nicomachean Ethics*, trans. Martin Ostwald (New York: Macmillan, 1962), 1155a22–32; and James V. Schall, "Friendship and Political Philosophy," *Review of Metaphysics* 50 (1996): 121–41.

3. J. R. R. Tolkien, "On Fairy-Stories," in *Tree and Leaf*, 2nd ed. (London: Unwin Hyman, 1988), 21; see also J. R. R. Tolkien, *The Letters of J.R.R. Tolkien*, ed. Humphrey Carpenter and Christopher Tolkien (Boston: Houghton Mifflin, 1981), no. 153, p. 188.

4. Tolkien also terms this genre "myth," and in a derivative sense, after the first of its specific functions, "fantasy." "On Fairy-Stories" is an essay that grew out of Tolkien's 1939 Andrew Lang Lecture at the University of St. Andrews and was first published in a 1947 collection of essays in honor of Charles Williams. See Tolkien, *Tree and Leaf*, preface, 5–6. It postdates *The Hobbit* and predates the completion of *The Lord of the Rings*, although it is contemporary with the writing of the latter. For a sense of Tolkien's assessment of the importance of "On Fairy-Stories," see Tolkien, *Letters*, inter alia nos. 89, pp. 100–101; 159, p. 209; and 163, p. 216.

5. See, for instance, the entry in *The New Lexicon Webster's Dictionary of the English Language* (New York: Lexicon, 1988), 338: "fairy tale: a story for children about fairies, or about magic and enchantment; a very improbable story; a lie."

6. Aristotle, *Nicomachean Ethics* 1094b28–1095a14; cf. 1179b4–35.

7. Plato, *The Republic*, trans. Allan Bloom (New York: Basic Books, 1991), 368a.

8. For more on this point, see Tolkien, "On Fairy-Stories," 36–37, hereafter "OFS," cited parenthetically in the text.

9. See Tolkien, *Letters*, nos. 52, 131, 132, 183.

10. We will return briefly to Tolkien's apparently antipolitical stance in the concluding part of the chapter. If we consider Tolkien's craft as he himself understood it, none of these apparently strong arguments carry the debate. See, for example, also Tolkien's poem "Mythopoeia" (in *Tree and Leaf*, 97–101), written in response to his

Oxford colleague C. S. Lewis's contention that "myths [and fairy stories] were lies and therefore worthless, even though 'breathed through silver'" (97; cf. "OFS," 50–51). For an interpretation of Tolkien's politics largely in the function of the literary aim of "escape," as a response to "political despair" evoked by the two world wars, see Lee D. Rossi, *The Politics of Fantasy: C.S. Lewis and J.R.R. Tolkien* (Ann Arbor: UMI Research Press, 1984), quoted phrases on 1.

11. Philip Norman, "The Prevalence of Hobbits," an interview with J. R. R. Tolkien, *Sunday Times,* January 15, 1967 (emphasis added).

12. Ibid.

13. He readily admits, however, that literary powers, like social and political powers, can be so misused. Cf. "OFS," 51–52.

14. Compare Aristotle, *The Politics,* trans. Carnes Lord (Chicago: University of Chicago Press, 1984), 1.2, with Tolkien's comments: "To ask what is the origin of stories (however qualified) is to ask what is the origin of language and of the mind" ("OFS," 20); "The incarnate mind, the tongue, and the tale are in our world coeval" ("OFS," 24); "To an inventor, that is to a storymaker, [other investigations regarding the origins of fairy-stories] must in the end lead back" ("OFS," 23).

15. Compare Thomas Aquinas, *Summa Theologiae,* trans. Fathers of the English Dominican Province (Allen, TX: Christian Classics, 1981), I–II, 61, 5; 72, 4; and 94, 2; with Tolkien, *Letters,* no. 109, p. 122: "a solitary art is no art."

16. Aquinas, *Summa Theologiae* I–II, 94, 2.

17. "OFS," 50–52; cf. 64–66. Tolkien originally expressed this idea in verse, in a stanza of "Mythopoeia" that closes with these lines:

Though all the crannies of the world we filled
with elves and goblins, though we dared to build
gods and their houses out of dark and light
and sow the seed of dragons, *'twas our right*
*(used or misused). The right has not decayed.*
*We make still by the law in which we're made.*
(Tolkien, *Tree and Leaf,* 98–99 [emphasis added])

18. Tolkien, *Tree and Leaf,* 99.

19. Aristotle observes this in his *Politics* 1262b20–24.

20. Tolkien, *Letters,* no. 89, pp. 100–101; cf. no. 154, p. 197, where the *elves'* anti-historical stance is contrasted and criticized.

21. Cf. "OFS," 39; and Tolkien, "Mythopoeia," 100.

22. Cf. "OFS," 52, with Aquinas, *Summa Theologiae* I, 16.

23. Cf. Aristotle's famous dictum opening the *Metaphysics,* that "all men by nature desire to know," and the continuation emphasizing the goodness of the senses, especially of sight or vision, "which makes us know and brings to light many differences between things" (980a). As we shall see, Tolkien counts a clearer, fresher perception of the *otherness* of beings as one of the chief benefits we can derive from fairy story. Aristotle,

*Metaphysics,* in *The Complete Works of Aristotle,* ed. Jonathan Barnes (Princeton, NJ: Princeton University Press, 1984).

24. Cf. Aristotle, *Politics* 1253a14–19.

25. See especially "OFS," 52–55.

26. Cf. Aristotle, *Politics* 1282b16–17, with *Nicomachean Ethics* 1155a22–28.

27. As quoted in Richard C. West, ed., *Tolkien Criticism: An Annotated Checklist* (Kent, OH: Kent State University Press, 1970), 25 (emphasis added).

28. References to *The Hobbit* are from J. R. R. Tolkien, *The Hobbit, or, There and Back Again,* rev. ed. (New York: Ballantine Books, 1966), and will be mostly in the form of parenthetical page numbers in the text and the notes. For a recent study exploring "*The Politics of Departure and Return*" through the lens of Homer's *Odyssey,* thus elucidating the import of the "*There and Back Again*" of *The Hobbit's* full title, see Patrick Deneen, *The Odyssey of Political Theory: The Politics of Departure and Return* (Lanham, MD: Rowman and Littlefield, 2000). On Homer's impact on the young Tolkien, see Tolkien, *Letters,* 172; on some Homeric aspects of Tolkien's tales, see *Letters,* 154, 159, and 201.

29. See Tolkien, *Letters,* 145. Also see Tolkien's *Letters,* no. 131, p. 145, highlighting the *humanity* and down-to-earth nature of *The Hobbit,* and the *Sunday Times* interview, emphasizing the *naturalness* of a hobbit's-eye view of the world. In *The Hobbit* itself, the author stresses the ordinariness of hobbits: "There is little or no magic about them, except the ordinary everyday sort" (16).

30. Tolkien, *Letters,* 158, second note at bottom of page.

31. The Shire is the land where most Hobbits dwell. Tolkien (significantly, as will become apparent in the conclusion of the chapter) specifies that its government is a form of "mixed regime: half republic, half aristocracy." *Letters,* no. 183, p. 241.

32. The reader who has studied political philosophy will note many parallels between *The Hobbit's* narrative and the dialogue of Plato's *Republic,* especially books 1 and 2 in their examination of property, justice, and friendship. Tolkien's theory of fairy story seems, appropriately enough, more Aristotelian, while his actual stories in their plots appear more Platonic in inspiration. This chapter focuses on how reading Tolkien's tales can benefit students of political thought, but one could reverse the inquiry and explore in greater detail how Tolkien has been influenced as a writer by reading political philosophy and theology. For discussions of Platonic influences on Tolkien, see John Cox, "Tolkien's Platonic Fantasy," *Seven* 5 (1984): 53–69; and Mary Carmen Rose, "The Christian Platonism of C.S. Lewis, J.R.R. Tolkien, and Charles Williams," in *Neoplatonism and Christian Thought,* ed. Dominic O'Meara (Albany: State University of New York Press, 1982).

33. See Aristotle, *Nicomachean Ethics* 1155b1–1157b4.

34. Cf. Aristotle, *Politics* 1280a6–22. The dispute is not resolved even in J. R. R. Tolkien, *The Fellowship of the Ring,* vol. 1 of *The Lord of the Rings,* 3 vols. (New York: Houghton Mifflin, 1954), 295, when this ancient falling-out between the two peoples is recalled among the Fellowship and the dwarf Gimli and the elf Legolas dispute where

the "fault" lies. Their growing friendship seems rather to replace the elusive answer concerning absolute right or strict justice.

35. The inability to perceive others as they are and to care for them for their own sakes is one of the chief forms of harm that the One Ring works over time on its possessor. For one illustration in *The Lord of the Rings,* see the telling description of heir-to-the-Ring Frodo's misperception of Bilbo on account of the Ring: "To his distress and amazement he found that he was no longer looking at Bilbo; a shadow seemed to have fallen between them . . . [and] he felt a desire to strike him." Tolkien, *Fellowship of the Ring,* 225–26.

36. On Tolkien's alteration of Gollum's character for *The Hobbit*'s second edition, see Bonniejean Christensen, "Gollum's Character Transformation in *The Hobbit,*" in *A Tolkien Compass,* ed. Jared Lobdell, 2nd ed. (Chicago: Open Court Press, 2003), 7–26.

37. Balin is the dwarf who developed the strongest affection for Bilbo for the hobbit's own sake; cf. Tolkien, *The Hobbit,* 194, 203–4, 218, with 96–98.

38. Ibid., 286. In *The Lord of the Rings,* friendship also appears as the chief sign and constituent element of the public welfare, among as well as within peoples and their polities. To give just one illustration, in a critical moment the Fellowship discovers that the password into Moria, the ancient and greatest city of the *dwarves,* was the *elvish* word for *friend;* the instructions carved into the secret entranceway are simply "speak, friend, and enter," or rather "say 'friend' and enter." The simplicity of the code, the relative ease of "border-crossing," and the content of the password all bespeak "happier days, when there was still close friendship at times between folk of different race, even between Dwarves and Elves." See Tolkien, *The Fellowship of the Ring,* 295–300.

39. Hence Tolkien, a Christian, concurs with poet Gerard Manley Hopkins's considered judgment that "the only just literary critic is Christ, who admires more than any man the gifts He Himself has bestowed." See the revealing epistolary exchange between Hopkins and Richard Watson Dixon as recounted by Tolkien in a letter to C. S. Lewis. Tolkien, *Letters,* no. 113, pp. 127–28; cf. also Augustine's *City of God against the Pagans,* trans. and ed. R. W. Dyson (Cambridge: Cambridge University Press, 1998), 19.18–19 and 21.

40. Tocqueville sees this "propping" afforded us by Greek and Latin literature to be a purely literary benefit, training modern democrats to be writers and readers sensitive to detail and to beauty and to forms, but *not* assisting in their social and civic education. Their aristocratic spirit is, on this account, too radically opposed to our democracies' needs. If this is indeed Tocqueville's final word on the matter, it seems an excessively reductive assessment of the classics' value. Compare Alexis de Tocqueville, *Democracy in America,* ed. and trans. Harvey C. Mansfield and Delba Winthrop (Chicago: University of Chicago Press, 2000), 452, with 482–84, 506–9, 511–14.

41. Ibid., 445–50.

42. Ibid., 469–72.

43. Ibid., 448–49.

44. See Kathleen Dubs, "Providence, Fate, and Chance: Boethian Philosophy in *The Lord of the Rings*," *Twentieth Century Literature* 27, no. 1 (1981): 34–42. See also Helen Theresa Lasseter, "Fate, Providence, and Free Will: Clashing Perspectives of World Order in J. R. R. Tolkien's Middle-Earth" (PhD diss., Baylor University, 2006).

45. Tolkien in these respects anticipates fellow poet Václav Havel's call for an "antipolitical politics" premised on a recovery of personal conscience and responsibility, transcending the anonymity of bureaucracy, striving to cultivate courage and humility in the service of country and humanity. Cf. Havel, "Politics and Conscience," in *Open Letters: Selected Writings, 1964–1990* (New York: Knopf, 1991), 269.

46. Tolkien, *Letters*, no. 52, pp. 63–64; see also no. 53, pp. 65–66.

47. In Tolkien's case, it is greatness when tempered by humility: cf. *Letters*, no. 5, pp. 9–10, and no. 52, with Tocqueville, *Democracy in America*, editor's introduction, xxxii–iii.

48. See Auden, "Hero Is a Hobbit."

49. Norman, "Prevalence of Hobbits." See also Tolkien, *Letters*, no. 131, pp. 158–59 and notes; no. 131, p. 160.

# 13

# "JUST GIVE THEM THE INTERNET"

## Social Media and the Promise of Liberal Democracy

*Joseph J. Foy*

On June 6, 2010, Khaled Mohamed Said was sitting at a table on the second floor of a cybercafé in Sidi Gaber, a neighborhood in Alexandria, Egypt. Two detectives from the local police station entered the café to arrest Said. After binding his hands behind his back, one of the detectives smashed Said's face on the edge of a marble tabletop. The officers then dragged his body out of the café and into an entranceway of another establishment across the street. There the men beat him, repeatedly striking his head against the iron doorway, the walls, and the stairs. They allegedly continued beating him long after his body was lifeless.[1]

When Khaled Said's family was allowed access to the morgue to view his body, his brother discreetly took photos of the beaten, disfigured corpse of the nearly unrecognizable twenty-eight-year-old. He then e-mailed the photos out, and they soon went viral on the Internet. Among the recipients of the gruesome images was Internet activist Wael Ghonim. In response, Ghonim and four others created and administered the Facebook page "We Are All Khaled Said." They used the page to post images of Said, condemn the brutality of the dictatorial regime of Hosni Mubarak, and organize the January 25, 2011, event "The Day of the Revolution against Torture, Poverty, Corruption, and Unemployment." The instructions were for people wishing to engage in the protest to wear all black and stand five feet apart (so as to comply with Egyptian laws against public demonstrations) while making no noise and carrying no signs. More than eighty thousand people clicked "yes" to the event, indicating their plan to participate, and eighteen days later, Mubarak, who had assumed control of Egypt in 1981, resigned his position as president.[2]

Internet technology has been rapidly revolutionizing the way information is both communicated and consumed and has given rise to what is known as "social media": Web- and mobile-based forms of interactive communication that allow users to generate and share electronic content through a variety of applications. Social networking sites such as Facebook, Ning, and Google+, as well as microblogging applications such as Twitter and Qiaku, allow individuals to connect with other users all over the world. People can engage in interactive discourse and information sharing, which leads to the creation of alternative communities and an electronic form of civil society.

The popularity of social media has spawned much discussion and speculation as to whether such technologies substantively and meaningfully alter the meaning of community and human relationships. In the realm of politics, much of the public attention has been directed to the possibility of social networking as a means of mass mobilization and as a tool of democracy, with analyses of national (2008 American presidential elections), international (the revolutionary activities taking place in countries from Iran to Egypt), and local (the mobilization of political protests in Madison, Wisconsin) events at the forefront of public scrutiny and popular punditry. And while such empirical case studies are vital for exploring in greater depth, from a theoretical perspective there is an even greater, global transformation that is occurring in both democratic and nondemocratic societies. Put simply, the Internet and social media are transforming the public sphere in a way that fulfills the long-standing promises of liberal democracy.

## Liberal Democracy in Form and Practice

A first step toward fully appreciating the role that Internet technologies and social media play in helping to secure the full potential of liberal democracy is to establish and understand the framework for such a system.

Democracy is an essentially contested concept, with many different understandings, conceptions, and applications, which lack universal agreement. For instance, in the classical, Athenian (508–322 BCE) sense, democracy was a system wherein the common people (*demos*) popularly shared in political rule or power (*kratos*). In that system citizens directly participated in collective deliberation and decision making, selecting governmental positions in the city-state through the process of lottery (citizenship was limited to adult males who had completed military training, thus excluding a majority of the population). By contrast, in the Roman tradition (509–527 BCE), democracy was defined in a republican sense; citizens were represented by elected officials, and political authority was divided in different governmental institutions through a defined separation of powers. Both systems, though procedurally quite different, are considered democratic because the public had a role in making or directly influencing political decisions that were binding on the community at large. As Pericles noted in his famous funeral oration eulogizing the Athenians, who were among the first to fall in the Peloponnesian War (431–404 BCE), "[Athens's] administration favors the many instead of the few; this is why it is called a democracy."[3]

During the Enlightenment period of the eighteenth century in the West, liberal-democratic theorists such as John Locke (1632–1704) conceived of democracy as resulting from a system of natural rights that empowers the individual by placing limitations on governments, constraining them to the "will" of the people, the "consent of the governed." Baron de Montesquieu (1689–1755) later expanded Lockean notions of division of power, so as to separate administrative functions of government through the establishment of legislative, executive, and judicial bodies and imposing further limitations on government. These early forms have become known as systems of "classical liberalism," emphasizing the right of the individual to be free from the coercive influences of the state. More contemporary political theorists and activists have begun incorporating economic rights into their conceptions of democracy. The modern liberal thinker John Rawls (1921–2002), for example, articulates the necessity of social programs to ensure meaningful participation, choice, and quality of life in a democratic society; his is a form known as "egalitarian liberalism" or "welfare state liberalism."

No matter which form a liberal democracy takes, the modern liberal consensus is that democracy requires the guarantee of certain rights and freedoms in order to sustain it in a meaningful sense. Along these lines, democratic theorist Robert Dahl established procedural criteria for what he calls "polyarchy," a modern, working democracy. Dahl states that seven features are necessary to qualify a system as democratic: control over governmental decisions about policy must be constitutionally vested in elected officials; elected officials must be peacefully selected and removed through the process of frequent, fair elections; there must be nearly universal adult suffrage; most adult citizens should have the right to run for elected office; citizens must retain the right of free expression and criticism; there needs to be access to alternative forms of information, such that the flow of information is not monopolistically controlled by government or another entity; and people must be given the right of association and participation.[4] If a system falls significantly short on any one of these dimensions, it fails to meet the necessary requirements to be considered within the rubric of democracy.[5] Thus, although democracies may take a variety of forms and incorporate different procedural and institutional mechanisms for political activities, all must provide a framework for citizen participation and public control of political authority.

Along with the institutional and procedural requirements for a liberal democracy, there is a growing recognition of the importance of democratic culture, to produce significant progress toward popular sovereignty. Ronald Inglehart, a professor of comparative political development, has famously argued that cultural patterns, once they are established, have a significant impact on political and economic decision making.[6] Recognizing the role of institutional liberalization in advancing cultural change, Inglehart does not dismiss the interplay institutions have in the shaping of culture through processes of socialization. However, central to his argument about substantive democracy is the recognition that if democracy is to exist in a meaningful sense, there must be a democratization of the mass public and culture, not just the liberalization of political institutions.

But what of those societies that have become culturally habituated to illiberal, undemocratic activities? Are they doomed to remain suppressed by the tyrannical abuses of power because circumstances have not allowed for the development of more open political institutions? When and if such institutions are liberalized, do the lack of a democratic experience and the societies' underdeveloped democratic culture threaten the consolidation of democracy? As American pragmatist philosopher and liberal theorist John Dewey once noted, "Full freedom of the human spirit and of individuality can be achieved only as there is effective opportunity to share in the cultural resources of civilization."[7] It is here that the Internet and the expansion of social media play a critical part.

## Liberal Democracy's Fourth Revolution

The history of liberal democracy to date might be summed up in three distinct movements: the rejection of political centralization, the rejection of economic control, and the rejection of social hierarchy. Each of these movements has attempted to expand the notion of freedom and participation in a meaningful sense, thereby democratizing institutions of public authority and broadening notions of liberty.

Arguably the first wave of liberal democracy occurred in the seventeenth and eighteenth centuries in the struggle against the unchecked power of oligarchic rule. England's Glorious Revolution in 1688 is but one example. The overthrow of King James II and the subsequent drafting of the English Bill of Rights imposed limits on the previously absolutist power of monarchy, establishing the foundations of modern democracy. The first wave, therefore, rejected the concentration of political power in the hands of the one or the few and formulated a theory of liberty as freedom from tyrannical authority through the development of constitutional limitations on the power of the state.

The eighteenth and nineteenth centuries saw the second wave of liberalization, which corresponded with the economic and social transformation resulting from the Industrial Revolution. Workers' movements began challenging the authority of the corporation through the formation of trade unions and demands for political recognition and the power of collective bargaining. New institutional arrangements that worked to advance liberty for laboring classes through the regulation of industrial practices and the establishment of social welfare expanded the principles of liberalism from strictly political to economic matters as well. And as an outgrowth of such a rejection of economic control, the third liberal wave arose in the form of mass movements that began in the nineteenth and twentieth centuries, rejecting principles of social hierarchy. Numerous civil rights movements sought to empower gender, racial, and ethnic minorities through the institutional expansion of the right of suffrage and of franchise.

Each liberal movement in history responded to changing social and economic conditions, altering the fundamental understanding of what is meant by freedom and equality. However, each of the movements focused on institutional reforms concentrated within the traditional realm of the public sphere, an arena in which matters of significance are discussed and outcomes are determined by the quality of argument. The first wave provided limitations on the power of the state, the second wave on the economic power of industry, and the third on eugenic principles of social hierarchy. The expanded principles of liberty in each case empowered individuals through greater inclusion into public deliberation and participation, democratizing institutions to advance evolving notions of liberty.

What we are now witnessing is a fourth wave of liberal revolution, culminating in the rejection of cultural control. In the late twentieth century, the rapid rise of Internet technology exploded the canon of identity, community, and what counted as the public sphere. This fourth wave is, in essence, a democratization of the public. Rather than pushing for de jure forms of institutional liberalization and the systemic opening of society, social media provide a framework for mass communication and interactive media that undercuts the cultural monopolies and levels hierarchical models of information distribution. Social media eliminate the long-standing barriers between citizen and journalist, private citizen and public activist; they offer the possibility for pluralistic contributions to public dialogue and debate regardless of a person's status or position. The political rights that give each individual the same input in political decisions as the next person regardless of background or status are thereby extended to all realms of social and cultural activities. To some, the elimination of these commercial, economic, political, intellectual, and cultural hierarchies is a source of great dismay and skepticism. However, within liberalism there has always been a fundamental tension between freedom and equality.

In addition to the transformative effect of Web-based access to information and expression and social media applications on institutions of culture in liberal societies, these technologies have a profound impact on cultural systems within closed societies. In those countries where open participation is suppressed and communication and information rigidly controlled by the state, there is a lack of opportunity for individuals to become acculturated with principles of diversity, tolerance, and collective action in the advancement of publicly defined goals. The existence of Internet technology has allowed for the development of what might be considered "parallel societies," ones in which groups willfully segment themselves from the dominant political paradigm in order to carve out a space for autonomous (or at least semiautonomous) social, cultural, and individual pursuits not otherwise tolerated. Social media provide for more pluralistic contributions to public dialogue and debate by not only fostering the development of alternative publics but allowing access to, and interaction within, those publics in ways not previously possible. For these reasons, social media are helping to carve out new frontiers of democratic participation and engagement and transforming cultural frameworks by democratizing the mass public.

## Social Media, Smart Mobs, Side-Stepping Censorship

As opposed to traditional media sources, social media and other Web-based applications make it possible for people to interact with information, posting reactions and insights and follow-up commentary. Whereas in earlier years, "debate" could occur asynchronously in the opinion columns and letters to the editor on the back pages of newspapers or through telephone calls to radio talk shows, now, through the use of blogs, user comment spaces at the end of news stories, online insta-polls, and more, people can instantaneously react to information, and they can continue to interact with others who comment on the same source. Although these forums often set boundaries in terms of deleting abusive language and threats, they are not subjected to the same kinds of editorial controls and screening as other forms of media. Likewise, they often allow for easy sharing of information through "like," "recommend," and "share" buttons that repost links and summaries of articles to social networking feeds. This feature not only enhances the democratic possibility of public discourse; it helps expand the notions of alternative sources of information and free expression, as well as of principles of association.

More overtly, social media have become a forum through which political activity is conducted, advanced, and reinforced, since it allows for quicker, easier dissemination of information as well as coordination of public action. Social and media critic Howard Rheingold refers to this power of electronic media as the creation of "smart mobs": technology's ability to organize and facilitate social and political action.[8] With a handheld device that is linked to a social networking application, a person can remain mobile while keeping in contact with a larger group. As Rheingold explains, "These devices will help people coordinate actions with others around the world—and, perhaps more importantly, with people nearby. Groups of people using these tools will gain new forms of social power, new ways to organize their interactions just in time and just in place."[9]

An example of the smart-mob effect was enacted in February 2011 in my home state of Wisconsin. After the passage of a budget bill that called for the elimination of collective bargaining rights for public employees throughout the state, the largest public protest in the state since the Vietnam War descended on the state capitol building in Madison. On Friday, February 11, Governor Scott Walker announced the proposed legislation, and by the evening of that day people had already begun protesting. The following

Monday, more than 1,000 University of Wisconsin students marched against some of the recommended changes announced, and Tuesday, February 15, an estimated 3,000 people occupied the capitol rotunda while 10,000 more marched outside. The following day, the number of protestors doubled, adding 5,000 more on Thursday, and the numbers swelled to more than 68,000 by the weekend.

Mass public protest of this kind is not unheard of in the United States, but the degree of coordination, communication, and facilitation of activities using social networking technologies altered the way organization and mobilization were occurring. Twitter updates from sources like *Mother Jones,* which posted, "Sources in Madison say riot police have been ordered to clear protestors from capitol at 2 am," helped followers who occupied the capitol stay current with information from outside the building, and through social networks people were able to witness in real time what was happening throughout the capitol. Facebook pages also began popping up for the dissemination of information and the coordination of a public response. Almost instantly, sites such as "Facebook Cause Page: Vote No on Walker's Budget Bill," "Thank You Wisconsin Dem Senators," "WI Public Employees against Walker's Attack on Workers' Rights," "Virtual Wisconsin State Employees Unions Solidarity Vigil," and "The Scott Walker Watch" appeared.[10] Supporters of the governor and the proposed legislation initiated responses such as the Americans for Prosperity Web page "Stand with Scott Walker" and the Republican Governor's Association's "Stand with Scott" site, which also organized a Twitter feed, "#standwithscott."[11] In this way, protests and public debate, dissent, and discourse were occurring not only at the capitol but also in the virtual spaces of the Internet.

Additionally, the rapid, often viral dissemination of video and sound files, art, music, infographics, books, blogs, and a host of other communication forms means that argumentation and identity formation is no longer hegemonically controlled by elite sources of production and information. Online messaging offers a meaningful challenge to cultural monopolies in the forms of political and social institutions and news and entertainment media; it also expands what counts as political discourse.[12]

Social media not only level the hierarchy of cultural control but also wreak havoc on attempts at censorship. For example, in response to an online petition following an open letter issued by 303 Chinese writers, lawyers, scholars, peasants, former party officials, and workers calling upon the Communist Party of China to relinquish its monopolistic hold of political authority, to liberalize the country and open prospects for political self-determination for the people, the Chinese government issued a major crackdown of speech on the Internet.[13]

The Cao Ní Ma, or "grass-mud horse," was a meme (a cultural artifact transmitted via repetition) that spread throughout China as a form of dissent from the government's control and censorship of the Internet. The grass-mud horse, its name derived from words that sound like a profane insult in Mandarin dialects but using characters that are harmless so as not to set off Chinese censors, is a mythical form of alpaca that received an entry in the Baidu Encyclopedia, an online encyclopedia that is edited collaboratively in a manner similar to Wikipedia. Dissidents used a variety of sophomoric puns, including another dirty pun in reference to the "difficult environment" in which the grass-mud horse lives, as a means of skirting antipornography laws and resisting increased efforts by the Chinese government to restrict open communication. Likewise, dissidents used a variety of Web-based technologies and social media applications to spread their message. The "Song of the Grass Mud Horse," which went viral on YouTube, celebrates the mythical alpaca for defeating the "River Crabs" (censorship) and protecting its grasslands (free speech).

Although risqué puns and dirty song lyrics may seem like a feeble response to authoritarian rule, they reveal not only the potential for widespread activism in otherwise closed systems and the difficulty Internet technologies create for illiberal political systems that seek to censor the free dissemination of ideas and forums for public activism. Soon after the grass-mud horse began galloping across the Internet—with YouTube videos of the original song, and others like it, drawing several million viewers over the years—T-shirts, dolls, toys, posters, and movies featuring the animal became available across the world. This phenomenon created an alternative public outside of the centralized systemic politics of China, allowing individuals a means for engaging in activism, protest, and expressions of solidarity. Such dissent was not institutionally allowed, but the democratizing effects of social media and Web technologies on the public created a space parallel to the closed institutions.

## iPod Liberalism and the Critique of Social Media

Internet technologies and social media are not without their detractors. Media analysts and social critics have long expressed a general concern that people use these technologies for mere escapism and self-indulgent enter-tainment.[14] More recently, broadcast and cinematic arts professor Peter B. Orlik has warned against the possibility of "unabated absorption" in online networks such as "Second Life" and "sci-fi sojourns" (presumably referring to multimember online role-playing games such as *World of Warcraft* and *Star Wars: The Old Republic*) that insulates and distracts individuals from participation in traditional public activities.[15]

Some traditional media sources, and ironically titled blog entries like "Real People Don't Have Time for Social Media," attempt to respond to the concern about the amount of time "wasted" with social media by pointing out that dedicating time to amusing ourselves is not by any means unique to Web-based technologies.[16] Just as the printing press allowed for the escapism of the pulp novel, radio for pop music, celluloid the summer blockbuster, and television the sitcom, individuals use social media as a means of pleasure and entertainment. Orlik explains, "Individual media 'programs' do not cre-ate escapist harm. It is only the unvaried aggregation of such programs that can turn gratification to dependency."[17] Besides this uniqueness argument, defenders of social media point out the creative and interactive potential of social media that does not exist within traditional media. It allows for the development of communities and the practice of social behaviors that continue even as individuals seek entertainment.

Of course, one problem resulting from the formation of alternative publics is the loss of any unifying public sphere that makes the necessary coordination, compromise, and cooperation of democracy possible. With the rise of more and more "closed publics," individuals either intentionally or unintentionally create an echo chamber in which their worldviews are constantly reinforced as the truth and all others are marginalized and dis-missed. These closed publics shelter individuals from dissent and insulate them from information or ideas they find to be uncomfortable.

Once again, these criticisms are not unique to social media. When one examines broadly the pluralistic nature of participation in liberal socie-ties, the tendency of individuals to seek like-minded others to collaborate with in an attempt to achieve mutually desired outcomes is endemic to democracy. In *Federalist No. 10*, James Madison argued that all free and open societies deal with the formation of "factions," which he described as "a number of citizens . . . who are united and actuated by some common impulse of passion, or of interest, adverse to the rights of other citizens, or to the permanent and aggregate interests of the community." These groups, which take the contemporary form of interest groups, advocacy networks, political parties, unions, and trade associations, among others, segment political activities around particular interests. Madison postulates that "the latent causes of faction are . . . sown in the nature of man; and we see them everywhere brought into different degrees of activity, according to the different circumstances of civil society."[18] The factionalization of the public into like-minded communities is therefore the by-product of associational freedoms allowed within open systems. Rather than being caused by social networking, the formation of these groups is an expression of the liberal freedoms inherent in the Internet.

Unlike traditional avenues of political engagement that connect almost entirely with already in-tune, mobilized groups, social media also help break down the barriers of disengagement. Because users can share political and nonpolitical content, as well as opening forums for immediate responses and feedback from other individuals within their networks, people are more commonly exposed to public engagement than they might be through traditional political activity. One may not attend a political rally or public forum in a conventional sense, but engaging in public discourse with a variety of family, friends, and followers in social media habituates norms of open communication and exposes people to overt political messages and information that they might not seek outside of these electronic communities.

A more direct criticism of social media's democratic potential comes from Evgeny Morozov, a renowned scholar and social critic. Morozov disparages the popular claims that the Internet will usher in a wave of liberal democratization. Dismissing what he refers to as "iPod Liberalism," which he labels as the deterministic assumption people have that the spread of technology will produce more open societies, Morozov contests that the mere existence of technology does not automatically lead to increases in liberalization in closed regimes.[19] On the contrary, although he sees the democratic possibilities inherent within Internet technologies, he criticizes the notion that advancements in technology will necessarily yield democratic outcomes.[20] Likewise, he argues that authoritarian regimes often use Internet technologies to their advantage, creating new means of surveilling dissenters and spreading progovernment propaganda. Morozov sees in the Internet a potential for further stifling opposition and suppressing dissent; he does not expect it necessarily to exert a democratic and liberalizing impact on societies.

Such a perspective is problematic for a number of reasons. First, Morozov acknowledges that the Internet has promoted the flow of information not only across open societies but also into and out of more closed, authoritarian states. And he grants that new generations of political dissidents are turning to social media to organize and structure oppositional movements. He even goes so far as to claim that "if anything the speed and ease of Internet publishing have made many previous modes of samizdat obsolete; the emerging generation of dissidents may as well choose Facebook and YouTube as their headquarters and iTunes and Wikipedia as their classrooms."[21] To that extent, Morozov agrees with the democratic prospects of the Internet and social media. His concern, however, is for the notion of "technological determinism," the idea that the Internet will necessarily yield democratization in any system in which it is introduced; he notes that these technologies can be used as easily by despots as by democrats. This criticism, however, places too high a threshold for any form of political activism. By introducing such a standard, claims that the printing press helped to advance democracy and promote the spread of liberal ideas could be dismissed by the fact that the print media did not help topple every closed regime in which they were introduced; or that authoritarian regimes have used these traditional forms of media to promulgate rigid party or state discipline; or that because art was used as a form of propaganda by the Communist Party of the Soviet Union or the National Socialist Party in Germany, we should reject the democratic prospects of artistic expression as being unable to produce a meaningful understanding of democracy. Thus, while it is true that social media do not necessarily result in immediate regime change across authoritarian states, by Morozov's own admission they can be important tools in the oppositional arsenal.

Additionally, Morozov's critique misunderstands the essence of what liberal democracy entails. Democracy does not mean that only "proper or agreeable" ideas will be allowed to surface, or that only certain groups ought to have the power to utilize tools of expression to further their agenda. Democracy requires a commitment to the ideals and procedures that allow for mass empowerment and the genuinely free and open participation of all. Such a system carries with it the possibility that illiberal voices will be heard and supported rather than those calling for greater openness and transparency. Democracies around the world have been known, in fact, to elect dictators. The problem Morozov has with social media, therefore, is a problem he would find with an open society itself. Democracy is a dangerous proposition. The radical opening of society by social media is also dangerous, but this is not an argument against its democratic potential. Theoretically and empirically, the democratizing potential of social media cannot be evaluated in terms of whether or not they are used in ways acceptable to a particular vision of a good society.

Finally, Morozov overlooks the fact that social media are not directly focused on producing regime change and promoting systemic liberalization. Systemic liberalization may be a likely outcome over time (it is important to note that in his 2009 article, one regime he cites as having a lot of technological advancement without a corresponding movement toward liberalization is Egypt), but the true power of Internet technologies is in the democratizing effect they have on the mass public, allowing a large number of individuals a means to view a diversity of information that is difficult for the state to suppress, as well as the opportunity to connect with other individuals and express solidarity and a common identity where no viable means previously existed. This access not only familiarizes and acculturates individuals to core aspects of democratic life—freedom of information, expression, and a form of assembly—it enables them to practice those aspects directly in ways that in all other forms are being suppressed. The Internet and social media help to create a democratic culture through the organization of alternative publics that can organize and communicate outside the bounds of traditionally defined political space, giving people an opportunity to experience and practice democracy even in situations where democracy is nonexistent in systemic politics. This opportunity can be far more critical than the mere creation of electoral institutions or what might amount to superficial avenues for representation. As Alexis de Tocqueville describes in his study of America, democratic societies do not have their roots in institutions but in culture.[22] Lacking a democratic culture, the creation and imposition of democratic institutions often fail or become distorted because of a lack of democratic experiences, habits, and ways of life.

## Facebook, Twitter, YouTube, and the Blogosphere: The "End" of Democracy

Social media and the Internet are reframing our understanding of the public sphere and of communities. In doing so, this technology is fulfilling the promise of a liberal democratic politics. Like other revolutionary moments in the history of liberal democracy, social media are pushing for the opening of traditional institutions and the establishment of a stronger, more expansive framework of democratic participation. Expanding on these movements, the social media revolution is not merely targeting external, institutional arrangements to bring about a more liberal democratic society, but it is part of a liberal revolution that is democratizing the public itself. Internet technologies may in fact be ushering in a new, and perhaps final, frontier in the creation of a more global civil society in which traditional feelings of association with a geographically defined scope of culture give way to a transnational sense of common identity. The image of a twenty-one-year-old Egyptian protestor in Tahrir holding a handmade sign saying, "Egypt Supports Wisconsin Workers" and "One World, One Pain," which was reported on by Lila Shapiro of the *Huffington Post,* and the photo of protestors in Madison, Wisconsin, carrying Egyptian flags around the capitol building are just two very small examples of the potential for a reconception of citizenship, democracy, and the public sphere in an electronic age.[23]

In specific cases, Web-based technologies and social networking applications are introducing fledgling forays into democratic activities by individuals who have otherwise had such freedoms suppressed within closed political systems. In the now immortal words of Wael Ghonim, "If you want to liberalize a society, just give them the Internet."[24] From a political-theory perspective, however, this tool for mass communication and public interaction may go beyond just advancing a traditional understanding of liberal democracy. Instead, social media and other Web-based applications and forums represent the fulfillment of liberal democracy. Not only do they allow for all individuals to engage in the dissemination of ideas and decisions; they break down elite controls over what counts as an important issue for social consideration.[25] The continued tension between freedom and equality within this framework will continue, as well as debate about whether too much democracy might not be the utopian conclusion many political theorists were hoping for. However, those debates will continue to add to the vibrant tradition of democratic theory and political philosophy for years to come, and perhaps represent the ultimate end in the long progress of democracy.

## Notes

1. Paul Schemm, "Egypt Café Owner Describes Police Beating Death," *San Diego Union-Tribune,* June 13, 2010, www.signonsandiego.com/news/2010/jun/13/egypt-cafe-owner-describes-police-beating-death/ (accessed August 27, 2011).

2. John D. Sutter, "The Faces of Egypt's 'Revolution 2.0,'" *CNN*, February 21, 2011, www.cnn.com/2011/TECH/innovation/02/21/egypt.internet.revolution/index.html (accessed June 17, 2011).

3. Thucydides, *History of the Peloponnesian War*, ed. M. I. Finley, trans. Rex Warner (Toronto: Penguin Classics, 1954).

4. Robert Dahl, *Democracy and Its Critics* (New Haven, CT: Yale University Press, 1989).

5. Several thinkers within a reformist tradition of Marxism, most notably Vladimir Lenin (1870–1924) and Mao Zedong (1893–1976), advocate what is known as a "people's democracy"; a system of political and economic dictatorship by a single communist party that is said to represent the largest and the single true class, the proletariat. In such a system, alternative political parties and contestation for public office are often suppressed in the name of eliminating the vestiges of capitalism or monarchy so that true economic equality and public ownership of, and democratic determinations regarding, the means of production can be established. However, such systems stray far from the notion of self-determination in a broad sense, as communication, competition over political decision making, protest, participation, and engagement are removed from the mass public and placed in the oligarchic hands of a single-party state.

6. See Ronald Inglehart, *Culture Shift in Advanced Industrial Society* (Princeton, NJ: Princeton University Press, 1990).

7. John Dewey, quoted in Carl Cohen, *Communism, Fascism, and Democracy*, 2nd ed. (New York: Random House, 1972), 501.

8. Howard Rheingold, *Smart Mobs: The Next Social Revolution* (Cambridge, MA: Basic Books, 2002).

9. Ibid., xii–xiii.

10. At the time this was written, many of these and other Facebook pages dedicated to the protests remained active, and some of them had turned their attention to supporting recall efforts throughout the state. Likewise, the Web site "Defend Wisconsin" (www .defendwisconsin.org/, last accessed August 28, 2011) continues to post a schedule of protest-related events and activities, as well as providing links to stories, videos, sound files, and public forums dedicated to ongoing mobilization in the state.

11. "Stand with Scott Walker," Americans for Prosperity, http://americansforprosperity .org/walker/ (accessed August 28, 2011); "Stand with Scott," Republican Governor's Association, www.standwithscott.com/ (accessed August 28, 2011).

12. My colleague and coeditor Timothy M. Dale makes the case for an expanded view of the public sphere in his essay "The Revolution Is Being Televised: The Case for Popular Culture as Public Sphere," published in *Homer Simpson Marches on Washington: Dissent through American Popular Culture*, ed. Timothy M. Dale and Joseph J. Foy (Lexington: University Press of Kentucky, 2010), 21–35.

13. "Charter 08," December 9, 2008, Human Rights in China, www.hrichina.org/ content/238 (accessed August 27, 2011); Michael Wines, "A Dirty Pun Tweaks China's

Online Censors," *New York Times*, March 11, 2009, www.nytimes.com/2009/03/12/world/asia/12beast.html (accessed August 28, 2011).

14. See Elihu Katz and David Foulkes, "On the Use of Mass Media as 'Escape': Clarification of a Concept," *Public Opinion Quarterly* 26, no. 3 (Autumn 1962): 377–88.

15. Peter B. Orlik, *Electronic Media Criticism: Applied Perspectives*, 3rd ed. (New York: Routledge, 2009).

16. Bernhard Warner, "Is Social Networking a Waste of Time?" *Times Online*, March 12, 2008, http://technology.timesonline.co.uk/tol/news/tech_and_web/article3536749 .ece (accessed August 27, 2011); Sarah Perez, "Real People Don't Have Time for Social Media," *ReadWriteWeb*, April 16, 2008, www.readwriteweb.com/archives/real_people_ dont_have_time_for_social_media.php (accessed August 28, 2011).

17. Orlik, *Electronic Media Criticism*, 173. This is not to suggest that political messages are not found within these popular media, as illustrated by the contents of this book, as well as the previously released volumes in this series, *Homer Simpson Goes to Washington: American Politics through Popular Culture* and *Homer Simpson Marches on Washington: Dissent through American Popular Culture*. It is merely to show that just as there are criticisms of escapism and social media, technological changes have long carried a history of skepticism regarding their democratic potential.

18. James Madison, "Federalist No. 10: The Same Subject Continued: The Union as a Safeguard against Domestic Faction and Insurrection," *New York Daily Advertiser*, November 22, 1787, available in General Records of the Department of Justice, Record Group 60, National Archives Building, Washington, DC.

19. Morozov delivered his comments, ironically, at the TEDGlobal conference in Oxford. TED, which bills itself as a forum for "riveting talks by remarkable people, free to the world," is an online database of lectures delivered by scholars, innovators, and a host of other notable people to advance social dialogue and open discourse about important ideas in society, economics, and politics. His talk, "How the Net Aids Dictatorships," can be found at www.ted.com/talks/lang/eng/evgeny_morozov_is_the_internet_what_ orwell_feared.html (accessed August 27, 2011).

20. Evgeny Morozov, "Texting towards Utopia: Does the Internet Spread Democracy?" *Boston Review*, March–April 2009, http://bostonreview.net/BR34.2/morozov.php (accessed August 20, 2011).

21. Ibid. "Samizdat" was the practice of reproducing and distributing censored materials by hand as a means of dissent in the former Soviet Bloc.

22. Alexis de Tocqueville, *Democracy in America*, ed. J. P. Mayer, trans. George Lawrence (Garden City, NY: Doubleday, 1969).

23. Lila Shapiro, "Wisconsin Protests Draw Thousands of Workers Fighting for Key Union Rights," *Huffington Post*, February 21, 2011, www.huffingtonpost.com/2011/02/21/ wisconsin-protests-_n_826246.html?page=1 (accessed August 28, 2011). There has been some speculation that the photograph was a fake, an issue that is addressed by "Politirature," the young man holding the sign in Tahrir, in his blog http://politirature

.wordpress.com/2011/02/19/from-tahrir-to-wisconsin/ (accessed August 28, 2011), where he claims he first became aware of the struggle for workers' rights in the state of Wisconsin via friends on Facebook. Another interesting example in the Wisconsin case is that of Ian's Pizza in Madison, which began taking orders for pizzas to be delivered to the protestors at the capitol. They reported receiving orders from fifteen countries, including South Korea, Egypt, and Denmark, and all fifty U.S. states. The restaurant used the social networking sites of Facebook and Twitter to list areas from which donations were given. See Maggie DeGroot, "Worldwide Donations Send Hundreds of Pizzas to Protestors," *Daily Cardinal*, February 21, 2011, www.dailycardinal.com/news/worldwide-donations-send-hundreds-of-pizzas-to-protesters-1.2007689 (accessed August 28, 2011).

24. Quoted in Micha L. Sifry, "Did Facebook Bring Down Mubarak?" *CNN*, February 11, 2011, http://articles.cnn.com/2011–02–11/opinion/sifry.egypt.technology_1_egypt-internet-access-revolution/2?_s=PM:OPINION (accessed August 28, 2011).

25. There remains a problem of access for low-income individuals, communities, and societies all around the world, an argument that can be made about any number of social and economic resources vital to meaningful participation in a democracy. However, with the continued proliferation of Internet technologies and resources around the world, as well as greater provisions of public access, the large and regrettable gap between the technological "haves" and "have nots" is not insurmountable. The problem here is not one of too much technological spread but of not enough.

# ACKNOWLEDGMENTS

The editors are indebted to the kind support of Anne Dean Watkins, Bailey E. Johnson, and all the good people of the University Press of Kentucky. Your support and guidance on this project are enormously appreciated. We could not ask for a better group of people to work with. We would also like to extend a special thank you to Margaret Weis for her willingness to share her wonderful insights and perspective. Your work has touched millions, and we are so excited you agreed to be a part of this project. Finally, we would like to thank the contributors to this volume for making the collection possible.

Joseph J. Foy would like to thank his colleagues and friends in the University of Wisconsin Colleges. Your support and collegiality have been greatly appreciated. Thanks also to Dean A. Kowalski. I will never forget a lunchroom conversation that opened up so many opportunities for me. I am forever indebted to you for your friendship, your guidance, and your really excellent taste for magnificent hops. Thank you to Shawn, Keri, Leah and all my nieces and nephews for your love and support, and also to my in-laws Luann, Kari, and Ryan. To my parents, Sue and Jim, to whom this book is dedicated: from *Sesame Street* to *Superman* to *Star Wars*, I will never forget how you helped me understand the narratives that breathe life into the stories. Read these pages carefully, and you will hear your own voices. Most of all, thank you to Kristi, Connor, and Keira. Your lives have made the lessons spoken through the ages all the more meaningful to me. Thank you for teaching me so much.

Timothy M. Dale would like to thank his colleagues, mentors, and friends at the University of Wisconsin–La Crosse and the University of Wisconsin–Green Bay. I have greatly appreciated your advice and support through many meaningful conversations, thoughtful suggestions, and heated debates about movies and television shows. Thanks to Fred Dallmayr, whose inspiring model of intellect and compassion continues to encourage me to approach texts with generosity and an open mind. Thanks also to Andrew Kersten for his wise guidance and valued friendship. I especially want to thank the members of my family, both immediate and extended, for their patience and encouragement. To my parents, Carlynn, Mike, Carol, and Doug, you made this book (and so much more) possible. Greatest of all, thanks to Amy, Ellie, and Ian, for the happiness and perspective that every day brings.

# Contributors

CARL BERGETZ is adjunct professor at John Marshall Law School in Chicago. His research interests are in the fields of political theory, popular culture, and political communication, with a particular emphasis on civic engagement, partisanship, and liberal democracy. As a practicing attorney, he focuses on election law, public law, and government affairs.

TIMOTHY M. DALE is assistant professor of political science at the University of Wisconsin–La Crosse. His research interests include democratic theory, political messaging in popular culture, and the scholarship of teaching and learning. He is coeditor of *Homer Simpson Marches on Washington: Dissent in American Popular Culture* and coauthor of *Political Thinking, Political Theory, and Civil Society.*

DENISE DU VERNAY is coauthor of *The Simpsons in the Classroom: Embiggening the Learning Experience with the Wisdom of Springfield.* She has written numerous articles on cultural and media studies, including contributions to *Breaking Bad and Philosophy* and *SpongeBob and Philosophy.* Du Vernay has been teaching courses on writing, literature, speech, and *The Simpsons* since 1999.

SUSANNE E. FOSTER is associate professor in the Department of Philosophy at Marquette University and assistant chair of the department. Foster specializes in ancient philosophy, ethics, and environmental ethics and has published several articles in *Philosophical Inquiry, Philosophia, Environmental Ethics, Mythlore,* and the *American Catholic Philosophical Quarterly.*

JOSEPH J. FOY is associate campus dean and a member of the Department of Political Science at the University of Wisconsin–Waukesha. He won the John G. Cawleti Award for editing *Homer Simpson Goes to Washington: American Politics through Popular Culture* and *SpongeBob SquarePants and*

*Philosophy: Soaking Up Secrets under the Sea.* Foy also coedited *Homer Simpson Marches on Washington: Dissent through American Popular Culture* and has contributed chapters on the philosophical significance of *The Hunger Games, The X-Files, True Blood,* eco-horror movies, the music of The Rolling Stones, and the works of Joss Whedon, Steven Spielberg, JJ Abrams, and Ang Lee. Foy serves on the editorial board of the *Journal of Popular Culture.*

ERIC T. KASPER is associate professor of political science at the University of Wisconsin–Barron County. Kasper is author of *To Secure the Liberty of the People: James Madison's Bill of Rights and the Supreme Court's Interpretation* (2010) and coauthor (with Benjamin Schoening) of *Don't Stop Thinking about the Music: The Politics of Songs and Musicians in Presidential Campaigns* (2012). He also serves as the municipal judge in Rice Lake, Wisconsin.

MARY M. KEYS is the author of *Aquinas, Aristotle, and the Promise of the Common Good* and of articles appearing in the *American Journal of Political Science, History of Political Thought,* and *Perspectives on Political Science.* Her research and teaching interests span a broad spectrum of political theory, with a special focus in Christianity, ethics, and political thought. She has a National Endowment for the Humanities Fellowship that supports her ongoing research project on humility, modernity, and the science of politics. Keys has been a visiting scholar at the University of Chicago and Harvard University.

DEAN A. KOWALSKI is associate professor of philosophy at the University of Wisconsin–Waukesha and chair of the Department of Philosophy for the University of Wisconsin Colleges. He is the author of *Moral Theory at the Movies* and *Classic Questions and Contemporary Film* and has edited and contributed essays to *The Philosophy of the X-Files, Steven Spielberg and Philosophy,* and *Big Bang Theory and Philosophy.* He has also contributed chapters to *James Bond and Philosophy, The Philosophy of Martin Scorsese,* and *Homer Simpson Goes to Washington* and has published articles in *Philosophy and Theology, Philosophia Christi, Teaching Philosophy,* and *Filosofilm.*

S. EVAN KREIDER is associate professor at the University of Wisconsin–Fox Valley. He is a coeditor of and a contributing author to *The Philosophy of Joss Whedon* and a contributing author to *The Philosophy of the X-Files.* His philosophical interests include ethics and aesthetics, and his papers have appeared in journals such as the *International Journal of Applied Philosophy* and *Philosophical Papers*.

MATTHEW D. MENDHAM is assistant professor of political thought at Christopher Newport University. His articles on the history of ethics leading up to Immanuel Kant and Alasdair MacIntyre, as well as on Jean-Jacques Rousseau and the rise of modern capitalism, have appeared in such venues as the *Journal of Religion, History of Political Thought,* and the *American Journal of Political Science.* He regrets that his future scholarly endeavors are not likely to bring him back to Schrute Farms anytime soon.

MARK C. E. PETERSON is professor of philosophy with the University of Wisconsin Colleges. Peterson began his career with a focus on nineteenth-century Continental philosophy, including that of Kierkegaard and Marx but emphasizing Hegel's natural philosophy and the history of science and technology. These interests eventually constellated around the question of how humans are related to nature, and his conference and invited papers have centered on the topics of ecofeminism and social ecology. More recently, years of practicing *taijiquan* and Kundalini yoga have pushed his research interests in the direction of how the relation between practice and theory can be used to unearth unexamined assumptions in our scientific, philosophical, and spiritual relationship to nature.

C. HEIKE SCHOTTEN is associate professor of political science at the University of Massachusetts–Boston, where she teaches political theory, feminist theory, and queer theory. Her research interests lie at the unlikely intersection of Nietzsche studies and queer theory, where she attempts to construct a theory of radical political transformation that does not fall prey to the pitfalls of modernity's seductive yet inevitably disappointing revolutionary desire. She is the author of *Nietzsche's Revolution: Décadence, Politics, and Sexuality,* and her most recent works include "Reading Nietzsche in the Wake of the 2008–09 War on Gaza" and "*Ecrasez l'infâme!* Nietzsche's Revolution for All and (N)one," in *Nietzsche's Ecce Homo,* edited by Duncan Large and Nicholas Martin.

JAMES B. SOUTH is chair of the Philosophy Department at Marquette University in Milwaukee, Wisconsin. He is the editor of *Buffy the Vampire Slayer and Philosophy* and a coeditor of *James Bond and Philosophy* and has written several essays on movies, comic books, and popular music. His research is primarily in late medieval and Renaissance philosophy, but he is making increasingly regular forays into writing about popular culture.

JAMIE WARNER is a professor in the Department of Political Science at Marshall University, where she teaches political theory. Her work has appeared in both political science and communication studies journals, such as *Popular Communication,* the *Electronic Journal of Communication, Polity,* and *Politics and Gender.* Her current research interests revolve around the theory and practice of political marketing and the intersection of political theory and popular culture, especially the *Harry Potter* series and the HBO drama *The Wire.*

# INDEX

CPSIA information can be obtained at www.ICGtesting.com
Printed in the USA
BVOW082016160413

317979BV00002B/2/P